The World of Columbus and Sons

by

Genevieve Foster

Illustrated by the Author

Beautiful Feet Books

Sandwich, Massachusetts

Many of the drawings in this book are based on
paintings, prints, cartoons, and maps
of the period

Library of Congress Catalog Card Number 98-071430
© Copyright 1965 Genevieve Foster
All rights reserved. No part of this book may be
reproduced in any form without the permission of Beautiful Feet Books.

ISBN 0-9643803-8-2

Published by Beautiful Feet Books
139 Main Street
Sandwich, MA 02563

www.bfbooks.com
508-833-8626

For John, Genevieve and Kate

CONTENTS

Part I

WHEN COLUMBUS WAS A BOY IN GENOA

Telling how Mohammed II, Sultan of Turkey, captured Constantinople and blocked the way to India . . . The printing press was perfected by Johann Gutenberg . . . Young Isabella became heir to the crown of Castile and managed to marry Ferdinand of Aragon . . . Prince Henry the Navigator sent explorers to search for a new route to India and the Portuguese reached Africa . . . Manicongo and other Negro rulers received the Portuguese . . . Young Leonardo da Vinci began to study painting in Florence . . . Young Lorenzo de Medici was being trained as a statesman by his grandfather . . . The Wars of the Roses started in England . . . Ivan, Duke of Moscovy made himself the first "Tsar" of Russia . . . etc.

Part II

WHEN COLUMBUS WAS IN PORTUGAL AND SPAIN

Telling how a three-year-old Duchess of Austria and her twelve-year-old husband Charles VIII became King and Queen of France . . . A twelve-year-old King of England was escorted to London by his uncle Richard III . . . Henry Tudor received Richard III's crown on the battlefield and was declared King of England . . . Queen Isabella first heard from Columbus about his great plan to sail west . . . Bartholomew Dias rounded the Cape of Good Hope and opened the Portuguese sea route to India . . . Baber, the Mongol conqueror of northern India, then five years old, was growing up near Samarkand . . . Young Michelangelo began to study sculpture and live with the Medici family . . . etc.

Part III

WHEN COLUMBUS WAS SAILING FROM SPAIN

Telling how Isabella, after sending Columbus away, called him back and approved his voyage . . . The Nina, the Pinta and the Santa Maria made the voyage across the Atlantic in 35 days . . . The Santa Maria was wrecked in Haiti on Christmas Eve and turned into a fort . . . Erasmus of Rotterdam wrote his first book and went off to study in Paris . . . Martin Luther, a German schoolboy, was struggling with Latin . . . The monk Savonarola was burned on the Piazza in Florence . . . Diego and Ferdinand Columbus became pages at the court of Queen Isabella after their father's triumphant voyage . . . John Cabot discovered Newfoundland for England . . . Vasco da Gama reached India and visited the Rajah of Calicut . . . Young Copernicus left Poland to study astronomy in Italy . . . etc.

Part IV

WHEN COLUMBUS MADE HIS FINAL VOYAGE

Telling how fourteen-year-old Ferdinand went with his father on the fourth voyage . . . How the New World happened to be called "America" . . . Henry VIII, the popular young King of England, and Catherine of Aragon spent their happy honeymoon . . . Magellan started from Spain on his voyage around the world . . . Michelangelo painted the ceiling of the Sistine Chapel in Rome . . . Leonardo da Vinci went home with Francis I to spend his last years in France . . . Thomas More wrote his famous book *Utopia* . . . Martin Luther's books were burned and he was excommunicated by Pope Leo X . . . Diego Columbus became Governor of Hispaniola . . . Isabella's grandson became the Holy Roman Emperor Charles V and signed an edict against Martin Luther at the Diet of Worms . . . Ferdinand Columbus built his house in Seville and collected his library . . . etc.

INTRODUCTION

IT WAS EARLY SPRING in Spain of the year 1539. Seated beside a window in his country house just beyond the walls of Seville, a portly Spanish gentleman might have been seen slowly turning the pages of a manuscript which lay in two neat piles before him on the broad surface of a massive carved desk. The words he read were those of a book he was writing but would not live to see published. This was the last year of his life. In July he was to die and be buried in the great cathedral of Seville. There an engraved stone in the floor is still to be seen, giving his name, Fernando Colon, and the dates of his birth and death.

This, however, was a late afternoon in spring when he sat rereading and correcting his manuscript. The sun had set, but beyond the river the west was still gold and crimson and the room aglow with light. In it Ferdinand's white hair, which reached the shoulders of his velvet coat, took on a tinge of its original reddish gold, resembling that of his father. The handwritten pages also became golden in the light as he lifted each that he had finished reading and transferred it gently from one pile to the other, lining up the edges with delicate care. He handled the pages as something very precious to him, as indeed they were. They were the making of a book. And all books were precious to Ferdinand Columbus.

For years he had traveled through the various cities of Europe buying and collecting until he had a library of over 15,000 books and manuscripts, one of the finest, most remarkable collections of his day. In recent years he had come upon several books about the discovery of the New World. Since none seemed to him truly faithful to the story and life of his illustrious and beloved father, he had decided to write the *Historie* as he felt it should be told, using only the Admiral's own writings and letters and what he himself had observed. The *Historie* which he had almost completed begins with these words:

"I, being the son of Admiral Christoper Columbus, a person worthy of eternal glory for his discovery of the West Indies, it seems fitting that I, who had sailed with him for some time and who had written of lesser things should write a history of his life and marvelous discovery of the New World. . . ."

In 1492 when Christopher Columbus made that marvelous discovery, he was forty-one years old, and his son Ferdinand was four. An older son, Diego, was twelve. Their lives together cover eighty-eight years from 1451, when Columbus was born in Genoa, to 1539, when his son Ferdinand died in Seville. Those were eighty-eight years filled with great adventures and deeds of extraordinary people whose imagination and courage changed the world in which they lived. This book tells the story of that wonderful, changing, reawakening world, the world of the Renaissance and the Reformation—The World of Columbus and Sons.

Part I

begins in Genoa in the year

1451

People who were living when

Isabella of Castile (born 1451) made her first appearance at court

Gutenberg developed the art of **Printing** and made the first printed Bible

Leonardo da Vinci (born 1452) near Florence was learning to be a painter

The **Wars of the Roses** began in England after the **100 Years War** with France ended in 1453

Edward IV Duke of York became King of England in 1461

red rose

white rose

Richard III (born 1452) was learning to be a brave knight.

Henry Tudor who was to be Henry VII was born in Wales in 1457

Louis XI of France "the Spider" became King in 1461

and some important Events that

Columbus was growing up in Genoa

Lorenzo de Medici
(born 1449) was studying Greek and reading Plato

Mohammed II
captured Constantinople in 1453 and held the trade routes to India

محمد الثاني

Ferdinand of Aragon
(born 1452) was going to marry Isabella in 1469,

Cosimo de Medici
of Florence "Father of his country" (died 1465)

Francesco Sforza
made himself ruler of Milan 1450 ; (died 1466)

Nomi Mansa
African ruler on the Gambia welcomed the Portuguese explorers.

Prince Henry the Navigator was searching a sea route to India by way of Africa
(died 1460)

Ivan III
Duke of Muscovy made himself the first Tsar of Russia,

took place between 1451 and 1474

States of Italy

Milan

Venice

Genoa

Florence

Statue of the Pope

Rome

Adriatic Sea

Kingdom of Naples

The Mediterranean Sea

ST. CHRISTOPHER'S NAMESAKE

IT WAS A JUNE DAY in Genoa. St. Christopher's Day was almost here. One red-haired boy of nine was counting the days until its celebration. Seated on a shady courtyard step just outside the weaving-room door of his father's house, he was dreaming over the miracle of the giant saint for whom he, Cristoforo Colombo, had been named.

This morning, as usual, Christopher was carding wool. With a sharp brush he was cleaning dirty tangled pieces, combing the fibers straight, and letting the small twigs and burrs drop between his bare feet. The wool would then be ready for spinning into yarn.

5

Bartholomew, his younger brother, sat beside him. As little Bart was just learning to card, he kept running inside for their mother's approval. Each time Christopher heard the noisy clatter of the loom stop for a moment, then begin again louder and faster as his busy mother, Susanna, picked up her shuttles and resumed her weaving. A certain length of material had to be delivered by nightfall.

Domenico, the master weaver himself, had sauntered off an hour or so before and disappeared down the street. By now, no doubt, he and his friends were discussing the last or next meeting of the Clothiers Guild, why selling wine and cheeses might not be more profitable than weaving, or some other one of their favorite topics. Drawn out and enlivened by many glasses of wine, the day might be far spent and his ready coins gone before the sociable master weaver returned.

But on St. Christopher's Day, the boy knew his goodhearted father would think only of him, his oldest son, and of helping celebrate the feast day of his patron saint, and might even have a few coins in his pocket for a present.

In honor of the day there would be High Mass at the cathedral, and the family would be going. To enter the cathedral on any day was like entering another world. How mysterious the silence was when the church was almost empty, with only a few souls kneeling there in prayer! How marvelous and beautiful it would be on St. Christopher's Day when the priest chanted the High Mass. The music, the incense, the flickering candles, the procession of priests in gold-embroidered robes, carrying the cross to the altar bearing the crucifix. "Christ-bearer," the boy thought. That was what his name, Christopher, actually meant. "Christ-bearer."

He stopped working, holding the brushes and wool loosely between his knees, and sat gazing across the courtyard thinking over again this miraculous, wonderful legend of St. Christopher.

In the beginning Christopher, a very strong man, had been a servant to the King of his country, but he was not happy. He wished to serve a master who was stronger than he was, and fearful of no one. So he left the King to serve the Devil, because the King was fearful of the Devil. Then he found that the Devil was in fear of the Cross so he left off serving the Devil and set out to find and serve Him whose symbol was the Cross, the Lord Christ. On his way he came to a holy hermit.

"Fast and pray," the hermit told him, "and perhaps the Lord Christ will show himself to you."

"I cannot fast," said Christopher, "and I know not how to pray. Is there nothing else that I can do?"

"Do you know," said the hermit, "that wide river which has no bridge and which people cannot cross without fear of drowning?"

Christopher nodded. He knew the river.

"Go, then," said the hermit. "Build you a cabin by the river's bank. Live there and carry travelers across the deep water on your broad shoulders."

Christopher did as the hermit said. One night, asleep in his cabin, he heard a child crying.

"Christopher, Christopher, come, carry me across."

The giant rose, took up the tree trunk he used for a staff, lifted the small child to his shoulders, and waded into the river. At every step the child's weight grew heavier, until the man was barely able to stagger across to the far bank.

"Ah," said he, "if I had had the whole world on my back, it could not have been heavier than thou."

"Marvel not," the child replied, "for thou hast borne upon thy back the whole world and Him who created it. I am the Christ. Thou servest me in doing good."

This story, which was one of the first that little Christopher of Genoa ever heard, foretold in a way the deed he was to perform. The desire of the boy became that of the man, to serve Christ by carrying His Cross and His Word to far lands and people across the unknown western sea.

YOUNG ISABELLA

ON A DAY in the year 1462, a small boy of nine, astride a high-stepping white horse, and a blonde, blue-eyed girl of eleven, seated on a lowly mule, were riding side by side out of a little walled town called Arevalo. They were leaving behind them the only home they could remember. The boy was Alfonso, Prince of Castile, and the blonde, blue-eyed girl who sat so straight and rode with such dignity on the humble mule was his sister Isabella. Escorted by a small cavalcade of messengers and retainers, they were on their way to Madrid to the court of their half-brother Henry IV, who was King of Castile.

Why their brother, the King, had suddenly sent for them, the children did not know. His word to their mother had been that they would be better educated at the court.

At the thought of what their education would be at her stepson's vile court, the Queen Mother had dissolved in tears. They

8

would be ruined—her two pure, lovely children whom she had reared so carefully. Why but to save them from such evil, had she left the court when their father died? Why else had she brought them, baby Alfonso and little Isabella, to live in this old fortress castle, though it was no fit residence for a Queen? An ancient run-down Alcazar deserted by the Moors, with broken tiles and rusty iron bars—she had wept at the sight of it, her tears mingling with those she shed in mourning for her husband, the King. The sad Queen scarcely ever ceased weeping except to pray, teaching her little daughter to pray as she did, spending long hours on her knees. Her mother's constant melancholy distressed Isabella.

On this day of farewell, it had been hard for her to leave her mother in tears as they rode away. But soon the little walled town lay far behind them. And Isabella was wondering what lay ahead. What did the future hold? What did her brother, the King, plan to do with her? Would he have her wed the prince of some foreign country and become its Queen? If so, what country? Aragon, perhaps? Maybe Portugal? That she might ever be Queen of her own country, Castile, did not enter her mind. There was no reason for Isabella to think that she would ever inherit the throne.

Alfonso might. Someday Alfonso would become King of Castile, if Henry, their brother, died without a child. Henry was nearly forty years old. He had had two wives, but so far no child. Some people said that he never could have one. But so many strange and ugly things were said about the King, they could not all be true. Isabella did not remember Henry, but he was her brother and she had made up her mind to love him if she could.

Little as she expected to be Queen of Castile, much less could Isabella have imagined being Queen of Spain. No such nation existed. The country later spoken of as Spain was then divided into four independent little quarreling nations: Castile, Navarre, Aragon, and Granada. Granada belonged to the Arabs and would remain in their possession for many years to come—until 1492 to be exact. That year, just before she helped Columbus realize his dream, Isabella was to conquer Granada and unite the parts of Spain into a nation, which was to become the richest nation in Europe.

The children traveled on, reached Madrid, passed through the gates and the doors of the royal palace, and soon stood on the threshold of a strange new life.

The King had left orders that upon arrival they were to be dressed and groomed like other fashionable children at the court, so the ladies-in-waiting began at once to help them out of their dusty traveling clothes. After Isabella had been bathed and perfumed, her hair was combed and restyled. Then out came a beautiful new gown, every bit as beautiful, she thought, as the one worn by the Madonna at home in the Easter procession.

Isabella was enchanted. She whirled about in the full rustling skirt of heavy blue silk, swung its long pointed sleeves to show the crimson lining, and stood admiring her image in the mirror. How different she looked. How beautiful! Not like herself at all. She touched her forehead where her hair had been shaved back to make her face look long and narrow, in the latest fashion. All that dark powder around her eyes made them look tremendous. She was fascinated. For days thereafter, she gazed at herself in every mirror until . . . suddenly she was struck with a pang of conscience. She was vain. And Vanity was a sin!

Overwhelmed with remorse, she rushed to her father-confessor to admit her sin, do penance for it, to say six paternosters night and morning, and whatever else he prescribed.

If love of beautiful clothes could be called a sin, it was the only one that Isabella acquired. Otherwise her mother needed to have had no fear that she would be ruined by the evils of the court. Isabella remained as unspoiled as she came. At the same time she observed what went on about her, storing up for future use all that she learned about the ways of people, good or bad.

WHO IS HEIR TO CASTILE?

IT WAS at a royal christening that Isabella, in her most beautiful gown, made her first public appearance in Madrid. As the young godmother she stood at the font while an infant girl eight days old was given the name Joanna. A few steps away in a magnificent court robe, heavy with fur and gold, stood King Henry IV who claimed to be the infant's father. The Archbishop of Toledo, resplendent in his costly clerical vestments, dipped his fingers in the holy water, but was convinced that the infant whose forehead he touched was not truly the child of the King.

The King insisted that she was. And two months later, despite the fact that many agreed with the Archbishop, Henry summoned the Cortes (Senate) and demanded that all nobles and churchmen take the oath of allegiance to the Infanta Joanna, as heir to the throne. They did as they were commanded, knelt and kissed the baby's hand, but many were seething with rage at having this infant foisted upon them. The one and only legitimate heir to the throne of Castile, they said, was the young Prince Alfonso.

The argument over the question grew so heated that by the time Joanna was three it was about to burst into civil war.

The King and the Queen saw that it was no longer safe to keep Joanna or Alfonso or even Isabella there at court. So, after Joanna's third birthday party, the three were sent away with nurses, ladies, and guards to a secluded spot near the border of Portugal, where they lived in a forester's lodge.

Isabella took with her a small missal, in which she began reading and painting the pictures of the saints which had been left blank to be filled in. One day as she was painting she heard a call echoing through the forest, and then the sound of hooves. Soon a troop of soldiers came galloping up, jumped from their horses, and shouted:

"Long live Crown Prince Alfonso!"

The soldiers had come for Alfonso, they said, and for the Princess Isabella. By orders of the Archbishop of Toledo, they must leave at once. Brother and sister were quickly dressed for the journey, not knowing why or where they were being taken. A crucifix was set up under the trees. The company knelt in prayer for the blessing of God. Then they were off, riding eastward till they came to a town called Avila.

There on a plain outside the walls a weird ceremony took place. A wooden platform had been built. On it, seated on what looked like a throne, was a lifesize image of King Henry made of sticks and straw, dressed in a cloth sewn with fake jewels and wearing a tinsel crown. Soon drummers were beating out the slow rhythm of death. Rebel soldiers stood ready. At a nod from their leader, they jumped to the platform, tore the crown from the King's image of sticks and straw, and threw it in the dirt, crying:

"Down with King Henry! Long live King Alfonso!"

Turning to Alfonso, they led the eleven-year-old boy to the platform and to his amazement placed him on the throne and crowned him King, crying, "Long live King Alfonso of Castile!" Now, truly, with two kings in the land, civil war began in earnest.

Opposing the forces of King Henry was the army of the Archbishop of Toledo, who was more of a warrior than a priest.

For the next three years the whole country was in a state of anarchy. Neighbors were enemies. Neighboring towns were fighting each other; even neighboring streets in the same town were at war. There was but one actual battle, which accomplished nothing. It only whipped up the rage of the people to further bloodshed and fury until the death of young Alfonso ended the war.

It was on a summer day, when he was fifteen. Isabella reached the village where he lay stricken just in time to have him die in her arms. He had been poisoned, most people believed by poison placed in a trout that was served to him.

So the war was over. But Alfonso was dead. Why, thought Isabella, had God let Alfonso be killed? It must be that their cause was wrong and so God had punished them.

Heartbroken, Isabella fled to Avila to be with the nuns in the Convent of the Holy Virgin. There, dressed in the white gown of mourning, living in a cell as the nuns did, she spent the rest of the summer quietly doing needlework.

One day a flurry of excitement swept through the convent as the news spread from cell to cell that a famous visitor had arrived—the Archbishop of Toledo—with an important embassy including a deputation from the city of Seville. The Princess Isabella met the bishop in her simple mourning dress of white serge. The Archbishop had come, he said, to offer her the title of Queen of Castile. This was a great honor. Expecting the girl to accept it thankfully, he was astonished to hear her refuse it, with a very firm No.

"While my brother lives he is the King," she said. "No one else has any right to the throne. If I am ever to be Queen it must be by lawful means—not by war." The nobles and churchmen might continue to rebel against Henry and fight among themselves, but she would not be part of it.

MOHAMMED CAPTURES CONSTANTINOPLE

THE YEAR that Columbus and Isabella were born, Mohammed II became Sultan of the Ottoman Turks. Two years later, in 1453, he captured Constantinople. A wave of shock and an unbelievable terror swept across Europe. For a thousand years Constantinople had been the capital of the Roman Empire of the East—the firm stronghold of Christianity. Constantine, Rome's first Christian emperor, who had built the city, had chosen for his new Rome, as he called it, such a strong site that no one believed it could ever be captured. All through the Middle Ages, that was true. So long as men fought with crossbows and battle-axes, its walls had been impregnable. But those days were now gone. Gunpowder had now been discovered and a powerful new weapon invented that could shatter the walls of any medieval city. Constantinople was doomed. The last Roman Emperor, Constantine XI, had been killed defending its walls, and the Empire was gone.

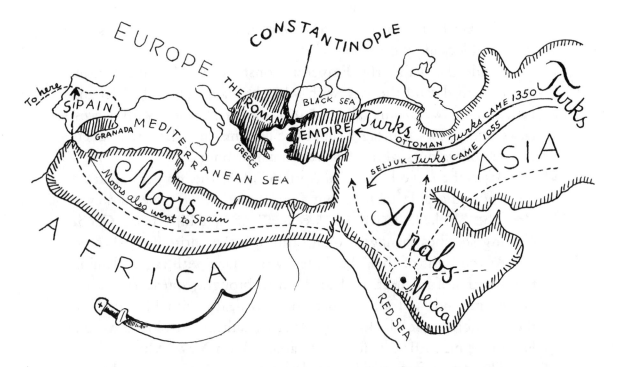

Mohammed II, the conqueror, was a Turk of the Ottoman tribe which, like all Turks, had come out of central Asia. In a little more than a hundred years after leaving their homeland, the Ottomans had conquered all of the Roman Empire of the East, except the city of Constantinople, which had been left standing like a lone island of Christianity in a Moslem sea.

As may be seen on the map, the Arabs, who were the first Moslems, or followers of the prophet Mohammed, had conquered an original empire that reached far into Asia and almost to the northern border of Spain. Though they had been driven back by the Spaniards, the Arabs, together with the Turks and Moors whom they had converted, still occupied a vast territory—around the Mediterranean from Granada to Greece.

Mohammed II was twenty-one years old when he became the Sultan. Full of purpose, he began at once to prepare for the grand attack on Constantinople. Gunsmiths were hired to cast for him the largest cannon yet made which hurled stone balls weighing 600 pounds. He had a force of 160,000 men and a fleet of 150 ships ready to blockade the harbor.

Inside the walls, the Emperor Constantine XI, a brave man, prepared to defend the city with what he had, but he had far too little. There were only about 5,000 soldiers, armed with lances, bows, and arrows, a meager supply of firearms that shot lead bullets the size of walnuts, and a few very small cannon.

After the siege began on April 6, 1453, the Emperor had no hope of being able to hold out long. Some relief came, however, after the blockade lasted six weeks. Four warships from Genoa carrying supplies managed to slip through the entire Turkish fleet.

At the sight of this, the Sultan went crazy with rage. Blaming the Admiral of his fleet, he had the man brought, spread face down on the ground, and almost beat him to death with his cane. He then reinforced the blockade and after consulting astrologers as to a lucky day, planned to make the final attack on May 29th.

The day before, inside the doomed city, Constantine, having proudly scorned Mohammed's offers to surrender, attended the final services in Santa Sophia. For 1,000 years Santa Sophia had been the most beautiful Christian church in the world. Now the Emperor promised honor and glory in heaven to all who should die defending the holy place.

An hour or so after midnight came the first assault, followed by wave after wave of troops thrown against the walls. Huge wooden towers had been rolled up and murderous flaming oil poured down on the city. By dawn the cannon had done their work, the walls were breached in several places. The Turks were fighting their way across the moat, heaped with dead bodies, its waters red with blood. The Emperor galloped to the Roman gate, shed his cloak, and fought like a common soldier. The Turks came pouring in, he fell, and was trampled. Later he was found, crushed beyond all recognition except for the golden eagles on his boots.

Inside the walls the Turkish soldiers rushed to Santa Sophia, burst open the doors to plunder and murder the Christian refugees who had sought shelter there. At high noon the Sultan himself arrived, gave one look about, and fiercely ordered an end to the massacre and destruction. He even killed one drunken soldier who was trying to crack up the marble floor. After all, that beautiful marble floor was now his! Santa Sophia was his. All that had once belonged to the Caesars now belonged to him! The Caesars were gone. Their palace was empty. At the thought, the perfect words of a Persian poet came to his mind:

"The spider's curtain hangs before the gate of Caesar's palace
And the owl stands sentinel on the towers. . . ."

Suddenly Mohammed's mood changed. He was again the ruthless conqueror. All who had opposed him must be punished. The Spanish consul and the Venetian consul who had helped the Emperor were to be executed. He ordered the Grand Duke, the highest officer under the Emperor, beheaded and all of his family, and had their heads heaped like a pile of fruit on his dining table.

Mohammed II had captured the Christian city, turned the Christian church of Santa Sophia into a mosque, but he had no intention of prohibiting the Christian religion. In fact, having heard of a scholar, Georgios Scholarious, highly respected in the Christian community, he had him found and brought into his presence to be honored. In the Church of the Holy Apostles, before the assembled Bishops, the Sultan invested Scholarious with the rank of Patriarch, the highest order in the Greek Orthodox church, saying:

"The Holy Trinity which has bestowed upon me the Empire, promoteth thee to be the Patriarch of the new Rome."

He then gave the newly made Patriarch a pastoral staff studded with diamonds, and also the Turkish rank of Beyler Bey, which meant that wherever the Patriarch went he was to be preceded by a standard bearer holding a pole from which three horse tails hung.

17

Mohammed II also laid down the rule that a Christian subject was to be held equal to a Moslem.

Mohammed II, sometimes called "the Parrot" because of his beaklike nose, was a strange mixture of bloody-handed Turk and classical scholar. He enjoyed all the arts, and was soon planning a palace garden, buying sculpture and paintings. Speaking five languages, he started a library of books on science and geography and sought out philosophers who could translate them into Arabic for the benefit of Turkish scholars.

In his dining hall he had hung a map of all the known world. On it, when he was not too drunk, he could mark with complaisance what an immense territory he and his Ottoman forebears had acquired. And yet not enough to satisfy him.

Europe tempted Mohammed. Hungary lay on his western border. On the map his eyes traced the Danube River from the Black Sea to the city of Belgrade, the next city to besiege and conquer. Fifteen days of blockade should be enough to starve the inhabitants of Belgrade into surrender.

Three years later, in 1456, Mohammed's army of Turks was moving into eastern Europe, bound for Hungary. They reached the walls of Belgrade with just as many cannon as the Sultan had used against Constantinople. He might well have made good his boast to take the city in fifteen days had it not been for one man, a brave Hungarian hero by the name of Hunyadi—János Hunyadi—whose name lives on in Hungarian songs and poems.

As the siege began, the citizens, preferring to die in battle if need be than to starve, rushed from the city, led by the bold Hunyadi. They destroyed the Turkish fleet and defeated the enemy so badly that Mohammed II withdrew to Constantinople.

Eastern Europe was still free, but all Europe was uneasy, not knowing when or where the terrifying Turks would make their next attack. With Constantinople gone, Europe was no longer safe.

MAN OF VISION

UNTIL 1453, when Constantine XI died in Constantinople, there were two Caesars, or Roman emperors, in Europe, one in the East and one in the West. The one in the west was German or Holy Roman Emperor, Frederick III. He had come to Rome to be crowned by Pope Nicholas V, the year before Constantinople fell. This was twelve years after the Emperor had been elected, according to custom, by the German princes. He had not dared to come sooner because the German princes of both Church and State were feeling very unfriendly toward Rome.

The German bishops had long contended that they should have some say in the government of the Church, rather than accept the absolute authority of the Pope. Three great Council meetings had already been held, at which delegates from Rome had met with the Germans to try to work out some kind of compromise.

Pope Nicholas V, who was most sincere in his wish to bring about an understanding with the German bishops, sent the wisest man he knew, his good friend Cardinal Nicholas of Cusa, to one of the great Councils.

Nicholas of Cusa was a true philosopher, one of those men who love truth more dearly and see it more clearly than most men of the age in which they live. Nicholas of Cusa had been born in France,

19

educated in Holland, and studied in Germany and Italy. He had also visited Constantinople where he studied the ancient Greek philosophers, searching for truth wherever he could find it.

"We should always seek for truth and knowledge," he said, "but we should remember that knowledge and wisdom are of worth only if we let our lives be governed by them."

In 1453, the year Constantinople fell, Nicholas of Cusa wrote a *Dialogue of Peace,* in which he pleaded for peace and understanding among all the different religions—Moslem, Hebrew, and Christian. He saw them all as various rays of light coming from one Eternal Truth.

This is the man whom the Pope sent to Germany and who appeared there, it was said, "like an angel of light and peace amid darkness and confusion."

As a loyal Cardinal, Nicholas of Cusa upheld the supreme authority of the Pope, but made this proposal: that members of the Council who were in touch with the needs of the German people give recommendations to the Pope, by which his decrees might be guided. If a Pope was bad, he should be deposed by an international Council and replaced, "since," said Nicholas of Cusa, "by nature all men are free and every government exists solely by agreement and consent of the subjects."

Nicholas V was a good Pope, and the words of Nicholas of Cusa might have led to a peaceful reformation, if those Popes who came later had not been a disgrace to the high office which they held. Dissatisfaction, however, quieted off for a time in Germany. Though it kept on smoldering it did not reach a crisis until many years later. Then the German Emperor was to be Charles V, the great-grandson of Emperor Frederick III, and also the grandson of Queen Isabella. As he was a friend of Ferdinand Columbus, and was still Emperor when Ferdinand was writing the story of his father, Charles V will bring to an end this story of the world, now beginning with his great-grandfather, Frederick III.

THE POPE AND THE PRINTING PRESS

FAR MORE IMPORTANT than the fall of Constantinople or of any other city in the history of the world was the invention of the printing press. The earliest example of printing now in existence is a copy of the indulgence issued by Pope Nicholas V in 1454, the year after Constantinople fell, and printed in Germany by the inventor, Johann Gutenberg of Mainz.

Good Pope Nicholas had been heartsick that he had not been able to save Constantinople. Despite all the appeals he had sent out to the kings and princes of Europe to join in a Crusade, he had been unable to rouse them. After the city fell, he sent out still

21

another appeal for a Crusade against the Turks, offering this inducement: Anyone who would either fight or give money to fight against the infidels would be excused from performing all or part of the penance due for sins which had already been confessed. This was called an indulgence.

The terms of this indulgence were written on a sheet of paper like any other business agreement, with space left for the name of the person to be filled in after the money had been paid. Agents of the Pope started out with a supply of these papers and peddled them through the countryside. The agent traveling through Germany found the sales so good that by the time he reached the city of Mainz he had used up his supply. To his surprise he was told that new copies could be made by machine. There was in Mainz a man by the name of Johann Gutenberg who had a printing press that could turn out fifty or more copies in less time than it would take a man to copy one.

Quick to take advantage of that information, the agent was soon on his way to the print shop. There he saw a tall wooden affair about the size of a gate, with a large vertical screw and a long horizontal handle. Standing beside it was a man about fifty years of age examining a sheet of printing which a workman had just taken from the press. As Herr Gutenberg laid it down to look over the indulgence, the agent may have noticed that what lay on the press was not a solid block of wood like those from which pictures were occasionally printed.

There was a form made of single letters cast from metal, each one separate but held together in a frame. They were being used to print one full page in a Bible. Then they would be broken apart and rearranged to print another page.

Movable metal type—that was the great invention. It was an idea which had taken Gutenberg years of hard work and disappointment to perfect. And yet when done it seemed like such a simple thing it was a wonder that others had not thought of it. As a matter of fact, they had. As so often happens, a new idea does not occur to one man alone, but the credit must go to that one who has had the infinite patience to work it out. Credit for the printing press, therefore, it has been agreed, belongs to Johann Gutenberg.

News of the invention spread and artisans came from other cities and countries to learn the wonderful new process by which books could be made so fast and so cheaply that even ordinary people would be able to have one to read. Books, copied by hand, were so slow and costly to make that even the wealthy seldom owned more than one or two.

Nicholas Jenson, master of the mint which made coins for the King of France, was one of the first to be sent to Mainz. According to old court records:

"On the third of October 1458 the king having found that Sieur Gutenberg Knight living in Mayence Germany a man dexterous in making letter punches had brought to light an invention for printing with metal characters, sent Jensen to Mainz with instructions to inform himself secretly of the invention."

Three years later Nicolas Jenson returned to France but conditions had so changed that he felt it was better to go on to Italy. It was a wise choice for in France conditions grew worse.

Three pupils of Gutenberg later went to Paris and set up printing presses in the College of the Sorbonne. They did very beautiful work but when the people in general saw the pages all exactly alike they said it must be black art, the work of the devil. They would have burned the printers alive if the King had not stopped them. Later the clergy, fearing that reading books would lead to independent thinking and heresy, obtained a royal order limiting the number of printers in France to twelve, all to be chosen by the King. Anyone else daring to operate a printing press was to be hanged.

Nicolas Jenson had then gone to Venice, which soon became the great center of printing in Italy.

FROM VENICE TO PORTUGAL

ENICE, the exotic island city on the Adriatic, was the "Bride of the Sea." Under the protection of Constantinople she had grown rich and colorful dealing with the East. Palaces of pink and golden marble lined her limpid blue-green canals and were mirrored in the water. Slim black gondolas with canopies of crimson carried their elegant owners to the Bridge of the Rialto, the financial heart of the city. There the wealthy Venetians invested their golden ducats in private enterprise, or purchased shares in the state-owned galleys that sailed in fleets across the Mediterranean. All this prosperity was threatened now that Constantinople had fallen.

Before too long the great center of commerce on the sea would move westward to Portugal. But still for a while Venetian galleys would be seen in every harbor of the inland sea, picking up cargoes of spices from India, jewels, silks and perfumes from China, wheat from Thessaly, sugar from Egypt. All were purchased from the Arab merchants and carried back to Venice, or to the various ports of northern Europe.

In the year 1454, a merchant galley was leaving Venice for the Netherlands with a spirited Venetian aboard who had a share in the cargo and was setting out, he said, to seek his fortune "by any means possible." Alvise Cadamosto was the name of the young merchant. As it happened, in seeking his fortune he was to take part in the greatest adventure of his age, the search for a sea route to India. And he was to sail for one of the most outstanding men of any age, Henry the Navigator, Prince of Portugal.

Though his name was known, the Portuguese Prince was a man of mystery, almost a legendary character. Living for years on lonely Cape St. Vincent, the southwest point of Portugal, he had been sending out caravels year after year from the harbor of Lagos to explore the coast of Africa and discover a new route to India.

Cadamosto's ship, leaving Venice, was bound for the wealthy city of Bruges in the Netherlands, seat of the Duke of Burgundy. He had made the trip before with no difficulty. This time as they sailed through the straits of Gilbraltar and rounded Cape St. Vincent, a full blast from the Atlantic struck with such fury that it blew the ship into the harbor of Lagos.

There he was in Prince Henry's harbor. Rising above him was the huge sacred rock, scoured smooth by wind and waves. On top of the rock was the city which the Prince had built for the use of his captains, scientists, engineers, mapmakers, and his court. Nearby in the shipyards the Portuguese ships which Prince Henry had designed were being built.

Prince Henry was at his villa, three miles inland, where he often went to think and work, when he received word that a ship from Venice had taken refuge in his harbor. He sent his secretary to accompany the Venetian consul to the ship and reminded him to take products that might be of interest to the merchant captain.

Cadamosto was excited by what the visitors brought. They had samples of sugar from an island in the Atlantic called Madeira, discovered about thirty years ago and now colonized and cultivated with fields of sugar cane and vineyards. The sugar was a very fine grade. He fingered it and tasted it, and found it quite as fine as that which the Venetians brought from Egypt. The Arab traders charged so much for their sugar that only the very rich in Europe could afford to use it. Here was sugar at prices that Europeans could afford to pay.

Cadamosto had planned to stop at Madeira on his way back from Bruges. But when he heard about the wealth and adventure to be had in Africa, he gave up all idea of going on to the Netherlands. Let the ship go on without him; he would go to Africa!

How soon could he start? On what terms? What security would Prince Henry require?

The Secretary and the Venetian Consul said they would take Cadamosto to meet Prince Henry himself.

THE GREAT PRINCE

THIS IS PRINCE HENRY the Navigator as the young Venetian saw him that day in 1454, a man of sixty years, dark, thick-set, of medium height. His forehead was furrowed and his skin had the brown, weathered look of a seasoned mariner who had spent most of his life at sea. Actually, Prince Henry had rarely been to sea, probably never beyond the sight of land. His had been an adventure of the mind. Over the years he had planned the voyages, supplied maps and charts, furnished the ships, and strengthened the faith and purpose of the captains who sailed and won the glory.

Prince Henry was not concerned with glory. His satisfaction came from doing something well. *"Talent de bien faire"*—the power to do well—was the motto he had taken when as a young knight he had set out to test his sword on the battlefield. He had then gone with his two older brothers to fight against the Moslems in North Africa. Just across the strait of Gibraltar in Morocco, the three Portuguese Princes had attacked the Moors and captured their city of Ceuta, the first European base on the African continent.

Prince Henry stayed on as governor of the city for a number of months. The facts he learned about the great unknown continent were the beginning of his life work. Desert Arabs told him of caravan routes that led eastward to the Red Sea, of Bedouin tribes who lived on the edge of the Sahara Desert. They told of Berber tribes to the west and of Negro kingdoms deep in green jungles to the south.

All North Africa was Moslem as far as the Red Sea. Moslems also held all the harbors where European ships picked up spices from India. And there was no way by land of reaching Asia or India without going through hostile territory.

Why not try, then, to discover a sea route which would circle below the land of the Moslems, south around Africa?

Here Prince Henry encountered the belief that to sail south was dangerous. The ocean boiled and the searing heat would burn men black. The waters ran downhill, so no ship that went could ever come back. In this the Prince detected a grain of truth.

The way of the wind was such that a regular square-sailed vessel might have little chance of beating its way north again. But surely ships could be designed to overcome this problem.

On his return to Portugal, the King, his father, made him governor of the southern province. There, alone with his dream, he found the perfect place to develop his plans—the lonely Sagres or Sacred Rock known as Cape St. Vincent.

For many years after Prince Henry sent out his first explorers his efforts were ridiculed as being costly and absurd. The King continued to have faith in his son until he died. Not many years later, criticism and ridicule were replaced by admiration, amazement, and an eagerness to have a share in any and all of the companies the Prince formed. This right about face was due to an event that was no part of Prince Henry's purpose or desire.

In the summer of 1444 six ships from Africa had reached the harbor of Lagos loaded with slaves.

from an old print

SLAVERY

BRINGING NEGRO SLAVES to Europe started indirectly with the capture of a Berber chief who had been taken to Portugal by Nuno Tristam, one of Prince Henry's earliest and best explorers. Nuno Tristam sailed the first caravel that Prince Henry had built, and used the first manual ever written for the navigators, which contained "Rules for Observing the North Star."

Adahu, a tall Berber chieftain, and two young boys were captured on the coast of Morocco and taken back there a year or so later by another explorer. In exchange he was given gold dust and ten adult Negroes, the first Negroes ever taken to Europe.

Nuno Tristam, meanwhile, had gone out again, sailing this time as far as Arguin Bay, south of Cape Blanco. Near the mainland where Prince Henry later built a fort and a trading post, Tristam anchored his caravel. Negroes, curious to investigate the strange huge bird, paddled out in their canoes, and fourteen of them were seized and carried away to Portugal.

Other Portuguese captains were quick to see the profit to be made in the slave trade. On August 8, 1444, six ships filled with

African natives for sale were unloaded in the harbor of Lagos. A Portuguese chronicler described the sad scene.

"Very early because of the heat, the sailors began to fill the boats and take the captives ashore. It was an astonishing sight. Even the hardest heart would have been moved to pity seeing them gathered together; for some bowed their heads with their faces bathed in tears; others groaned and raised their faces to the heavens for help. Prince Henry was there on horseback. He parcelled out his share, (as if) having no other pleasure than in thinking that these lost souls would now be saved. Hope was not in vain, for as soon as they understood our language they became Christians. And I who wrote this history have seen them in Lagos (and think) how great must be the reward of the Prince before God for having saved these souls."

None of the Africans brought to Portugal were ever mistreated. They learned trades, intermarried, and were soon looked upon as any other Portuguese peasant.

How could it not have seemed to Prince Henry that slavery under those conditions could be wrong? But how could he imagine a world without slaves? There had always been slavery since the beginning of time—in the days of the Romans, in the time of Christ. All Europeans who now sailed the Mediterranean might be captured by Moorish pirates and end their days in slavery. African tribes fighting one another sold the women and children they captured to Berber traders who went down from Morocco to the great inland trading center of Timbuktu.

Nuno Tristam was killed in 1446 by natives on the Gambia River, which he had discovered. In two small boats he and his men went upstream into the steamy green darkness of the jungle. Soon they were surrounded by canoes and struck by a blizzard of arrows, the heads of which had been steeped in poison.

Nuno died, and only five got back to the caravel, four boys and a young clerk. Not strong enough to pull up the anchor, they cut the chain and drifted out to sea. The Negroes salvaged the anchor and took it to their chief as a fine trophy.

The death of Nuno Tristam, who had been the ideal explorer, was a great loss to Prince Henry. Since the slave trade began it had been difficult for him to find captains who would carry on with exploration and not stop at the first possible place to pick up a load of slaves and hurry back home.

Now Prince Henry was hoping as he talked with the animated Cadamosto, that in the young Venetian he had at last found another true explorer. His constant fear was that the captains in their greed for slaves might try to take them by force instead of buying them. So he had laid down the rule that the men who sailed for him must never fight the natives except in self-defense.

All relations with the people of Africa, he explained to Cadamosto, were to be made "in good peace and with their consent" and peace was to be established "by tact and not by force."

In this year 1454, to his great satisfaction, Pope Nicholas had granted the Portuguese the monopoly of exploration as far as India and this very year might see the sea route opened, possibly by Cadamosto.

How and on what terms, the young Venetian inquired, might he undertake the expedition?

Prince Henry gave him two choices. Either Cadamosto could equip a caravel at his own expense and pay one-fourth of the profits to Prince Henry on his return, or the Prince himself would provide and equip the caravel and take one-half of the profits. Cadamosto chose the latter arrangement. Whatever extra money he had he spent on merchandise to trade.

Impatient to be off after what seemed, he said, like "many many days," he set out from Lagos in a brand-new caravel. His first stop in Africa was to be the Senegal River.

AFRICA AND THE AFRICANS

MIGHTY BUDOMEL was the Negro lord who ruled over the land bordering the Senegal River. His palace was a large palm-thatched hut in the inner and most sacred of seven circular courtyards which separated his subjects by rank.

One summer day, Budomel, being fanned by one of his many wives, sat in his inner sanctum, perplexed. His favorite horse was dead as well as seven others purchased not so long ago from Berber tribesmen at Timbuktu. He could not understand why horses that were lean and fine when they came from the desert, always grew

32

enormously fat and very soon began to wheeze and die in his keep.

As he was puzzling over the problem, a messenger crawled into his sacred presence, touched his forehead to the ground, threw dust on his head, and then crept to the exact distance from the haughty chief at which he was allowed to speak. Budomel did not deign to look at the messenger but found what he had to say of decided interest. A ship was anchored near the great palm at the mouth of the river. On it were horses for sale.

On board ship, waiting to sell the horses, was Cadamosto. It was not long before he saw Chief Budomel with his men riding up on the few fat horses they had left. The chief looked at the white trader, scrutinized his horses, nodded, and offered one hundred slaves for seven animals. The slaves would have to be brought from the village which was twenty-five miles inland.

Budomel urged the white chief to pay him a visit in the village, and Cadamosto accepted.

"I went quite as much to see and hear new things as to receive my payment," he said. What amazed him most was the abject reverence Budomel demanded or inspired in his subjects. "If God himself had been there I don't think He could have been treated with greater respect."

Budomel's God was Allah. He was a Moslem, recently converted with the rest of the Senegal tribes by the Azanegues, who lived north of the Senegal, closer to the desert. They were a tall, dusky brown people with long straight hair which they greased with fish oil; its odor announced their coming long before they were in sight. An Azanegue instructed Budomel in his prayers, to which Cadamosto was invited to listen. This he did, until he could keep silent no longer.

"Ours is the true religion," he blurted out, and then began an argument with the Moslem teacher, to the amusement of Budomel who finally ended it all with this wise observation:

"No doubt the Christian white man's faith is good. The

33

Moslem also good. God has blessed them with many things. But God is just. The black man has little here—the next world must be his."

Cadamosto bade farewell to Budomel and returned to the caravel. As he was leaving the Senegal going south, two other caravels joined his and the three proceeded together toward the Gambia River.

One bright night on the South Atlantic the sky looked strange to Cadamosto. Over the sea to the south rose new stars, one formation men from north of the equator had never before seen. It was the beautiful Southern Cross!

Cadamosto's caravel was at the mouth of the Gambia River. This he knew was the river on which Nuno Tristam had been murdered. The tribes along the Gambia were hostile and savage, not friendly like those along the Senegal, who were in touch with the Arabs. Cadamosto's crew had already had proof of their hostility. Each of the three caravels carried an African interpreter sent out by Prince Henry. All were Negroes who had been sold by their native lords, and carried to Portugal where they had learned good Portuguese and had been baptized as Christians. Each interpreter was paid with a slave of his own for his services. When he had four slaves, he was himself set free. About seventy miles south of Cape Verde one of these African interpreters went ashore to gather information from some natives in log canoes. The natives talked with the interpreter a long time and then suddenly killed him. The Portuguese would have sprung to their guns, but remembered the order of the Prince, not to fight except in self-defense. They were not being attacked, so they sailed on down the coast to the richly wooded shore at the wide mouth of the Gambia River.

"I have never seen a land more beautiful than this," exclaimed Cadamosto as his caravel, the first of the three, entered the shining, glassy waterway that wound silently on through the green walls of the forest. The tide carried them along for four miles. All was silent —not a sound—no sign of life. Suddenly the river was alive with armed canoes. At sight of the caravel the Negroes stopped moving and stared, holding their dripping paddles in the air. There were more than one hundred and fifty of them, fine tall men, in cotton shirts and headdresses topped with white plumes. As they stared up in wonder, the white men in equal wonder stared down upon them. "So we remained for a long time," said Cadamosto, "and neither did they attack us nor we move against them."

Then around the bend came the two other caravels. The Negroes dropped their paddles, seized their bows and affixed their deadly arrows. The men on board ship sprang to the bombards. Arrows sped through the air, while great stones hurled by the bombards splashed in the water. The roar went echoing through the forest. The blacks fled to a safe distance. The interpreter called to them in their own tongue.

"Why do you attack peaceful men coming only to trade? Take our merchandise, as much as you like, and give us yours in exchange."

They listened. They waited. Then one of them spoke:

"White men are man-eaters. The slaves they buy are for butchers' meat." They would not trade, they said. They would kill the white men and give all that they had brought to their chief.

Just then a breeze filled the sails of the caravels—the wings of these giant water birds that spit balls of fire! The Negroes fled in terror.

Cadamosto would have gone farther, looking for the source of the Gambia River, but the sailors objected. They were weary. They might have mutinied if he had forced them into further danger, so he turned back and headed for home.

As a memento, Cadamosto took Prince Henry some salted elephant meat, a hoof, and a tusk eight feet long. The Prince sent the hoof and tusk to the Netherlands as a present to his sister, who was the wife of Philip the Good, the Duke of Burgundy, the richest ruler in northern Europe.

DIOGO GOMES ON THE GAMBIA

I WAS the first Christian to make peace with the Gambia blacks,"
Diogo Gomes was proud of saying. Gomes had been a cavalero in
the royal household of Portugal and esteemed as a friend by Prince
Henry before he became an explorer.

Two years after Cadamosto returned, Diogo Gomes went to the
Gambia River, sailed about 500 miles upstream in a small boat and
made friendly contact with the three hostile Negro lords who ruled
the land along the river—Nomi Mansa, Batti Mansa, and Boor Mali.

BOOR MALI

Boor Mali ruled over the Gambia's north bank, which made him
the richest of the three. All the gold mines in the mountains to the
east were his, as well as the fabulous city of Kuka, where the Arabs
came from as far away as Egypt to buy gold. In front of Boor Mali's
palace there was said to be a hunk of gold to which he tied his
horse—a piece so huge that twenty men could not lift it.

Diogo Gomes did not reach Kuka to see this fabulous hunk of
gold with his own eyes, but he did get to the nearby city of Cantor
where he did some trading for gold, and saw the chief men from
Kuka, all wearing ornaments of gold in their noses. As news of his
arrival spread, natives came streaming in to Cantor to see the strange
white men who had come up the river in a boat. They were used to
the dusky brown Arabs and Berbers who rode in from the desert.

36

But these men were white as if their skins had been painted, and they had come by water from a place called Portugal.

Diogo Gomes wanted to go on to Kuka, but again the crew did not share the enthusiasm of the explorer. They were worn out from the heat of the steamy forest and glad to go back down the river toward the sea where the caravel itself had been anchored. They found only three men up and about. Nine had died and all the rest were ill with some kind of fever. Gomes now paid the native guide for the trip to Cantor and then sent him to arrange a meeting with Chief Batti Mansa whose land lay south of the river.

BATTI MANSA

Batti Mansa was shy and distrustful. He and his people, unlike the Africans near Cantor, were unaccustomed to seeing anyone at all outside of their jungle world. Yet he was curious and came to the meeting, though well protected by many men carrying poisoned arrows, spears, and shields.

Very cautiously he advanced toward the water's edge, keeping his back close to the tangled thicket.

"I walked up to him," said Gomes, "bringing my offerings and some of our wine, for they know only that of the palm."

The chief took a sip, nodded with pleasure, and drank it all. He then made Gomes a present of three Negroes, a man and two women, and swore, explained the interpreter, "By the living God I will never fight Christians any more."

NOMI MANSA

Nomi Mansa was lord of the lands at the mouth of the Gambia. His people had attacked Cadamosto and killed Nuno Tristam. He could make it difficult for Portuguese ships to enter the river.

"Therefore," said Gomes, "I worked hard to make peace with him and sent him many gifts. He accepted the gifts, and sent many men and women to me to see if I would do them harm."

Finally, Nomi Mansa felt it was safe to grant an interview,

which took place on the beach. Having seated himself with ceremony, his men lined up behind him and his Moslem priest beside him, he motioned to Diogo Gomes to approach and speak.

Nomi Mansa wanted to know about the white man's Prince and about his religion. So a cross-questioning began between the Moslem priest and Gomes, whose lightning success as a missionary suggests that the convert was quick to see material advantage in becoming a Christian. In no time Nomi Mansa declared himself converted. From now on he would worship no other God than the one worshiped by the great Prince Henry. He gave the Moslem priest three days to leave the country, and decreed that no one under pain of death should honor Mohammed any more.

Let Gomes baptize him at once—all of his wives, his courtiers also, and all of their wives. He told them to choose their new Christian names. He, for himself, chose Henry.

Who would be Diogo? Or Nuno? Or Tristam?

Gomes tried to explain that he could not perform that sacred rite. But to celebrate their conversion and friendship he invited them to dinner on board the caravel. Nomi Mansa, his eight wives, and twelve of his oldest courtiers accepted.

Chicken, meat, and red and white wines were served. With each serving the guests declared with added conviction "that there were no better people than Christians!"

Again and again, Nomi Mansa insisted upon being baptized. At last he had to be satisfied with Gomes' promise to ask Prince Henry to send a priest who would perform the ceremony.

And a falcon, added Nomi Mansa. Would the Prince also send him a falcon, and some sheep and ducks? And a pig, or two pigs? And two men to teach him how to build houses and a wall? He wanted a stone wall around his town. Gomes promised everything.

Then, as a parting gift for Prince Henry, Nomi Mansa brought forth a long treasured trophy. It was the anchor from Nuno Tristam's ill-fated caravel.

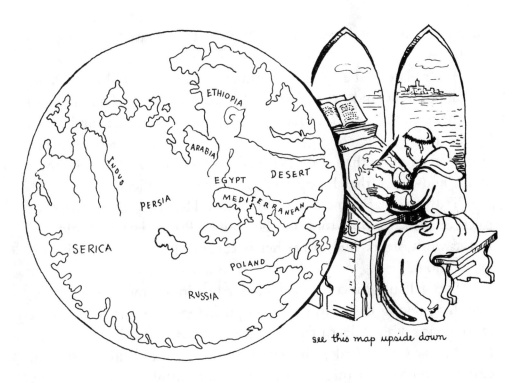

Labels on map: ETHIOPIA, ARABIA, INDUS, DESERT, EGYPT, PERSIA, MEDITERRANEAN, SERICA, POLAND, RUSSIA

see this map upside down

A MAP FROM VENICE

IN 1458, Prince Henry had a visit from his nephew, Alfonso V, who was now the King of Portugal. An impetuous young man of twenty-seven, he was far more interested in war and glory than he was in exploration. If he had had the money to do so, he would have led a crusade to the far ends of the Mediterranean against the Moslems. As it was, he had to content himself by fighting against the Moors in North Africa, where he was to win three victories and gain the honorary title of "El Africano."

Alfonso V was happy to see his uncle and to have a look at the place where the old man had lived and worked for so many years, hidden away like a saint or a hermit. He fell in readily with Prince Henry's desire to send to Venice and have a map of the world made showing all the most recent discoveries. This task was entrusted to Fra

Mauro, a Franciscan monk, one of the most celebrated cartographers of his day.

A year later, when the map came, it was all that Prince Henry had hoped it would be. All the information that he had collected was there, and also all that had been reported about Asia and China by the traveler Marco Polo of Venice. Although Marco Polo had crossed Asia more than 150 years before, his book was still the most recent knowledge that Europeans had about the Orient.

With the map came a letter to Prince Henry from the Doge, or ruler, of Venice, who wrote that he "hoped Prince Henry would find in the work of Fra Mauro further inducement to carry on with his explorations."

The gallant Prince needed no further inducement to carry on than his lifelong desire to reach his goal. One thing that was most encouraging was to learn from both Cadamosto and Diogo Gomes that below Cape Verde, the coastline of Africa definitely turned eastward. Next year might actually see the fulfillment of his hope. One of his caravels might reach India!

But his life span was running out and he knew it. In the summer of 1460 he made many final arrangements. Diogo Gomes, his good friend, was with him and wrote of those last days.

In the late autumn of 1460, when the caravels were "home from Africa and the islands," and their sails were furled, Prince Henry's life came to an end. Diogo Gomes wrote:

"King Alfonso and all the people of Portugal mourned the death of so great a Prince."

In his will the Prince had left instructions that he should be buried as he had lived, quietly and simply.

On his tomb were carved the words of his motto: *Talent de bien faire.* The power to do well. How great that power had been! The vision and work of this one man had opened the great Age of Exploration and Discovery and prepared the way for all who were to follow him.

IN THE HARBOR OF GENOA

CHRISTOPHER COLUMBUS was nine years old in the autumn of 1460, when Prince Henry the Navigator died. On almost any bright morning, the red-haired boy might have been seen running down a narrow street of Genoa, leaving behind the dark house with its clacking loom and heading for the wide, open harbor. His feet barely touched the cobblestones, he was so eager to see the big galley that had just come in.

There it was! Anchored at one of the busy wharves was a galley just in from the eastern end of the Mediterranean. Its three tall pointed sails were already furled, the oars banked, and it was being

41

unloaded. Sailors were coming ashore with bags and barrels out of the hold. The boy watched for a chance to slip aboard and peer about. He sniffed. The air was tinged with the most delicious smell —the scent of spices. Spices he knew came from a land called India and were hard to get and costly. Pepper was almost as good as gold. A small bag of peppercorns, his father said, would make a man rich.

The galley was armed. It had to be because of the terrible Turks, who held all the eastern end of the Mediterranean. What a thrill it would be to sail on such a voyage, and have a look at what was there to be seen! Why should he have to sit in an old court-yard carding wool and learning to be a weaver, when what he wanted to be was a sailor, as soon as he was old enough!

So far his only sailing had been on one of the little packets that carried wine, cheese, and wools to towns along the coast both ways from Genoa, but what did that amount to? Ships from faraway lands came into the harbor of Genoa; he wanted to see the places they came from, all the lands and seas and harbors of the world. He knew all the ships; he knew the cut of their sails, the shape of their prows, and how high they rode above the water. The Mediterranean galleys were long and slim, with triangular pointed sails. The Span-ish galleon was high and heavy with square sails and three masts. The Portuguese caravel had pointed sails set at an angle like the wings of a gull, and flew like a bird across the water.

On these caravels the Portuguese sailors had gone farther out into the Atlantic, he heard a mapmaker say, than any other sailors, and also farther down the coast of Africa. Maps were always being made in Genoa for these Portuguese explorers. How much farther would they, or could they, go? What would they find? What would there be to see? How he would love to go and see every part of the world!

Some of the old weatherbeaten seamen, who had been sailing the sea for a lifetime, shook their heads in disgust. They knew all they cared to know about this old world. They had seen it growing worse every year. Mediterranean trade was being ruined by the Turks.

A bad lot, those Moslems. The Arab traders in Egypt were bad enough, but the Turks were worse. They had captured Constantinople. Soon they would be trying to drive all ships but their own out of the Mediterranean. And what could be done about it? Where would ships go then? How then would good Christian people get their spices from India?

The boy standing on the wharf in Genoa was still too young to answer that question. Years later his answer, though wrong, would lead to an even greater discovery.

GALLEY

Another boy also born in Genoa, just a year older than Columbus, was to have the same answer—that ships could reach India by sailing west. Giovanni Cabato was his name, John Cabot. Until he was eleven, Giovanni had lived in Genoa; then his father moved to Venice. Young John was soon sailing back and forth across the Mediterranean on one or another of the many Venetian galleys belonging to the merchant fleet. Picking up spices from the Arab traders in various ports, he began to wonder exactly where in India those valuable spices came from, how the Arabs got them, and how they brought them to the Mediterranean.

Years later, John Cabot was to discover and claim for England a northern part of the great new world discovered by Columbus.

TWO PATRONS OF THE RENAISSANCE

ONE DAY in the fall of that year, 1460, when Prince Henry the Navigator died, a wealthy Italian banker, Cosimo de Medici, seventy-one years old, and his favorite grandson Lorenzo, who was eleven, might have been seen leaving the Monastery of San Marco in the city of Florence and walking slowly homeward toward a massive gray stone palace. Their pace was slow, not so much because the old gentleman was slightly lame as that the two were deep in an exciting conversation about Socrates and Plato.

The boy did most of the talking, using his hands in lively fashion and looking up often to his grandfather for a comment or question. The two were great friends, Cosimo de Medici, the unassuming but most powerful citizen of Florence, and the dramatic young Lorenzo de Medici, who was to equal if not excel his grandfather as a patron of art and literature.

About the time that Prince Henry sent out his first explorers,

Florence :~

1 Palazzo Vecchio
2 Piazza
3 Duomo - Cathedral
4 Baptistry
5 San Lorenzo
6 Medici Palace
7 Monastery San Marco

Cosimo de Medici had begun to make Florence a center for rediscovery of the wonderful art and learning of the ancient Greeks. Both this and the discovery of unknown lands were part of a thrilling change taking place in Europe. People were becoming interested again, as the ancient Greeks had been, in the nature of man himself and the marvelous world in which he lived.

For centuries the Church had taught that man's life on earth was but a dismal preparation for his death, a misery to be endured in the hope of Heaven or the fear of Hell. Now, as Europeans discovered the ancient, happier way of thinking, the change was so startling it was like being born again. And so those years in which the change took place were called the Re-birth or the Renaissance.

The boy Lorenzo, who was now entering the palace courtyard with his grandfather, had been brought up in the "new learning." In the center of the marble courtyard, stood a statue of David, made before Lorenzo was born by the sculptor Donatello, who was the age of Cosimo. The statue was especially important because it was

45

the first one made in modern times that could be viewed from all sides, like the ancient ones being discovered in old Roman ruins.

There at the statue the boy and his grandfather parted. Cosimo went to his study on the ground floor. Lorenzo bounded up the flight of marble stairs to the second floor where he was to have a lesson in Greek. His tutor was a Greek scholar, one of many who had fled from Constantinople seven years before, when their city had been captured by the Turks. They brought many rare old books and manuscripts for his grandfather's library, and he had put them all to work copying and translating and teaching.

Now that he was eleven, Lorenzo's training in public affairs was beginning. This summer, for the first time, his grandfather had had him stay in Florence instead of going to their country villa with his mother and sisters and younger brother Giuliano. Other summers he had spent riding horses and playing games. This was another kind of game he was learning, managing people and money.

Grandfather was growing old and tired and needed help. His gout was so painful that he often had to rest in the Monastery of San Marco. This morning after two days' rest he felt ready to cope with whatever foreign affairs needed his attention. The King of France, or England, or some other ruler of Europe, might be asking to borrow money for one of their never-ending wars.

Power lay in money and the clever use of it, Lorenzo could see that, and he knew that his grandfather used his money not to make war but to keep peace among the city-states of Italy. Once when Venice had threatened to attack Milan, he had loaned his good friend, Francesco Sforza, enough money to defend Milan and gain control of the Duchy. Another time when Venice and Naples combined against Florence, he called in so many loans made to men of those cities that they had no money to carry out their plot.

And who would do it when he was gone? That was what Cosimo de Medici often thought as he talked with Lorenzo, who was so bright, so gifted, but so young. Piero, the boy's father, was capable but he was an invalid and might not live until Lorenzo was old enough to manage.

Four years passed. Lorenzo was fifteen, spending another summer in Florence. Both his father and grandfather were in the country villa, both very ill. His father recovered, but on August 1, 1464, Lorenzo heard that his grandfather was gone. Piero was still too ill to come to Florence, so the boy took charge of all arrangements for the funeral. The Signoria, or City Council, had planned a magnificent ceremony, but Lorenzo told them that his grandfather had requested that the service be very simple and quiet. So it was. But a special honor was accorded the man who had directed the affairs of Florence and kept it peaceful and prosperous for so many years. On his tomb in the Church of San Lorenzo was engraved in Latin the words meaning, "Cosimo Medici lies here declared by public decree the father of his country."

COSIMUS MEDICI HIC SITUS EST DECRETO
PUBLICO PATER PATRIAE

Hardly was Cosimo de Medici in his grave than plots were being formed by other rich men of Florence to kill Piero, banish the family, and take over the enviable position of power. Young Lorenzo detected a conspiracy headed by Luca Pitti just in time to send a warning to his father and save him from being murdered. The Signoria passed a death sentence on the ringleaders, but Piero refused to have it carried out and merely had them banished from Florence. By his forgiveness he made his enemy a friend for life, and the Medici position stronger than ever in the government of Florence. By this act he also won the admiration of his son Lorenzo who made the wise remark that, "Only he knows how to conquer who knows how to forgive."

And so, although Florence was still called a Republic, Piero, like his father Cosimo, became the absolute ruler of Florence in everything but name.

GOZZOLI

BOTTICELLI SELF PORTRAIT

EARLY FLORENTINE ARTISTS

AS A THANK OFFERING for his narrow escape, Piero commissioned a painting for the church of Santa Maria Novella to be made by a young artist, Sandro Botticelli, whom he had invited to live as one of the family in the Medici Palace. Botticelli was just five years older than Lorenzo.

The painting which he made was called the "Adoration of the Magi," and was really a painting of the Medici family, showing Cosimo, Piero, and the young hero Lorenzo, as he is shown here, leaning on his sword.

Young Lorenzo was also shown as one of the Three Kings, riding through a fabulously beautiful land, in a painting by Gozzoli, ordered by Piero for the chapel walls of the Medici Palace.

DAVID BY DONATELLO

FRA ANGELICO: THE ANNUNCIATION

The old sculptor Donatello died in December, 1466. Piero was sad to hear that he was gone—the last of those great artists who had been friends of his father Cosimo.

There was Brunelleschi, who had designed the great Duomo;

Ghiberti, who had spent a lifetime on the magnificent bronze doors of the Baptistry;

Fra Angelico, who had decorated the Monastery of San Marco which Cosimo had built for the Dominican friars.

Donatello's last request had been that he might be buried near his lifelong friend and patron, Cosimo de Medici. Piero saw that his tomb was placed in the crypt of San Lorenzo. Almost the whole city of Florence walked in his funeral procession.

Among those who mourned was a former pupil, Verrochio, who was both a sculptor and a painter and who himself had just taken a pupil who would prove to be one of the most versatile and gifted men the world has ever known. He was a boy of fourteen by the name of Leonardo, who had been born in the little hamlet of Vinci not far from Florence, and so was called Leonardo da Vinci.

DAVID BY
VERROCCHIO

49

YOUNG LEONARDO

O N THE FIRST MORNING that young Leonardo came to the
studio with his father, Verrochio must have been struck
with amazement. Could this be his new pupil, or was it
young Apollo who had just stepped down from Mount Olympus?
Or had he come to pose for the Archangel Michael? It did not seem
possible that one so talented could also be so beautiful. Later Verrochio was to use Leonardo as a model for his statue of David.

Verrochio had already seen samples of the boy's work. Leonardo's father, Ser Piero da Vinci, who was a notary, had brought a
sheaf of his son's drawings to get an expert's opinion of the boy's
ability. He was anxious that Leonardo should be educated in that
for which he was best fitted. His own profession, the law, did not
seem to appeal to the boy, nor was he drawn to reading the classic
authors. In all the creative arts and sciences he showed a marked

50

interest and did everything easily and well. In mathematics, for example, he made such progress that after a few months his tutor confessed that he was dumbfounded by his questions. From the time he was a small boy he had stood spellbound by water wheels and mills, levers, cranes, and winches, with endless curiosity as to how they worked. He was always drawing everything he saw, although none of his drawings satisfied him. He would work hard on something, then look at it, turning his head this way and that, and then tear it up and begin over again.

What to do with this versatile boy was a problem. Unable to decide, Ser Piero had brought the drawings to Verrochio. Upon the master's encouragement he had signed the usual papers for Leonardo to become an apprentice in Verrochio's studio.

One of the first practice drawings Leonardo did was a study of folds and draperies on a seated figure. He first modeled the small figure in clay, then dipped a piece of cloth in thin plaster, arranged the wet cloth in folds, and when it dried and hardened, made a drawing of it with a fine pointed brush.

One of the first real assignments was to draw a cartoon, or pattern, of Adam and Eve in the Garden of Eden. This was for a tapestry to be woven in Flanders and sent to Alfonso V of Portugal.

In a busy studio like Verrochio's it was customary for an apprentice to fill in the background or even a minor figure in a painting begun by the master. Some time after Leonardo was with him, Verrochio was at work on a painting of the Baptism of Christ. Having done the two figures of Jesus and John the Baptist, he asked Leonardo to paint the kneeling angel in the lower corner and fill in the landscape, while he turned to some other commission.

Leonardo's angel was so superior to the figures that Verrochio had done himself that he saw at once that his pupil had surpassed him. As the story goes, he vowed he would paint no more, and from then on turned to his real forte, which was sculpture.

THE MEDICIS ADD A LILY

PIERO DE MEDICI conferred continually with his young son Lorenzo, especially on foreign affairs and matters of diplomacy. One day there was a letter to be answered from the King of France, Louis XI, to whom Cosimo had loaned vast sums of money, long overdue, and which the King could not, or did not care to repay at that time, though he made no mention of it. He began his epistle by addressing Piero, a man of middle class, as "Cousin," a term used by Kings only in addressing others of royal blood, a neat bit of flattery. Then he announced that he was conferring upon the Medici family the honorable distinction of adding the French fleur de lis to their coat of arms. That was all. But the spidery cunning paid off. The Medici, as he expected, considered the tinge of royalty worth the price of canceling the loan.

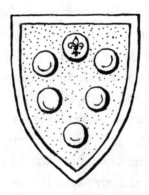

THE "SPIDER KING"

THIS IS LOUIS XI, who became King of France when he was thirty-eight years old and already more or less set in his odd ways. Though so sly and wily in his doings as to be called "the Spider" by his enemies, he was nevertheless a statesman and one of the most important kings in French history. For he actually formed the modern nation of France, by subduing the old feudal lords and uniting their lands under the crown.

Richest, most independent and powerful of those feudal lords was the Duke of Burgundy, Philip the Good, who far outshone the King at his coronation.

This took place in 1461 in the Cathedral at Rheims. In honor of the occasion, Louis, not one for needless display, did go so far as to get himself a velvet bonnet and coat and breeches of red and white satin. Usually he went about in an old pointed felt cap and gray dusty clothes like those of a pilgrim. Actually he did often make a pilgrimage to one of the famous shrines as he was very superstitious about the power of bones, teeth, hair and other relics of the saints, as well as intensely religious.

The night before the coronation he prayed in the cathedral from midnight until five in the morning. By nine o'clock he was back again on his knees before the high altar. There he remained until the sound of trumpets announced the arrival of the Abbot bearing the sacred oil with which he was to be anointed. Louis then rose and the solemn service began.

First, the Duke of Burgundy came forward, magnificent in cloth of gold and sparkling with jewels. He knelt and swore his allegiance. He was followed by the Duke of Brittany. These two great feudal lords were still completely independent. They were followed by the lesser peers who, each in turn, knelt, kissed the hand of the King, and swore allegiance as vassals of their royal lord.

The Archbishop then took the cruet of sacred oil and anointed the body of the King, who had been stripped to the waist. After this, wearing a sweeping robe of blue velvet embroidered in fleur de lis and carrying the scepter, Louis was escorted to the throne. The Duke of Burgundy again stepped forward, took the heavy gold crown, raised it high in both hands, held it a moment, then lowered it gently onto the now divinely royal head of Louis XI.

"Vive le Roy," cried the Duke in a loud voice, and through the crowded cathedral resounded echoing cries, "Vive le Roy," followed by the deafening blare of trumpets and the ringing of many bells.

In the coronation oath Louis had sworn to unite the parts of France into one nation. To him those were not just empty words. He had meant what he said, and was impatient to be about it—too impatient. So he was in for trouble.

In the first years of his reign, the new king started overly brash and hasty action against the feudal lords, not yet having perfected the technique of gaining his ends with cunning instead of force. The feudal lords, determined to preserve their old independence, took up arms against him, led by Charles the Bold, the new Duke of Burgundy.

Charles the Bold, a very different man from his genial father Philip, was an out-and-out warrior, reckless, daring, and fiercely ambitious. Although he owned all the rich and prosperous Netherlands, as well as Burgundy, he was not satisfied, but meant to seize another rich piece of French land. Charles was constantly on the warpath, and Louis had to be ever on guard against him.

England presented another problem for the French King. Louis had to keep a sharp eye on England. He meant to see that the English did not come back and start war on France as they had done off and on for the past hundred years. Louis had been eight years old when they burned Joan of Arc, after she had helped to crown his father. He was thirty in 1453, when the English had finally given up trying to conquer France and had gone home defeated. Since then they had been fighting at home among themselves.

This suited Louis to perfection since it kept them too busy to think about France. Louis' own cousin, Henry VI, had been King of England when the fighting started, but he had lost his throne, which made no difference to Louis. He did not care a whit who was King of England, so long as he left France alone. Whenever it looked as though this useful fighting in England might possibly be slowing down, Louis intended to give it a judicious poke here and there and get it started up again.

England : The Plantagenets

Edward III

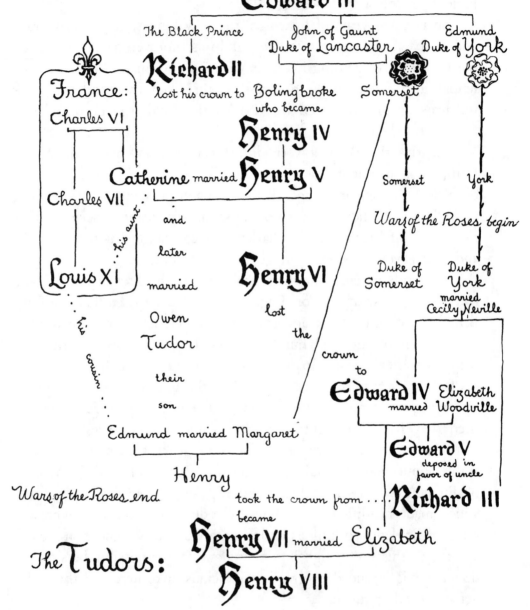

The Black Prince   John of Gaunt
Duke of Lancaster   Edmund
Duke of York

Richard II
lost his crown to   Boling broke
who became   Somerset

France:
Charles VI

Henry IV

Catherine married **Henry V**

Charles VII

and

later

Somerset   York

Wars of the Roses begin

Louis XI

married

Owen

Henry VI

Duke of
Somerset

Duke of
York
married
Cecily Neville

Tudor

their

son

lost

the

crown

to

Edward IV Elizabeth
married Woodville

Edmund married Margaret

Edward V
deposed in
favor of uncle

Henry

Wars of the Roses end   took the crown from . . . . **Richard III**

became

The Tudors:

Henry VII married Elizabeth

Henry VIII

THE WARS OF THE ROSES BEGIN

THE FIGHTING in England, which began when the English retreated from France, was to last for thirty years, up to 1485. It was a feud between two branches of the Plantagenet family —the House of Lancaster and the House of York—fighting for the crown. Since the white rose was the badge of York and the red rose the badge of Lancaster, it came to be known as the Wars of the Roses. It was a wild, crazy, treasonous business and in the end neither side won. After the final battle there was not a soul left on either side of the royal family to wear the crown.

Henry VI, the King who saw the wars begin, belonged to the House of Lancaster as did his Prime Minister, the Duke of Somerset.

To start it off, the Duke of York, a beefy, square-faced man of action, accused the Duke of Somerset of having lost the war in

France, either through treason or plain stupidity. He also claimed that by all that was good and holy, he should be King instead of Henry VI, whose grandfather had seized the crown and then forced Parliament to accept him.

The Duke of Somerset was furious at the Duke of York. The King was completely bewildered.

Henry VI, poor kind soul, as good and gentle a man as ever lived, had been king for thirty years. He failed to understand why now, after all these years, his right should be questioned.

"Why? Why?" he queried. "My father was King. His father before him was King. I have worn the crown from my cradle. How then can my claim to it be disputed?" This he could not understand.

Soon after his one and only son was born he completely lost his mind. He was talking with the Bishop about Eton College, which he had founded, when all of a sudden he could not speak. Doctors were called at once. They applied every known remedy, but with no result. The poor King remained insane for two years. During that time, the Duke of Somerset sat in prison while his rival, the Duke of York, acted as Regent and ruled the realm. Two years later Henry suddenly recovered his senses, and the tables were turned. Somerset was released from prison, and Henry VI was back on his throne.

The Duke of York, stripped of his power, rode home to his castle in Yorkshire to his wife, the Duchess Cecily, and their family of children. They were eight in number, from Edward who was thirteen down to three-year-old Richard. The older children were away, being brought up at other castles according to English custom, but the Duke enjoyed the younger ones in his hearty fashion, holding his youngest and prettiest daughter, nine-year-old Margaret, on his broad knee. Then with a farewell hug and kiss around the family circle, the Duke was off again—to war.

At the head of his private army of Yorkshiremen, he was soon galloping south toward the city of London. At the same time, galloping north out of London came the army of Lancaster, headed by the Duke of Somerset. The two armies met head-on with a crash of arms in the first battle of the war, near the town of St. Albans. The Duke of Somerset was killed.

The Duke of York then appeared before Parliament and bluntly demanded the crown. Dressed in a crimson doublet, he stepped up and laid a hand firmly on the throne reserved for the King.

That was too much for the Earl of Warwick. Warwick, the richest and most powerful earl in England, was a nephew of the Duchess Cecily, and up to this time had been his uncle's most loyal supporter. Now he was shocked by the Duke's demand.

"Neither the Lords nor the people will allow you to strip the King of his crown," Warwick said later, glaring down at the older man, who glared back so fiercely that it was obvious something had to be done to pacify him.

The Earl of Warwick therefore went to the King to arrange a compromise. Henry VI meekly agreed that if he were allowed to finish out his reign undisturbed, after his death the crown should go either to the Duke of York or to his son Edward.

Queen Marguerite, mother of the royal prince, was in a towering rage to think that Henry had allowed his own son and heir to be set aside. Being as fiery and high-spirited as the King was meek and mild, she rallied the forces of Lancaster, who met the forces of York near Wakefield and defeated them in a bloody battle. The Duke of York was killed. The Queen had his head cut off, crowned with a paper crown, and stuck up on a pike over the main gate of his own city of York.

Edward, eighteen, a golden-haired young giant, six feet four, now became the Duke of York. He carried on the war to avenge the death of his father and secure the throne for himself, and was highly successful. He won a decisive battle, and with the help of his cousin, the Earl of Warwick, who was to be known as "The King Maker" in this War of the Roses, he became Edward IV.

ENTER EDWARD IV

NINE-YEAR-OLD RICHARD was in the Netherlands when he heard the exciting news that his big brother Edward had been declared King by his cousin, the Earl of Warwick. After their father's death, the Duchess Cecily had sent her young sons, Richard and his brother George, out of the country to be under the care of the Duke of Burgundy where they would be safe. Now she wrote that Henry VI and Queen Marguerite had fled to Scotland; their brother was King. The happy boys, loaded with gifts, sailed for home to be there for the coronation, which took place on June 27, 1461. That was a wonderful day for Richard who rode in the procession from the Tower of London to Westminster Abbey.

A frail, undersized, serious little boy, Richard worshiped his big, handsome brother Edward who was everything he longed to be. In all of his nine years, the most thrilling day came when the new King Edward IV girded him with a sword and kissed him, saying, "Be thou a good Knight," and he had become a Knight of the Bath, a

Knight of the Garter, and also the Duke of Gloucester. Richard had chosen for his motto, "Loyalty binds me," and wanted more than anything else in the world to become a good knight and gain the approval of his wonderful brother. Six months later, his training in knighthood began.

On a November day Richard, astride a rather large horse, was approaching the huge gray stone walls and towers of Middleham Castle which belonged to the Earl of Warwick. He was about to enter his cousin's household to be trained in knightly courtesy and also to learn how to fight, since war was the actual business of a knight.

Other boys were also at the castle for training, as well as the Countess of Warwick and her daughters. The Earl had no son, just two little girls, one, Richard's age, and one who was five, a shy, pale little wisp of a thing with sad brown eyes whose name was Anne. At home Richard had played with his sister Margaret, or "Meg," who called him "Dickon." Meg was now fifteen, old enough to be married. And he, Richard, had no more time to play with girls; he was too busy learning to be a knight.

Even for boys who were strong and athletic, it was strenuous work to handle a sword, dagger, and massive battle-ax. For Richard, encased in a heavy armor of steel, it was little short of torture, but day by day he gritted his teeth and endured it.

The boys' day began at dawn when they rose, went to mass, and then broke fast with meat, bread, and ale. Studies came next—some Latin and French, a little law, mathematics, music, and penmanship. At half past nine there was a second breakfast. Then the boys went to the tiltyard where they practiced jousting, using long wooden lances, running at each other first on foot, then on horseback. At noon they struggled out of their armor to prepare for dinner in the Great Hall. As pages they had to wait on the lords, carrying ewers and trenchers, and cups of wine held above their heads so as not to breathe upon it. In the afternoon there was hunting, hawking, riding over the moors for stag or wild boar. Supper came at four or five, then a couple of hours of singing and dancing, after which Richard, for one, tumbled into bed exhausted.

The Earl of Warwick, himself, was almost never there. He was away with Edward IV, trying to subdue the still rebellious lords of Lancaster, who were unwilling to accept their defeat, and were determined to bring back the old King Henry VI.

Queen Marguerite, also determined to see her husband back upon his throne, had left King Henry waiting in Scotland and sailed for France to get help for him from his cousin, Louis XI.

During her absence, Henry foolishly crossed the border into England, was captured by men of York and taken prisoner to the Tower of London. So he was safely out of the way.

The possibility that Queen Marguerite might get help from the King of France looked like serious trouble both to the Earl of Warwick and Edward IV, but they disagreed on what to do about it. Edward favored making an alliance with Charles the Bold, Duke of Burgundy. Warwick, who was confident that he alone knew how to run the country and manage the King, proposed outsmarting

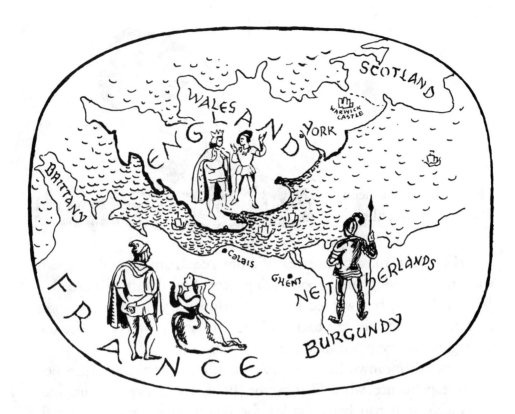

that "vile creature," Queen Marguerite, by going to France himself and making an alliance with Louis XI. This he did and as he hoped, the King of France proved agreeable to his proposition, provided that England, in return, saw fit to help him against the Duke of Burgundy. To seal the bargain, they agreed that a young relative of Louis XI should marry Edward IV. The Earl was elated with his success and rushed back to London to make his report to the King and the Council. Then came a shocking surprise.

The King was already married!

Now it all came out. On May 1, 1464, in a hunting lodge, Edward IV had secretly married Dame Elizabeth Woodville! Caught by her charm, he had married a widow five years older than he, who had two sons and a swarm of poor relatives trailing after her.

Warwick was horrified. He stalked off in such a furious mixture of rage, disgust, and humiliation as to turn a white rose red, and a good friend into a traitor.

This is the new Queen,
Elizabeth Woodville.

King Edward, growing yearly more good-natured and easygoing with much loving and good living, was not overly disturbed by Warwick's fury, but wanted to avoid an open break with his stormy cousin. So he let him go back to France to see what Louis would be willing to do, even without the marriage.

Edward, meanwhile, quite able to think for himself, had been in correspondence with Charles the Bold, the Duke of Burgundy. Warwick's ship had barely sailed for France when a ship from the Netherlands sailed into the Thames, bringing a half-brother of Charles the Bold to take part in a tournament. His opponent, equally skilled in the art of jousting, was Lord Rivers, a brother of the Queen —one of those numerous Woodville relatives.

It was a gala occasion with people streaming out from London to the grandstands, bright with flying flags and banners. The King appeared, clothed in purple, accompanied by Chancellors, knights, esquires, and his youngest Knight of the Garter, his brother Richard, who was then fifteen. At the sound of the trumpets, the two experts in the deadly art rode onto the field, and contended violently until, as the chronicler reported, "It became so perilous that the King in a high voice cried 'Whoa!' and brought it to an end."

The tournament thus concluded was not an end in itself; it was the celebration of a far more important event, the betrothal of the King's sister, lovely Margaret of York, to Charles the Bold, the Duke of Burgundy.

Mary of Burgundy

THE BRIDE AND THE PRINTER

CHARLES THE BOLD, Duke of Burgundy, was a widower who had no interest whatsoever in taking another wife. All he cared about were war, conquest, and power. He sent his mother and his daughter Mary, a dear young girl of eleven, to meet his bride when she arrived. Both found the new Duchess young, exquisite, and completely charming. Even the surly Charles was taken with her, in spite of himself. And the young bride, to everyone's amazement, seemed to find a way to temper the Duke's harsh nature, as no one else had ever been able to do.

The Duchess Margaret made a place for herself at once in the court of Burgundy, and captured the heart of her little stepdaughter Mary who was herself engaged to be married. Her father, possessed with the ambition to be a king instead of a duke, had approached the German Emperor Frederick III, who could bestow that title, and had arranged that his Mary should later marry the Emperor's eleven-year-old son Maximilian, the Archduke of Austria.

65

One person who was most happy over the treaty which brought Margaret of York to the Court of Burgundy was William Caxton, an English merchant living in Bruges who was to become known as England's first printer.

Shortly after the Wars of the Roses began, William Caxton had been sent as an ambassador to the Netherlands to look after the interests of the many English wool merchants living there, and to straighten out their difficulties with the Flemish weavers, who bought great quantities of wool from England for their famous tapestries.

This new treaty, sealed by the Duke's marriage, had settled so many of William Caxton's former worries that it had left him, he was pleased to say, "with no great charge of occupation."

Now he could browse to his heart's content in the Duke's library poring over the gorgeously illuminated manuscripts and books. One day he came upon a popular French romance laid in ancient Troy. "To

66

eschew sloth and idleness," as he put it, William Caxton began translating it from French into English.

Copying it by hand he found so tedious and so hard on his eyes that he gave it up for a time, until the Duchess Margaret urged him to finish it for her.

By that time he had learned of the German way of reproducing books by machine, and had heard that a printer who had learned the trade in Mainz had set up a shop in the city of Cologne. Soon Caxton went off to learn the new art. Three years later he returned to Bruges and set up a press of his own. With the help of a famous scribe, Colard Mansion, he designed and cut the first English type, a very black letter known as Old English. The first English book ever printed was Caxton's own translation of the story of Troy which he had copied for the Duchess. He sent a copy to Edward IV's Queen, Elizabeth Woodville, which contained this engraving showing him, William Caxton, presenting two volumes to his young patron, the Duchess Margaret.

Margaret had been in Bruges less than two years when two refugees from England arrived in a fishing smack—her two brothers, Edward and Richard.

Edward had lost his throne!

Betrayed on all sides, he had fled for safety to his sister and his ally, the Duke of Burgundy.

The Earl of Warwick, their cousin, had turned traitor!

It was true. Warwick, who had declared Edward IV King, had

gone over to Lancaster and acted as "King Maker" again; this time for his former enemy, Henry VI. This strange alliance was the clever work of Louis XI, King of France, who was no more pleased than Warwick over the marriage between England and Burgundy.

Queen Marguerite was still there at the French court when Warwick arrived, utterly furious with Edward. It was plain to Louis what might well be achieved with a bit of flattery. Addressing the Earl as "Prince" to begin with, he gradually led Warwick to join hands with the lady whom he had considered his "most vilest enemy," Queen Marguerite, who had been previously charmed by Louis into embracing the hated Earl. So the former enemies had combined forces and arranged for the marriage of their children, Anne, Warwick's sad-eyed little daughter, and the royal prince.

Warwick, then, had returned to England and, at the head of a Lancastrian army, had taken Edward completely by surprise. The captain of the royal guard had also betrayed the King. His brother George had been bought off by Warwick, the troops had deserted.

Edward had had to leap from his bed into the cold, foggy dawn and literally run for the shore. Closely followed by Richard, he had stumbled onto a small fishing smack and escaped. So there he was, at the Court of Burgundy—Edward, nine years King of England, now deposed. But he would be there only until he could assemble forces enough to fight his way back. It was then the fall of 1470.

Meanwhile in England, King Henry VI was again on the throne, and Warwick had become what he had always aspired to be—the actual ruler of England. He was in his glory.

As for poor gentle Henry! For five years he had enjoyed peace and quiet in the Tower of London, able to read and pray undisturbed. Now he had been dragged back again onto his throne, into the midst of wrangling and confusion, where as he complained, "They do so interrupt me that night or day I can hardly snatch a moment to be refreshed by any holy readings."

YOUNG HENRY TUDOR OF WALES

HENRY TUDOR of Wales was a boy of thirteen in that fall of 1470 when to the great joy of the House of Lancaster, meek, good, gentle Henry VI was restored to his throne by the Earl of Warwick. It was a great day for the tall, blond Welsh lad when he set out with his Uncle Jasper Tudor on a journey to London to pay a visit to the King.

It was the proudest day in the life of his determined little mother, Lady Margaret, who had come from Pembroke Castle to the harbor of Tenby to see them off. Only fourteen when Henry was born, she was still so young and so small that she looked like a little girl as she stood smiling and waving to her son and brother-in-law as they sailed away. Henry was her only child. His father, Edmund Tudor, had died two months before Henry was born. From the moment Margaret saw her son he had been the center of her life, her joy, the apple of her eye.

Henry knew how glad she must be that he was now on his way to meet the King, the head of the House of Lancaster to which she belonged. As long as Henry could remember, his lady mother had been telling him with pride that way back she had the same royal ancestor as the King. Henry's father did not.

The Tudors, she said, did not belong to the English royal family at all, even though his father and Uncle Jasper were half-brothers of the King. That, she explained, was because they had had the same mother. After King Henry's father died, his mother the Queen had secretly married Owen Tudor of Wales, which had caused a great scandal because Owen Tudor was not even a nobleman. Later Henry VI had kindly ennobled his two half-brothers, making Edmund the Earl of Richmond and Jasper the Earl of Pembroke.

Henry had been born in Pembroke Castle, and he and his mother had lived there, in the care of his Uncle Jasper, until the House of Lancaster lost the throne to the House of York and Edward IV had become King. That was 1461, and then for Henry Tudor, who was only four, the whole world had turned topsy-turvy.

Pembroke Castle had been captured and his Uncle Jasper had fled the country. And Henry himself had been hurried from one castle to another in Wales, until all the castles of Lancaster had been captured except Harlech, the strongest of all. And then, when Henry was nine, Harlech Castle fell. The new Duke and Duchess who came to live there took kindly care of Henry, but he knew that he was actually their prisoner.

But now he was free! Now it was 1470; those horrible years were over. The sun shone again on the red rose. The tables had been turned. The Earl of Warwick had changed sides. His daughter Anne had married the Crown Prince. King Henry, after five years as a prisoner in the Tower of London, was once more seated on his throne. Uncle

Jasper had come home from France. And he, Henry Tudor, was on his way to visit the King!

There are many conflicting stories as to where the two Henrys met, and what the gentle, weary King Henry VI said to the strong, good-looking boy of thirteen who, with the help of his determined little mother, was to become Henry VII. As the young Tudor was then so far removed from any claim to the throne it is most unlikely that the King mentioned his ever wearing the crown. It is agreed, however, that Henry VI was impressed by what he called the lad's "wit and likely forwardness."

Only six months later, in March, 1471, the tables had been turned once again. Henry VI had lost his throne, and the House of Lancaster was once more replaced by the House of York. Edward IV and his brother Richard, after six months in Burgundy, had returned with an army to attack their traitorous cousin, the Earl of Warwick.

Warwick had been killed in battle.

The Prince, son of Henry VI, had also died in the battle.

King Henry VI had been taken to the Tower and murdered.

Queen Marguerite had fled back to France.

Jasper Tudor hastened back to Wales.

The only soul left now in the Lancaster family who had any claim whatsoever to the throne was Henry Tudor. Though the claim was slight, Lady Margaret felt it was no longer safe for her boy to remain in Wales. She insisted that his Uncle Jasper take Henry overseas and find a refuge for him with Louis XI in France. Once more the tiny figure of Lady Margaret was to be seen standing on the pier at Tenby, waving farewell to her son, her heart filled with anxiety until she should hear that he was safely across the Channel.

Weeks later she heard that winds had blown his ship off its course, and Henry had landed not in France, but in Brittany. There for thirteen years Henry Tudor was to be kept under strict guard by the Duke of Brittany, well paid for doing so, by Edward IV.

ISABELLA CHOOSES FERDINAND

IN SPAIN, as in England, there was also a lull in the actual fighting between the King and his enemies, but no end to the scheming and plotting among the contentious nobles of Castile. Henry the King, and the lords who supported him, and his daughter Joanna were waiting for any excuse to take up arms against the Archbishop of Toledo and those nobles who supported Isabella.

On September 9, 1468, however, a truce had been signed, because Isabella insisted upon it. Even though the over-zealous partisans wanted to keep on fighting to the finish in her behalf, she insisted on making peace with her brother Henry.

Henry, not at all sure he might not be thrown from his throne, as his straw image had been hurled to the ground at Avila, was ready to make almost any concession, so long as he was assured of being King so long as he lived. This was granted, but the terms imposed on him were so humiliating that it is difficult to believe anyone expected him to keep them.

He was forced to divorce his wife, send her home to her brother Alfonso, the King of Portugal. He had to declare his, or her, daughter Joanna illegitimate, set aside any claim for her, and declare his half-sister Isabella his legitimate heir to the throne. He also had to agree that Isabella was not to be married against her will, but might choose her own husband, subject to his approval and the consent of nobles of the realm.

Choosing a husband for Isabella had been going on for years. When she was ten, Henry had selected one who was forty years old, Prince Carlos of Aragon. Prince Carlos had died suddenly, probably of poison. This was due, many believed, to the ambition of his scheming stepmother, the Queen of Aragon, who had her own nine-year-old son, Ferdinand, in mind for Isabella.

Henry did not favor Ferdinand.

Henry's next choice was his brother-in-law, Joanna's uncle, King Alfonso of Portugal. Alfonso was the nephew of Prince Henry the Navigator, who had gained the title of "El Africano" for his bravery in fighting the Moors in North Africa. Alfonso was a widower with a son, John, almost as old as Isabella, but what of that? Henry intended that Isabella should marry him, and regarded the matter as settled.

Alfonso, equally confident and elated by the prospect, sent a magnificent embassy headed by the Archbishop of Lisbon to arrange a betrothal. The Princess flatly refused to consider it.

"An Infanta of Castile cannot be disposed of in marriage without the consent of the nobles of the realm," said Isabella, knowing that there were many nobles who would not consent. Most important among them was the Archbishop of Toledo.

Ferdinand of Aragon was the Archbishop's choice. Isabella had liked what she had heard about Ferdinand. A messenger whom she had sent secretly to Aragon to see him reported that the Prince was a "very proper man with a comely visage and a brave spirit."

Henry was so enraged at Isabella for refusing to marry Alfonso that he threatened to imprison her in the fortress at Madrid until she consented. But the common people sided with the Princess. They paraded the streets with Aragon banners and sang ribald songs contrasting the widower of Portugal with the young Prince of Aragon.

All this was before Henry had been forced to make peace with Isabella. As heir to the throne, she instantly became more valuable property and suitors popped up in every country.

Richard, Duke of Gloucester, brother of King Edward of England, was one of them. Richard, who was just the age of Ferdinand, offered to come to live in Castile, if Isabella would have him as her royal husband.

The King of France, Louis XI, proposed his brother, the Duke of Guienne, sending as his ambassador, a French Cardinal famous for his oratory. Isabella was ready for him. She knew all about the French candidate. The same messenger she had sent to Aragon had also gone secretly to France. He reported that the Duke was "weak and feeble with watery eyes and limbs so skinny as to be almost deformed." Isabella listened politely, however, while the Cardinal praised the Duke as a model of charm and grace. Then she dismissed France with the same firm legitimate excuse that she had given Portugal.

Having made her decision, Isabella sent another secret messenger to the King of Aragon to arrange a betrothal with Ferdinand. The marriage contract was signed at Cervera near Barcelona on the seventh of January, 1469.

Isabella had then gone to stay with her mother in Madrigal. Soon she learned that Henry had sent word that any help given to Isabella would be punished as treason, followed shortly by orders for her to be seized by force and taken into custody. Somehow, the determined girl managed to get word to her good friend, the Archbishop of Toledo. He hastened to the rescue and carried Isabella off to the loyal city of Valladolid. From there messengers were sent to Ferdinand bidding him come at once or all would be lost.

The moment word came from Isabella, Ferdinand was ready to start. This marriage was his chance to get his hands on the throne of Castile, a much larger kingdom than that of Aragon. He did not mean to lose this chance, nor did his royal parents who had struggled to bring about the marriage.

In a matter of days, plans were complete for his departure. Secrecy was all-important, since the border was being guarded. Six knights, disguised as traders, went with the Prince. Ferdinand was dressed as their servant, sleeping in the stable with the mules at each inn where they spent the night. On October 15th, travel-stained and dirty, but safe, he was near enough to Valladolid to send word to Isabella. At midnight there came a pounding on the castle door. The massive door swung open in the torchlight, to reveal the Prince and four servants.

"Ese es. Ese es. It is he!" cried one of the courtiers.

The Archbishop of Toledo, roused from his bed to welcome the young man, suggested that he wait until morning to see Isabella. The impatient Prince brushed the suggestion aside. So Isabella was awakened, hastily dressed, and saw for the first time the young man she had heard and thought so much about. There he stood—Ferdinand of Aragon. A sturdy young man with swarthy face and brown hair, not quite so tall as she—this was the husband she had chosen for herself, and to whom she was to be a devoted and loving wife for the rest of her life.

On October 19, 1469, the Archbishop of Toledo performed the marriage ceremony of Ferdinand and Isabella, uniting Aragon and Castile, the first step toward a united Spain.

Ferdinand was seventeen—Isabella, eighteen.

THE YEAR that Isabella was married, Christopher Columbus was also eighteen. That year, 1469, or the next, it is believed he made his first real voyage on an armed galley or galleass, owned by his native city of Genoa. Genoa owned so many of these armed galleys that foreign rulers often engaged both the ships and the brave Genoese soldiers to fight their battles for them. It was on such a mission that Columbus was enlisted.

"It happened to me," he wrote later when he had become an Admiral, "that King René (whom God hath taken) sent me to Tunis to capture the galleass Fernandina."

This sounds as though Columbus had been the captain which, of course, was impossible.

"King" René was actually the Duke of Anjou, ruler of Provence. René often chartered Genoese galleys to defend Provence against the Moorish pirates of North Africa. In 1469 he was at war with the King of Aragon. Therefore, as the galleass to be captured was named the Fernandina, it most surely belonged to the King of Aragon, whose son Ferdinand had just married the future friend of Columbus, the Princess Isabella.

René was the father of the former Queen Marguerite of England. After the death of her husband and son, her ransom of 50,000 crowns had been paid by Louis XI and Marguerite had gone home to Provence. In return for all the help he had given her, the wily "Spider" demanded that she give up the rights to the inheritance of her father. So that was how Provence was added to Louis XI's ever-growing nation of France.

from Botticelli's "Primavera"

PERPETUAL HOLIDAY IN FLORENCE

ONE FINE DAY in June, 1469, just four months before the simple wedding of Ferdinand and Isabella, for which they themselves had to borrow the money, a most costly and elaborate wedding had taken place in Florence. The whole city was decorated; every street, shop, and gateway was bright with flags and banners for the wedding of Lorenzo de Medici.

The bride, Clarice Orsini of Rome, had been carefully chosen by Lorenzo's parents. As his father, Piero, was far from well, Lorenzo's mother had gone to Rome, to "look closely at the girl," before they signed the final contract. She had written her husband that she could see no fault in the young lady, save shyness, and that "she does not carry her head as proudly as our girls do, but pokes it forward a little."

Young Lorenzo did not care at all how Clarice carried her head or what she looked like. If she suited his parents he would marry her. He could not be bothered to think about her. He was much too busy having a gay time with his brother, their friends, and the pretty girls

77

of Florence, especially his sweetheart, darling Lucrezia Donati.

Since December, when he had been married by proxy in Rome, Lorenzo's mother-in-law, the Countess Orsini, had been urging him to come to Rome and honor them with a visit. He had had to keep thinking up excuses why he could not get away.

The tournament in February was far too gay and exciting ever to have been missed. He had worn the colors of Lucrezia and she had crowned him with a chaplet of violets. Every month, every week, every day, there was something too joyful to lose in thinking about the future. Lorenzo put his happy thinking into verse:

> "Dance and play
> In the future come what may
> Youths and maids enjoy today
> Naught ye know about tomorrow
> Fair is youth and void of sorrow
> ...keep perpetual holiday."

So in perpetual holiday six months rolled by and Lorenzo did not get to Rome, before Clarice Orsini, who was prim and proud and rather dull, arrived in Florence for the wedding. Though she did not approve of unbridled hilarity, she was pleased to be the center of proper wedding festivities.

For days handsome gifts had been pouring into the Medici Palace. Wagonloads of produce had been coming in from the country —meats, wines, vegetables, fruits, and sweets to be distributed among the common people when the feasting began. There were five formal banquets for the invited guests, at which tons of sugar plums and hundreds of casks of wine were consumed.

Clarice sat among the young ladies. Lorenzo dined with the young men. The older people sat apart where they could hear and watch the music and the dancing. The ceremonies started off with an exhibition of dancing in front of the Medici Palace, after which an olive tree, symbol of a peaceful marriage, was hoisted into an upper window, with many cheers and good wishes.

THE NEW RULER

Lorenzo's wedding mass was celebrated in the Medici Church of San Lorenzo. Six months later friends and relatives returned for the funeral services of Lorenzo's father Piero, who died on December 3, 1469. During Piero's last illness, everyone had been worried about the future government of Florence—everyone, that is, except young Lorenzo, the future ruler, himself.

Aside from the grief of seeing his father suffer and die, Lorenzo was composed and self-confident. To his great good fortune a powerful kinsman, Tommaso Soderini, who had been urged to assume control, remained loyal to Lorenzo and persuaded the heads of the powerful Florentine families to follow his lead.

"The second day after my father's funeral," Lorenzo wrote, "the principal men of the city and of the state came to our house to condole with us on our loss and to encourage me to take care of the city and state as my father and grandfather had done... I consented to it unwillingly but I did so in order to protect our friends and our property; for it fares ill in Florence with any one who possesses wealth without any control in the government."

Lorenzo might have been unwilling at first because he hated to use time for work that might have been more happily spent in writing poetry, discussing Plato, visiting painters' and sculptors' studios, hunting and horse racing, or just dancing and singing songs. But Lorenzo wanted everything that life had to offer and that included power.

Lorenzo loved power, and he showed at once that he knew how to handle it and how to keep it.

"The new ruler of a government must make his position secure within the first four days," he said, and proceeded to do so.

First he called in his most powerful rivals for conferences and overwhelmed them with honors, sending one or more of them on some very special mission to a faraway court. This got them out of Florence, and also increased the reputation of his government at those foreign courts. Though he often traveled himself, he always returned to Florence to supervise the drawing of names for the Signoria. The Signoria, or Council, was made up of eight tradesmen and merchants, and was changed every two months. At every inauguration he gave a speech of welcome to the "magnificent and illustrious" newly elected members, and a celebration in their honor of horse races and dancing on the Piazza.

As for the average workmen of Florence, Lorenzo did not believe as Plato did, that they were interested in government—unless it interfered with their happiness. So he planned more amusements for them, and better ones. Even though many friends told him the common people wanted only coarse, rough, slapstick and horse play, he believed they would appreciate and respond to something better.

Every feast day he gave them beautiful pageants and tournaments. For months ahead he had artists designing elaborate floats and costumes, and poets writing verses and composing music to be sung. Beautiful girls posing as Venus and Aphrodite rode in chariots or on the backs of horses dressed in the skins of lion and tigers, led by Hercules or Apollo, and accompanied by groups of singers and dancers. It was like a festival in ancient Athens, the Golden Age brought to life again in Florence. That is how Lorenzo thought of Florence—as the center of a Golden Age, a lighthearted city of art, learning, love, and laughter. For one of the tournaments he took as his motto, "Le tiem revient," the time returns, as Spring returns after a long winter.

Botticelli expressed the idea in a famous painting made for Lorenzo, called the "Primavera," or "Return of Spring." Botticelli had just opened his own studio, and was seeing much of Verrochio's former pupil, Leonardo da Vinci, whose name was enrolled for the first time in the year 1472 in the famous Red Book listing the painters of Florence.

That year, also, an Italian goldsmith brought into Florence a queer machine from Germany for making books. He cast his own type, set up shop, but printed only one book.

No one in Florence, certainly not Lorenzo, had any use for an ugly book made by machine. He took pride in his beautiful hand-lettered, illuminated books. They were works of art on which he spent thousands of ducats a year. If everyone could get books for little or nothing, what would books be worth?

And if books were printed by machine, what would copyists, scribes, illuminators, do for a living? They would be out of work.

Oh, no. Lorenzo was not interested in this machine for turning out inferior books, "made among the barbarians of some German city" in the backwoods.

ANOTHER ROME, ANOTHER CEASAR

IVAN III, the Grand Duke of Muscovy, was the first Russian to take upon himself the ancient time-honored Roman title of Caesar (or Tsar), though the idea did not originate with Ivan. It was suggested to him by a plump, strong-minded little woman named Zoë, or Sophia Palaeologus, who became his second wife.

In 1472 Sophia, with chests full to bursting with beautiful clothes and jewels, was leaving Italy for the practically unknown land of Muscovy on the border of Asia. She was going to marry the ruler of Muscovy, of whom she knew nothing except that he belonged to the Greek Orthodox Church. That, to her, was enough.

IVAN III

Zoë Palaeologus was Greek. Her uncle had been the last emperor of Constantinople, Constantine XI, who had died so bravely defending the city where she had been born. He was the last of the Caesars, the last one of her family which had held the proud title for eight generations.

Sophia had been but a small girl in 1453 when Constantinople fell and she had been sent off to Rome to be under the protection of the Pope. There she had been brought up and converted, so her Roman teachers believed, from her own Greek Orthodox faith to that of the Roman. They mistook Zoë.

Her plump little figure might be all curves and softly rounded, but her mind was firm and her wits sharp. She knew what she wanted

83

and held out for it. She had often heard it said that Greeks in Constantinople preferred to be under the Turkish turban than the Pope's crown. She refused all offers of marriage with European princes who belonged to the Roman church, making one excuse or another, until the proposal came from Ivan III of Muscovy. His form of Christianity was Greek Orthodox, the one which she had inherited.

That was why, little as she knew about this mysterious land to which she was going, Sophia was setting out with hope and purpose on the long tedious journey up through northern Europe and across the Polish border into Russia. She was riding in a litter accompanied by a large retinue on horseback, led by a Roman Cardinal appointed by the Pope.

Pope Sixtus IV fondly imagined that this marriage would result in bringing the Greek Orthodox Church of Moscow under the rule of Rome. Rome had tried to do this with the Greek Church in Constantinople, but never succeeded. The break between the two churches was of too long standing, having originated in the days of Constantine.

The Cardinal, however, wasted no time in trying to bring this union about. He began as soon as they crossed the Polish border.

At the first Russian town they came to, he entered at the head of the procession carrying the Roman crucifix. Since their Greek cross had no human figure on it, this looked strange to the townsfolk who had gathered at the gate to welcome the new Duchess with bread and salt, the old symbol of hospitality.

Festivities had also been planned for the distinguished guests by the city fathers, beginning with a visit to the cathedral whose onion-shaped dome rose above the surrounding rooftops. As they were entering, the Cardinal whispered to Sophia not to follow the Orthodox priest in bowing to the Magi, a coaching which she promptly disregarded. This may have disconcerted the Cardinal a bit, but did not alter his approach.

At every other Russian town they entered, he went first, carrying the Roman crucifix, until they got to Moscow. There, outside the heavy wooden gate, the Cardinal was halted and informed that he must not enter the Holy City carrying that cross.

Runners had gone ahead to report to the Grand Duke how and when the Cardinal who was bringing the bride would be entering the city. Ivan III had summoned the Council of Boyars for advice on what to do in this embarrassing situation.

The Metropolitan, head of the Church, put the decision squarely up to Ivan with these words:

"If you allow that messenger with his crucifix to enter this our Holy City of Moscow, by one gate, straightway do I, your father in Christ, depart by another."

So, without the Roman Cross, and with all the bells ringing and clanging in the Russian Orthodox churches, the new Grand Duchess entered Moscow. There she was. She, Sophia Palaeologus, brought up in luxury and comfort, now found herself in a wooden city with mud streets, a frontier town on the edge of a pine forest, an outpost of Europe on the border of Asia.

Except for the three-cornered fort of brick, called the Kremlin, which overlooked the river, all the buildings were made of wood. Even the old church with the loudest of the many bells that were ringing, was built of wood. The huge square market place was crowded with peasants and also with queer-looking people who must be Tatars from Asia. Around the Kremlin were wooden houses in which the noblemen, who were called Boyars, lived. All of them wore long robes, heavy with fur, immense fur hats, and long black beards.

The Grand Duke Ivan III, whom Sophia had come to marry, proved to be quite acceptable. He was actually rather distinguished looking, though he dressed much like his Boyars. He also lived, as did they, in a wooden palace scarcely larger or better than any one of theirs. And he slept on a bed of hay or straw, Sophia found out later, after their marriage.

The wedding festivities, due to the chests filled with costumes and jewels and other royal trappings which the bride had brought with her, were so magnificent that the primitive Boyars stood about in tongue-tied amazement. Never before had there been such a dazzling affair in Muscovy.

Ivan III went about among the Boyars, to Sophia's dismay, as if he were one of them. That was no way, she told him later, for an absolute monarch to behave, as if his subjects were his equal. He, the Grand Duke of Muscovy, who intended to make himself the Sovereign of Russia, should behave like an emperor who was—or should be—the new Emperor of the East.

That was her ambition. Now that Constantinople had fallen, Moscow should take its place as center of the Eastern Empire, and head of the Greek Church. Constantinople had been the second Rome, the third should be Moscow! And he, Ivan, Grand Duke of Muscovy, should take the title of Caesar.

Eventually Ivan III complied, but not without consideration. He was a cool, cautious, calculating man, who did not hasten into things. He kept trying out various combinations, and finally decided upon Tsar of all Russia as the best-sounding title—Tsar being the Slavic form of Caesar.

The Boyars mumbled and grumbled in their beards. They hated this foreign innovation and saw in it a serious threat to their independence.

The Metropolitan, on the contrary, and the patriarchs of the Church, looked upon this rise in the status of their Duke, their city, and themselves, with high approval.

Later, to prove Ivan's claim to the title of Caesar, they invented a legend tracing the descent of his ancestor Rurik, the first Russian Prince, back through fifteen generations, to none other than Caesar Augustus, the first Roman emperor of them all!

So now again there were two Caesars or Roman Emperors in Europe: Frederick III of Austria and Ivan III of Russia—the "Kaiser" and the "Tsar."

Part II

begins in Portugal in the year

1474

People who were living when

Ferdinand and **Isabella**
became King and Queen 1474
Infanta Isabella was born 1470
Juan 1478   Maria 1480
        Juana 1479
Catherine of Aragon 1485

Diego Columbus
was born in
1480

Muley Hussan
defied the Spanish sovereigns
and War to conquer Granada
began in 1481

Tudor rose

Wm Caxton
began Printing
in England 1476

Henry VII   Arthur, his
                 first son.
won the Wars of the Roses in 1485 and
founded the royal family of Tudor

The **Emperor Maximilian** of Austria
married Mary of Burgundy 1477
Philip (born 1478) was to marry
Juana and be Philip I of Spain

and some important Events that

Columbus was in Portugal and Spain

Portugal

INDIA

Bartholomew Dias
discovered and rounded
the Cape of Good Hope in
1488

John II
of Portugal renewed the search
for a sea route to India,

Queen Isabella
heard in 1486 of Columbus's
plan for sailing west to India

Ferdinand Columbus
was born in
1488

born 1483
Martin Luther
German schoolboy of Eisleben was
struggling with Latin grammar

Michelangelo
(born 1475) was a pupil in the
gardens of Lorenzo de Medici

Henry VIII
was a year old in 1492
just learning to walk

Baber (born 1483)
first Mongol ruler of India
was reading Persian poetry.

Lorenzo de Medici
died six months before the
discovery of the new world

took place between 1474 and 1492

COLUMBUS IN PORTUGAL

IT WAS AUGUST 13, 1476, toward nightfall. A raging battle at sea had lasted all day. Black clouds of smoke from burning ships thickened the still air. Hundreds of seamen had been drowned, and young Columbus was wounded, with a bullet lodged in his leg. The ship on which he fought was on fire and sinking fast. There was but one thing to do. He leaped from the sloping deck into the sea, afloat with wreckage, and disappeared. As his head rose again above the waves, he saw a long oar floating nearby. Clutching it, he pushed off toward land, dimly visible miles away. In spite of his wounded leg, God willing, he believed he would reach it. If so, he would be in Portugal.

The ship on which he had been sailing was one of a merchant fleet of five bound for the Netherlands. Four of the ships belonged to merchant bankers of Genoa. The fifth came from the Netherlands and flew the flag of Burgundy, which caused the disaster. As the fleet rounded the tip of Portugal, the flag was sighted by the commander of a French war fleet. Since his King, Louis XI, was at war with Charles the Bold, Duke of Burgundy, the French commander immediately gave the order to fire and the battle began. Three ships from Genoa went down. The other two, badly battered and burned, struggled into the nearest port for repairs. This was the harbor of Lagos, made famous by Prince Henry the Navigator. So it was here, by chance, that Columbus was washed ashore in Portugal, at the very spot where the work had been done that made his future voyage of discovery possible.

It took Columbus many days to recover, but as soon as he was able, he made his way to Lisbon to find his brother Bartholomew. Some years earlier when work was scarce in Genoa, Bartholomew, who had become a mapmaker, had sought employment in Lisbon. Columbus found Lisbon what Genoa had once been, a bustling harbor with ships and seamen out of ports all the way from Norway to Africa.

Bartholomew, his brother, was doing well in his chart and map-making shop, being industrious and very skillful in his art. He would have been more than glad to have Christopher join him in the business, but the less practical older brother was not ready for that. He still dreamed of visiting far parts of the world that he had never seen. Shortly after the New Year his chance came.

A trading ship was leaving Lisbon with merchandise for Iceland, then called the Island of Thule. Columbus signed up for the voyage. On the way the ship stopped at Galway in Ireland. And it may have reached the shore of Greenland, for he wrote later: "I sailed in the year 1477, in the month of February, 100 leagues beyond the island of Tile (Thule). To this island which is as big as England, come the English with their merchandise."

Columbus was back in Lisbon by spring, sure of what he wanted to do, and what he needed to learn. So far, he had learned little if anything from books, only from experience. Now he intended to read all that had ever been written about navigation, exploration, and geography, even though to do so he had first to learn Latin, as well as Castilian and Portuguese. No matter. He must learn. And this was the place to learn—here in Portugal which led the world in exploration and discovery. Someday a Portuguese captain would return to Lisbon with the great news that he had rounded the end of Africa and found the passage to India. So far no one had succeeded. Perhaps Columbus himself could not say exactly when, after he began to read and study, the idea came to him that it might be easier to reach India by sailing west. It had, however, occurred to Portugal's King Alfonso.

There was a physician in Florence, Italy, by the name of Toscanelli, who was also a mathematician and an astronomer. The King had written to him, asking about a new route to India.

In reply, there came a letter from Toscanelli dated June 25, 1474, in which he wrote that he was delighted to hear that the King was interested in a "shorter way of going by sea to the lands of spices." He enclosed a chart of the course for a ship sailing westward from Portugal which, he said, would bring it to China, empire of the Great Khan. Another course would pass the "noble island of Cipangu (Japan), most fertile in pearls and precious stones, where they cover the temples and palaces in solid gold."

Nothing, however, was done with this information. Alfonso V, who had never shared his famous Uncle Henry's zest for exploration and was far more excited by battles and victories such as he had won in North Africa, had let it drop.

At present he was about to engage in a fascinating war with Castile, whereby he fully expected to become its King, ousting that impudent girl, Isabella, who had snubbed his proposal of marriage and now, upon the death of her brother, had become Queen.

Alfonso V

Alfonso had received a letter from the Archbishop of Toledo, who for years had been Isabella's most loyal supporter. Now the Archbishop had turned against the young Queen and hatched a plot with the supporters of Joanna. According to the letter, which Alfonso read with mounting enthusiasm, he was to marry his niece Joanna, invade Castile with an army, and make good her claim to the crown. All the nobles of Castile, the Archbishop assured him, would rally to his cause. The victory would be won. Joanna would be declared Queen and he, Alfonso, would be King of Castile. What a prospect!

Alfonso, with his usual optimism, allowed no doubt to cross his mind that the nobles would support him. He ignored the fact that the Pope might not grant him permission to marry his own niece. He believed what he wanted to believe.

And in May, 1475, according to plan, he crossed the border for the great adventure. At the town of Plasencia he met Joanna, the pawn in this game of politics, and on a high platform in the center of the town the so-called wedding took place, followed by a blare of trumpets and the loud voice of the herald proclaiming:

"Castile for Dom Alfonso of Portugal and Queen Donna Joanna, his wife and the rightful owner of this kingdom!"

94

ISABELLA MEETS THE CHALLENGE

ISABELLA was at Valladolid with Ferdinand and their small daughter, the five-year-old Infanta Isabel, when Alfonso crossed the border. Quite naturally, she had been distressed over the Archbishop of Toledo's desertion, which she knew was caused by his jealousy of the Cardinal, her new Prime Minister. Although she had seen him storm off in a rage, Isabella could not forget the days when he had been like a father to her, protected her from her brother, and made it possible for her to marry Ferdinand. She felt she must go to him, even though friends told her that it was useless and also foolish to humble herself.

"But I must do it," she replied, "or I should forever blame myself for not having tried to make him change his course."

Leaving Ferdinand to gather forces along the border, Isabella set out on horseback for the Archbishop's palace at Alcala, sending a count ahead as they approached to announce her arrival.

"Isabella!" snorted the Archbishop. "Let her come in by one gate of this palace and I leave by the other."

Disappointed, Isabella continued on to Toledo to recruit more forces, to meet Ferdinand there and to consider how, without any money, to fight this war that was being forced upon them. The treasury was empty. Henry IV had stripped it. There was no money to buy arms, ammunition, or even food for the soldiers.

A meeting of the Cortes was called and the problem presented to them. Isabella's steadfast courage in the face of danger was always to inspire trust in her. Bishops of the Church came forward and offered half of their silver plate, the amount of its value to be paid back in three years. Many nobles, moved by her unwavering courage, now deserted the rebellious Archbishop of Toledo and again declared their allegiance to Isabella.

What a shock that was for Alfonso! How far this was from what the Archbishop had led him to expect! Where were all those nobles who were so sure to rally around him?

Alfonso was then at the Spanish fortress of Toro, which had been turned over to him by a disloyal governor, when he first crossed the border. And it was on a wide plain about five miles away in February, 1476, that the deciding battle was fought in this foolish war on which he had so blithely embarked. The fighting was hand to hand and so fierce that after some hours the Portuguese troops weakened and gave way and were utterly defeated.

Still Alfonso was not ready to give up and make peace. Leaving his son John in Lisbon in charge of the government, he rushed away to France to have a talk with King Louis, who was supposed to be his ally, but had been of no real help. He found the old "Spider" at Tours, his favorite residence. Louis embraced Alfonso like a long-lost brother, but then cut short any talk of war with the curt remark that he had done his part. Alfonso hung about, trying in vain to get another word with the cagy old King, also waiting and hoping for permission from the Pope to marry Joanna. Finally he became so disgusted that he decided to give it all up—the war, his bride, everything, even the crown of Portugal—and go on a pilgrimage to the Holy Land.

On the impulse he sent word to Lisbon, with the result that when he got home he was astonished to find that he had been taken at his word. His son John had been proclaimed King!

Prince John, who was known as the "Perfect Prince," readily handed back the crown to his father. Alfonso then called off his marriage with Joanna and signed the peace treaty with Isabella, whose right to be Queen was never again challenged.

Ferdinand and Isabella now had a year-old son, Juan, the joy and pride of his royal parents. Joanna was given the choice of marrying him eventually, or becoming a nun. As she was then sixteen, she chose to become a nun in the order of Santa Clara.

To seal the treaty, another wedding was arranged. The Infanta Isabel, who was nine, was engaged to marry Prince John's son Alfonso when he should become fourteen.

1479

It was September 24, 1479, when the treaty was signed at Alcantara on the border of Portugal. From there Isabella rode on horseback, two hundred miles to Toledo, where in November her third child was born, her poor unfortunate little daughter, Juana, who was to have such a very tragic life.

That same year in Lisbon, Portugal, a marriage was recorded in the parish register between a foreign mapmaker from Genoa, Cristoforo Colombo, and a Portuguese lady of the aristocracy, Dona Felipa Perestrello y Moniz.

OF MAPS, BOOKS AND DRIFTWOOD

DONA ISABEL, Felipa's mother, laid a faded old map of the Madeira Islands on the table in front of her new son-in-law, Christopher Columbus. Folding her small plump hands in her black-silk lap, she sat back then and beamed upon him with satisfaction. She was delighted by the interest Christopher took in her late husband's charts and writings, as well as in all the tales she had to tell of early life on the Madeiras. Her husband, Don Bartholomew Perestrello, she said, had gone out on the second colonizing expedition, appointed by Prince Henry as the hereditary captain of the Island of Porto Santo.

Columbus had never been to Porto Santo, but the year before he was married he had gone on business to Madeira and seen its marvelous vineyards and fields of sugar cane. He had been sent to buy sugar for a merchant in Genoa. Although the agent in Lisbon had given him but a fraction of the purchase price, Columbus went, made a contract for 60,000 pounds of sugar to be delivered when the balance was paid. The money had not yet arrived when the ship came to load the sugar and the Madeira merchant would not release it. Columbus had to sail to Genoa with the small amount paid for, explain to his employer, and even go to court to have the facts recorded before he could return to Lisbon.

After that brief business venture, Christopher had gone back into the shop with Bartholomew, making or selling maps and charts and poring by the hour over books on geography and travel.

The Book of Ser Marco Polo was his favorite, the marvels of the Far East told by the famous Venetian traveler who had made his journey 200 years ago. Starting out in 1271 as a boy of seventeen with his uncle and his father, Marco Polo had traveled across the vast width of Asia to China, the Empire of the Great Khan. The most interesting thing to Columbus was that Marco Polo gave to Asia much greater width than did Ptolemy.

Ptolemy was a Greek astronomer and mathematician who had lived in Egypt around the year 150 A.D. Ever since his geography had been rediscovered, it was accepted as the absolute truth.

Marco Polo, Columbus knew, was no scholar, but he had actually traveled around Asia, and should know how far he went.

If Asia was that much wider, then the western ocean must be just that much narrower. And if so, China could not be more than 5,000 miles from Portugal. Therefore, by sailing west from Portugal one could reach the Empire of the Great Khan!

The chapel in which the Columbus brothers attended mass adjoined the Convento dos Santos, a boarding school for the daughters of noble Portuguese families. One day, coming out of chapel or through the bars of the convent window, somehow or other Christopher met Dona Felipa. He must have made a favorable first impression on her mother Dona Isabel. He was a foreigner, to be sure, not the son of one of the first families of Portugal whom Dona Isabel would have chosen for her daughter. But after all Felipa was twenty-five, well beyond the age when she, poor child, would have been married had her mother been able to provide a suitable dowry for a young nobleman. Here was a young man, intelligent, well mannered, who would no doubt succeed in the merchant marine business. And so they were married in the chapel: Dona Felipa Moniz and Cristoforo Colombo.

After living for some time with Dona Isabel in Lisbon, the young couple went to make their home on the island of Porto Santo, where Dona Felipa's brother was the captain general. There, in 1480, a son was born and given the name of his father's younger brother, Diego.

What did Felipa think of her young son's father? Did she realize that Columbus would never be satisfied with quiet life on the islands? Her brother had shown him a piece of driftwood blown in from the west, carved like another picked up near the Azores. Could she see then how strong her husband's desire was to find the lands from which it came—a desire so strong that nothing could ever turn him aside until he had accomplished his purpose.

A FATEFUL MARRIAGE

THIS YOUNG COUPLE are Maximilian and Mary, son of the German Emperor and daughter of the Duke of Burgundy. Their marriage in 1477 was by far the most fateful marriage of their day, affecting the history of Europe for centuries to come, bringing war after war, down to 1917.

For a time it looked as though the wedding might never take place. The nobles, who had not wanted the young Hapsburg of Austria to marry their Duchess, did their utmost to prevent it.

Charles the Bold, Mary's father, who had arranged the marriage, died suddenly. The States General had the royal palace in Ghent immediately surrounded by guards, making Mary a prisoner and separating her from her stepmother, the Duchess Margaret. Meanwhile, they sent a delegation to France to confer with Louis XI and arrange for the marriage of Mary to the King's son, although the Dauphin Charles was but eight years old and the Duchess Mary twenty.

Mary, sweet thing, was frightened to tears, but managed to smuggle out a letter to Maximilian, to whom she had long been betrothed and who, from all she had heard, was such a brave knight that he would surely come to her rescue. The Duchess Margaret also sent him an appeal for help. Nothing could suit Maximilian better than this—to be the brave knight rescuing the fair maiden, especially when he found the maiden so sweet, so utterly lovable as Mary.

That was a most happy day when Maximilian appeared to claim his bride. The perfect knight of a maiden's dream, he came clad in armor of shining silver, with a wreath of precious jewels encircling his blond hair.

The French-speaking bride could not reply to his German greeting, but as it was never any trouble for the charming "Maxi" to pick up another language, he was soon expressing his love for her in French. And they found many tastes in common.

Hunting, for example, was Maximilian's favorite sport. Mary, too, loved the chase and had a beautiful well-trained falcon, also a pet greyhound that always slept by her bed and soon included Maximilian in his affection.

"If we had peace," said the happy young husband, "we would be living in a garden of roses."

Peaceful life in a garden, had it been possible, would hardly have been a life for that restless romantic knight, with his love of adventure and excitement. Maximilian was soon in his silver armor again, speeding off to war. Upon the death of Charles the Bold, Louis XI had been quick to reclaim the original French province of Burgundy, delighted at last to get that long independent part of

France under the rule of the crown. Maximilian made it his business to try to recover it, and resumed his father-in-law's endless war against the French King. This only resulted in further antagonizing the States General; not only had the nobles no interest in Burgundy but they were sick of raising money for the war.

Maximilian was away on the field of battle when both of his children were born: first a son and then a daughter, who were eventually to marry a son and daughter of Ferdinand and Isabella.

The boy, born in 1478, was named for Mary's grandfather, Philip the Good. The baby sister, two years younger, was named for Duchess Margaret who, though only thirty-three, was now a grandmother and to be called the "grand lady," or Madame la Grande.

In 1482, when the children were two and four, their father, to Mary's joy, was home again. One day when the weather was mild, the young couple went hunting with their ladies and nobles. Jumping a ditch, Mary's horse stumbled and fell upon her. She died a few days later, leaving Maximilian and Madame la Grande, who had both loved her so dearly, stricken with grief.

According to Mary's will, Maximilian was to act as ruler of the Netherlands until her heir, four-year-old Duke Philip, was old enough to rule. To have had to accept the Hapsburg as Mary's husband had been distasteful enough to the States General and the people of the Netherlands. To have to accept him as their ruler was so intolerable that they proceeded to block him in every possible way. First, by cutting off the money they put a stop to Maximilian's expensive war against France. Then, in spite of his objection, they sent a delegation to make peace with Louis XI, and seal the treaty with the marriage of two-year-old Margaret with the Dauphin Charles, to whom they had first wanted to marry her mother. They offered as her dowry the provinces of Artois and Franche-Comté, to the delight of the old King, and promised him as soon as spring came and the roads were passable to send the little girl to France to be given an education suitable for a future queen.

MARGARET OF AUSTRIA, QUEEN OF FRANCE

THIS IS LITTLE MARGARET HAPSBURG in her wedding hat. Three years old, she was leaving home in April, 1483, to marry the son of her father's greatest enemy. Her young grandmother was in tears. The little girl rode away on the lap of her nurse, seated in a golden coach hung between two broad-backed Flemish horses. An elegant escort of ladies and nobles were going with her to the border. There, Madame Anne of France, the King's oldest daughter, with her husband, the Duke of Beaujeu and a large French escort, were to meet their future Queen, take her to Paris, and from there to her new home, the Castle of Amboise.

On this April day the little Duchess of Austria was starting out on a most amazing life, to be checkered with alternating fortune and misfortune. First she would be Queen of France; next the Infanta of Spain, married to Isabella's son; then the Duchess of Savoy; and lastly the Regent of the Netherlands, when she would see her young nephew, the King of Spain, become the next German Emperor.

As the horses started, the little traveler leaned out as long as she could see, waving kisses to her dear Madame la Grande.

HER HUSBAND KING CHARLES VIII

LOUIS XI, the old Spider King, was now nearing the end of his life,
though he clung to it with every ounce of strength he had left,
and still carried on the government of France. What kind of king
his twelve-year-old son would eventually make was a disturbing question. But he was doing the best he could to pass on to Charles what
he had learned of the tricky business of ruling a kingdom, especially
the wastefulness of war.

The King closed a book from which he had been reading aloud
to Charles one afternoon and while the boy repeated what he had
read, studied him through half-closed lids, his old eyes still as bright
as bits of steel. They were an odd pair, the wizened old man wrapped
in a dark fur-lined cloak, and the boy in red satin, with a head so
large for his small frame and spindly legs that he looked more like
a gnome. They were in the Castle of Amboise where Charles lived
with his tutor, strictly guarded for his safety.

The old King had made the ten-mile trip from his own residence
at Tours to bring this beautiful book of maxims he had had made

105

especially for his son. Intended to teach Charles the value of peace, he had called it the *Rosebush of War* because, as he pointed out in the preface, "the counsel of wise men refresh the spirit like a fragrance—when you come to reign over this noble kingdom you must smell one rose from this rosebush every day."

Whatever slight comfort the old King could derive from the prospect of having to leave France to this young Charles was that his oldest daughter Anne would act as regent for her young brother until he came of age. Anne of France was twenty-three and so intelligent that her father called her "the least foolish woman in France," which for him was praise of the highest caliber.

As the shadow of death crept closer, Louis XI grew desperate to postpone the final day, and sent about here and there for some sacred relic or other mystical help. He got permission from the Pope to have the phial of sacred oil with which he had been anointed King brought from Rheims and placed on a chest where he could see it from his bed. From Lorenzo de Medici he heard of an Italian monk noted for his holiness, and prevailed upon the holy hermit to come to Tours and offer prayers in his behalf.

Up to the very end, the thoughts of the old King were centered, as they had always been, upon the welfare of France. In almost his last hour, he called for the Duke of Beaujeu, Anne's husband, and urged him to avoid war. He had made his last confession and was lying quite still. Suddenly he opened his eyes and called for his son-in-law, who hastened in and bent over the bed.

"Keep the peace," said Louis. "For five or six years at least there must be peace in order for France to grow strong."

Satisfied then, the old King closed his eyes and drifted away listening to the voice of the holy monk chanting the last prayer:

"Go forth, Christian soul, out of this world, in the name of God the Father Almighty who created thee."

And so Louis XI went at dawn on August 31, 1483, leaving his beloved kingdom to his twelve-year-old son who became Charles VIII.

GROWING UP AT AMBOISE

"DITES, AMANT VERT! Speak, speak!"

Margaret, Queen of France, now five years old, was talking to her parrot, whom she called her green sweetheart, and whose cage stood in one of the deep-set windows of the Castle of Amboise. She was trying to make him say her name, but he merely winked at her in silence, moving deliberately back and forth on his perch in and out of the sun, which turned the child's hair into a shower of gold. The little Queen, as usual, was wearing black. Madame de Segré, her governess who sat nearby hemming a doll's dress to match, thought black most becoming to the little girl's fair skin. Margaret went to sit beside her and hold the new doll which had just come from Paris, and look again at her beautiful new belt. Madame de Segré had had it made for her out of one of the heavy gold chains she had brought with her from Flanders. That seemed a very long time ago, the day Madame Anne, Charles's grown-up sister, had come to meet her at the border in that beautiful violet dress. Then his Majesty, the old King, was still alive and Madame Anne was not as busy as she was now. Now she had to govern France until Charles was old enough.

Charles would soon reach fifteen, though he was still not very big, not nearly so tall as some of the pages at his court. Once in a while his tutor brought him over to pay Margaret a visit. In his part of the

Castle of Amboise Charles had a household like his young Queen's.

The Grand Master of her court was Madame de Segré's husband. There were twenty ladies-in-waiting, six lords, a doctor, a priest, a secretary, and lots of servants, such as laundresses and cooks and valets. The only one who came from Flanders was her nurse.

Margaret remembered sitting on her nurse's lap and waving to dear Madame la Grande who was crying because she, Margaret, was going away. And maybe, too, because Madame's brother, Edward, King of England, had died and she would never see him again.

Louise said that Kings of England and their families always hated Kings of France and probably her grandmother did not want her to marry Charles and become a French Queen. That was Louise of Savoy, who was nine. Louise lived with Madame Anne and the Duke of Beaujeu, who was her uncle, because her mother was dead. And her father was very poor, even though his father was the Duke of Savoy. Louise knew everything—all about which people liked or hated each other and why, and what might happen to them. Louise said that if Charles should die, as sickly boys often did, the next person to be King would be Louis of Orleans, who was over twenty years old and big and strong. But if Louis of Orleans should die of poison or something, the next king would be the Count of Angoulême, and that was the man she, Louise, was supposed to marry as soon as she was old enough. And then she would be Queen, and she would have as much to say about things as Madame Anne did now.

Margaret hoped that nothing would happen to Charles. She wanted him to live a long time and take good care of the people as kings and queens were supposed to. Next week on Whit Thursday she was going to wash the feet of thirteen poor people and give each one a golden half ducat. That was fun, giving golden ducats away to make people happy, especially those who came to perform for her, like the singers and players and dancers, and that wonderful man who could twist himself all up in knots and untie himself again. That was fun to watch—wonderful, wonderful fun! It tickled her toes just to think about it. Jumping up, she went dancing and twirling around the room, humming a little tune and making up rhyming words to go with it, until the parrot joined in, shrieking her name as she whirled by his cage. Out of breath at last she plumped herself down beside dear Madame de Segré and gave her a hug and a kiss for finishing the lovely doll's dress.

France: the royal family of Valois

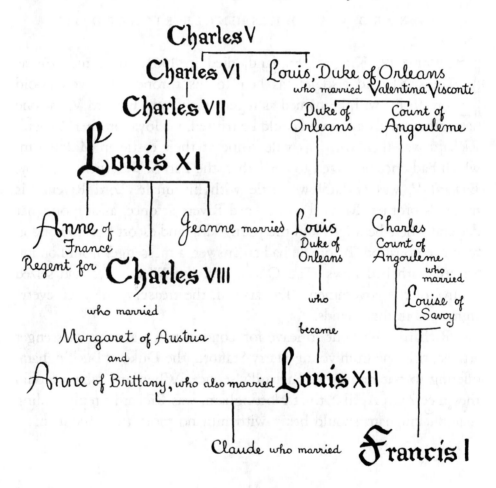

EDWARD V AND HIS UNCLE RICHARD III

EDWARD IV, King of England, died in 1483, the same year as Louis XI, and also left as heir to his throne a twelve-year-old son. In his will, he named as regent for young Edward V, the one person he had always found could be trusted, his loyal brother Richard. Richard was then with his wife Anne at their castle in Middleham, which had once belonged to her father, the Earl of Warwick. The boy, Edward V, was at Ludlow Castle with his uncle, Lord Rivers, his mother's brother. Richard wrote Lord Rivers at once, asking on what day and where he might join the young king and escort him to London for the coronation. Before he had an answer, a messenger from London arrived with bad news. The Queen and the Woodvilles had seized control of the government. The arsenal, the treasury, the fleet, everything was in their hands.

Richard was about to leave for London when another messenger arrived, this one from young Harry Stafford, the Duke of Buckingham, offering to put himself in Richard's service. When and where should they meet? On April 29th at Nottingham, was Richard's reply, adding that Buckingham should bring with him no more than 300 men.

Then Richard, dressed entirely in black, set out for Nottingham with 300 men of York. On the way he was met by a messenger from Lord Rivers saying that he and the young King would also meet him at Nottingham. Those were Lord Rivers' words, but not his intent. He intended to have young Edward in London before Richard got there, so that the Woodvilles would have the King as well as everything else under their control.

At the inn in Nottingham the two uncles met—Richard and Lord Rivers—but without young Edward who, Rivers explained, had merely gone on to Stony Stratford for the night, where there were better accommodations. Richard was suspicious at once, but made no comment.

Rushlights were flickering in the tavern, and they were halfway through supper when the young Duke of Buckingham came blustering in and opened a lively conversation which lasted until the hour was late. Richard said nothing until Lord Rivers departed to spend the night at another inn. Then he confided his suspicion of treason and his plan for dealing with it, sharply and quickly.

At dawn, Lord Rivers' inn was quietly surrounded by soldiers and he was put under guard, while Buckingham and Richard rode at top speed to Stony Stratford. There, as they suspected, young Edward sat astride his horse ready to leave for London—a boy in blue with blond hair hanging shoulder-length beneath a soft hat of black velvet.

Suddenly the prince saw two strange men in black come galloping up, followed by their troops. Reining in their horses, they dismounted and knelt before him. The smaller, older man, he learned, was his Uncle Richard, his father's brother, who was to take him to London to be crowned. The boy was not at all happy as they started out. At one of the inns, however, where they stopped on the way, his Uncle Richard helped him issue his first order as King. Then, feeling better, Edward was pleased to sign his name and new title on a scrap of parchment, under which his grown-up companions also signed their names and mottoes.

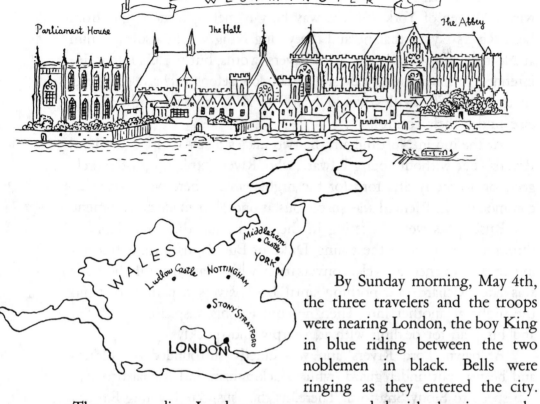

By Sunday morning, May 4th, the three travelers and the troops were nearing London, the boy King in blue riding between the two noblemen in black. Bells were ringing as they entered the city.

The narrow, dirty London streets were crowded with cheering people, all eager to see their new King, Edward V. At St. Paul's churchyard they caught a glimpse of the boy being escorted into the Bishop's palace. Later he was taken to live in the royal apartments in the Tower of London where his brother Prince Richard, who was ten, also went to keep him company. People passing by often stopped to watch the two princes playing ball or archery in the yard.

The coronation of Edward V, the twelve-year-old King, had been set for June 22nd. Buckingham, bursting with self-importance, was rushing about all over London giving orders for it when it was learned that the coronation was off. It would not take place. Edward V could not be King!

The Tower

Ricardus Rex

A long carefully guarded secret had come to light.

The Bishop of Bath broke the shocking news at a meeting of Lords in Westminster Hall. Prince Edward was illegitimate! So were his brother Richard, his sister Elizabeth, and all of his other sisters. All of Edward IV's children were illegitimate. The Queen, Elizabeth Woodville, had not been the King's legal wife. Before Edward IV had married her, he had been betrothed to Lady Eleanor Butler, and this, in the eyes of the Church, was the same as an actual marriage.

On June 25th a joint meeting of Lords and Commons was held. The two princes were declared illegitimate and their claim to the throne set aside. Richard of York was declared heir to the throne and a document drawn up asking him to accept the "crown and the royal dignity." The next day, June 26, 1483, Richard accepted the honor, rode to Westminster Hall, took the royal oath and became King of England, Richard III.

Westminster Abbey had never seen a more gorgeous coronation than that of Richard III, the last of the Plantagenets who had ruled over England for more than 300 years. Almost every nobleman in the kingdom was there, turned out in his most elegant attire. None was more spectacular than the Duke of Buckingham in blue velvet trimmed with golden cartwheels.

Trumpets sounded and the line began to move along a broad red carpet leading to the Abbey. After the heralds with their trumpets came the abbots and priests, walking behind a cross of gold. Then came the most noble lords and high officers of state bearing first the sword of mercy, then the sword of justice, then the King's scepter with its ball and cross, next the King's sword and last, his heavy bejeweled crown resting on a pillow.

Then came small, dark Richard in a purple robe, walking barefoot and bareheaded between two bishops in heavily embroidered robes who towered above him in their mitered crowns.

After the King, carrying the long train of his purple robe, came the Duke of Buckingham, plainly showing with each step that next to Richard, he knew himself to be the noblest peer in the realm, with some right to the throne himself. After Buckingham, in order of rank, came the earls, the barons, and the lords.

Then came the Queen. And who of all people was that tiny woman carrying the Queen's train? Lady Margaret, the mother of Henry Tudor who, at that very moment, was waiting in Brittany for a chance to return and seize the crown for himself. To everyone's amazement, Richard III had given her this honor, even though he was well aware that she had never stopped plotting for the downfall of the House of York and the final triumph of Lancaster. It seemed evident that by justice and fair play, he was hoping to end the Wars of the Roses that had been going on for almost thirty years, and to give England the peace that was so badly needed.

The war was to end, but not as he had hoped.

THE DUKE OF BRITTANY had been well paid by Edward IV to keep strict watch over Henry Tudor and see that he did not escape to England. Now, as a price for continuing to keep Henry under guard, the Duke of Brittany asked Richard to help him fight against France. Richard III refused, wishing to keep England at peace.

The Duke, therefore, in a huff turned completely about and joined in a plot to help Henry Tudor overthrow Richard, promising him 15 ships and 5,000 soldiers with which to return to England.

By early fall, only four months after Lady Margaret had walked in Richard's coronation, she and her supporters had plans well laid for her son's return. Henry Tudor was to sail from Brittany to the south of England. There he was to be met by a force of English soldiers and commanded by the man one would least expect—the one who had carried Richard's train in the coronation—the Duke of Buckingham!

After the coronation, as the Duke was riding home from London to his castle in Wales, the foolish fellow, spoiled by Richard with too many honors, became possessed with the notion of being King himself. And why not, he thought. Who by birth had a better right? Certainly not Henry Tudor, whose grandfather was not even a nobleman. He, Harry Buckingham, had royal blood on both sides of his family. And right there in his own castle was Bishop Morton, the very man to help him.

Bishop Morton, a wily, ambitious man, had been caught in an

earlier plot against Richard III. But instead of having him sentenced to death with the others, the King had let him be sent to Buckingham's castle to be kept strictly under guard. Buckingham was joyful to find the Bishop so sympathetic and understanding, as indeed he was. He understood the foolish fellow perfectly.

"Your claim to the throne is indeed good," began the wily Bishop. "But," he added, "your chance of gaining it is less than, let us say, that of Henry Tudor, who has his mother Lady Margaret working for him, as well as his stepfather, Sir Thomas Stanley."

Moreover, said he, Lady Margaret was arranging with the former Queen for Henry Tudor to marry her oldest daughter, the Princess Elizabeth. This would unite in bonds of matrimony the Houses of Lancaster and York and so bring blessed peace to England. In this worthy cause, no one, said the Bishop, could render greater service than he, Harry Buckingham. So, before he knew it, foolish Harry was deep in the plot to help, not himself, but Henry Tudor, to the throne of England.

In mid-October Richard III learned to his dismay that his friend had turned against him. With his usual speed he proclaimed Buckingham a traitor and opened a campaign against him.

The Duke's badly organized forces were already deserting him.

Seeing what a fool he had been, the miserable fellow tried to hide but was found, condemned for treason and beheaded.

Henry Tudor meanwhile had sailed just near enough to England to discover that the plot had miscarried. Turning cautiously about, he sailed back to Brittany to wait until his mother and friends had plans better organized for his return.

Bishop Morton, far too clever to let himself get caught, had slipped off to a hiding place in Flanders. There he kept an ear cocked for the latest news from England, to pass on to Henry. Very soon a rumor began to circulate that the two princes, Edward V and his brother Richard, living in the Tower of London, had been murdered by their uncle, Richard III.

Was that true? Had they been killed, or were they still alive, to be killed later by order of Henry Tudor after he had seized the throne and would have reason to fear them? That was a mystery that probably never would be solved.

Bishop Morton laid the blame for the "foul murder" on Richard III and blackened his name forever, since all historians under the Tudors copied what he wrote.

But why should Richard have murdered Edward's two boys? They had been set aside by an act of Parliament and were of no danger to him. And why, if he had killed them, would their mother, Queen Elizabeth, have put her five daughters under his care? Or why would she have written to her older son, their half-brother who was in Brittany, to leave Henry Tudor and return to the court of Richard III? Henry did not allow him to leave.

Henry Tudor needed every supporter he had. He had heard from Bishop Morton, on the lookout in Flanders, that the Duke of Brittany had now been paid by Richard III to keep him in strict custody again and that he must escape at once. Now or never!

Henry lost no time. One afternoon he and a few friends left the castle, casually, as if for a bit of hunting. No sooner had they entered the woods than Henry tore off his suit, got into a servant's smock, and rode like mad for the French border, crossing over just one hour ahead of the men sent in pursuit of him.

Bedraggled and destitute, he turned up at the elegant French court to beg Anne of France for protection, help, even enough to live on. This was humiliation which he was never to forget, and which was to develop later into a miserly passion for money.

Anne of France made the English refugee welcome and also helped him against Richard III. Remembering her father's policy of protecting France by keeping the English fighting at home, she promised Henry Tudor fifteen ships and troops enough to invade England when word should come from his mother that the time was ripe.

WAR WITH GRANADA BEGINS

ISABELLA had begun her reign with the firm determination to capture Granada, the last stronghold of the Moslems in Spain. By putting a clause in the marriage contract she had forced a promise from Ferdinand to help her.

Proud, tiger-hearted old Muley Hussan, the Sultan of Granada, scoffed at the idea of losing his kingdom to the young Queen of Castile and her inexperienced husband. To begin with, they had a hard enough time keeping control of their kingdom, without trying to capture his.

And how could his Granada possibly be taken? The land of Granada was studded with fortresses to the very border of Castile. Thick as seeds of a pomegranate they were scattered through the

118

valley. The city of Granada, which held his Alhambra, the most beautiful palace in the world, was built on a rocky height impossible to scale. Granada could never be captured, unless it be the will of Allah, from whose will there was no protection.

Having no fear of Ferdinand and Isabella, old Muley Hussan had not paid the annual tribute which Sultans for years past had been accustomed to send to the sovereigns of Castile.

His answer was ready and waiting for the day when the Spanish ambassadors should arrive and demand payment. That was a day in 1476. The old Sultan received them in the Audience Hall of the Alhambra, seated cross-legged on a large satin cushion. Above his black brows set in a straight line rose a tremendous turban decorated with an ornament of jewels. In scornful silence he watched the Spanish ambassadors approach. With no change of expression he listened to their suave and tactful request for the tribute to be paid their sovereigns. Then he gave his well-considered answer.

"Tell your sovereigns," said he, "that the Sultans of Granada who paid tribute to the Kings of Castile are dead. Our mint coins nothing for them now but scimitars and swords."

The Spaniards returned with the Sultan's answer.

Up to this time Ferdinand had been lukewarm about Isabella's proposed war with Granada. But when the ambassadors brought back no tribute money, nothing at all but an insolent answer, Ferdinand was for making war on Granada at once.

"I will tear the seeds from that pomegranate one by one," he snarled, using the word for pomegranate which in Spanish is *granada*. "That overbearing infidel should be wiped off the earth!"

Isabella finally calmed her irate husband and made him see that war with Portugal must be finished first before war with Granada could begin.

Their delay in answering his challenge made Muley Hussan still more scornful. His scimitars and swords were ready and sharp, and an army of faithful men and fierce was ready to use them against the Christian infidels.

One wild winter night in 1481 he made a surprise attack on the Spanish fortress of Zahara just across the border. He captured it with awful slaughter, taking the few Christians who survived back with him to Granada to be sold as slaves. Entering the city gates he was greeted with wailing and moaning as if this victory were the forerunner of disaster.

"Woe, ah woe," moaned a whirling dervish. "Now will come the fall of Granada—Woe, ah woe is our beautiful Granada."

The loss of the fortress of Zahara came as an unexpected shock to Ferdinand and Isabella. To retaliate, a Spanish army struck back at a Moslem fort on the border and captured it. Thereupon Muley Hussan surrounded this fortress, cut off all supplies from the Spaniards, hoping to starve them into surrender.

The Spanish generals were uncertain whether or not to burn the fort and desert it. The Royal Council believed the cost of holding it would be too great, both in money and in lives.

"Every war must have heavy costs," said Isabella firmly. "We are determined to conquer Granada. To surrender the first fortress we have taken would be weak and cowardly."

As always, the Queen's courage and determination carried the day. The Spanish held the fort.

Muley Hussan, having lost it, also lost the confidence of his people. This defeat added to the strength of an opposing party, who had long been sick of the ruthless tyrant and had already been plotting to replace him with his son Boabdil.

From then on it was to be father against son, with the Arabs divided, foolishly fighting one another instead of uniting against the Spanish, who might not otherwise have conquered them.

This mild young Arab with the melancholy eyes is Boabdil, "the Unlucky," whose misfortune it was to become the last Sultan of Granada. On the day of his birth, astrologers casting his horoscope had called him "the unlucky one." Whatever unhappy combination

121

of stars and planets shone above his cradle, the true misfortune of the young Sultan lay in his feeble character—his lack of inner strength and courage.

Zorayah, his mother, a beautiful Christian slave girl, had long been the favorite wife in Muley Hussan's harem. When she was replaced by one younger and more beautiful, she became jealous and fearful that her son might also be set aside by his father. So she became the center of a plot to depose Muley Hussan and seize the throne for Boabdil.

Muley Hussan soon discovered the plot and had the mild-mannered son and his scheming mother locked up in a tower. Zorayah knotted her colored scarves into a long rope one dark night and let Boabdil down to the river's bank below, where horses were waiting. He escaped to a town in the mountains where he remained until he had word to return in haste and be proclaimed the new Sultan.

That was a day which Muley Hussan had spent in a pleasure garden outside the city walls, with the latest beauty of his harem. At sunset, returning, he found the gates of Granada barred against him, and remembering an old prophecy, cried aloud at his fate:

"Allah Akbar! Such is the will of Allah. Allah Akbar!"

El Zagal, "The Bold," another relative, now entered the family feud. He was Boabdil's uncle, a really great old warrior, justly known as "the Bold."

El Zagal joined his exiled brother, Muley Hussan, and helped him establish a new capital on the Mediterranean coast at Malaga, a city so fair and lovely that the Arabs called it their "Paradise on Earth." High mountains encircled and protected Malaga. Nevertheless, with Muley Hussan there, the Spaniards made an attempt to scale the mountains and capture the city. The soldiers were urged on with promise of robbery and plunder. Fierce old Muley Hussan did not sit still in his Paradise and wait for the invaders. With a mere handful of men, he went forth to met them in the mountains and left so many dead that from then on the mountains of Malaga were known to the Spaniards as the "Heights of Slaughter."

Isabella could not understand this awful defeat. Why in her Holy War against the infidels had the Lord allowed it to happen?

A curate spoke the truth. Robbery and plunder—not the service of the Lord—had been the thought of the majority. "The good must be punished when they have neglected God."

The Moslems were giving thanks to Allah for the victory and such high praise to Muley Hussan that to even up the score, Boabdil could see that he also needed to win a victory. For this, he chose to attack the Spanish town of Lucena.

It was an April morning in 1483 when young Boabdil set out from Granada with his troops, a murky morning filled with evil omens. The first occurred in the gateway when his horse stumbled and he broke his lance. Later, crossing a field, a fox dashed in front of him and ran through the whole army, which was enough to make the bravest men jittery. At Lucena they found the Spanish governor so bold and defiant they feared that a huge army was behind him. At the first encounter, panic struck the Arabs. They fled in disorder and only a few escaped death. Boabdil was found and captured crouching under a bush.

Next day the watchtowers of Granada were packed with people waiting for a messenger to return with news of victory.

"How goes it," they cried, "with the Sultan and the army?"

"There they lie," gasped the man, pointing toward Spain. "The heaven fell upon them. All are lost."

"Upon that sad note," said an Arab chronicler, "wailing was heard from palace to cottage... All Granada joined to deplore their brave young monarch cut down in the promise of youth." Fugitives from the battle then came straggling in with the truth. How Granada railed then at the cowardly young Sultan who had allowed himself to be captured! Old Muley Hussan was again their hero. They threw open the gates to him and hailed him once more as their rightful Sultan.

Boabdil had been taken prisoner, but now that Ferdinand and Isabella had him, they did not keep him, knowing that it would suit Muley Hussan far too well. Instead, they sent him back to stir up more trouble. Boabdil had barely established himself in the seaport of Almeria when his brave uncle, El Zagal, attacked the town and tried to capture his nephew, miserable traitor that he was. Boabdil barely escaped. Then, not knowing where else to go, he scurried back to Cordova and begged protection of Ferdinand and Isabella.

The old Sultan, Muley Hussan, restored to Granada, kept the confidence of the people until he lost another fort to the Spaniards. Then another wailing swept through the city, and another outcry against him.

El Zagal now appeared as the only one of the royal family who could save the Arab people from disaster. They sent a message to him, and the brave old warrior entered Granada in triumph to be hailed as the new Sultan.

Muley Hussan soon became ill and died, which again left but one Sultan in Granada, a peaceful situation which Ferdinand and Isabella could not allow to continue.

Boabdil was shipped home again, with enough money and men to regain his throne and keep the country once more upset and divided. In return, Boabdil weakly promised to surrender the capital city of Granada, as soon as Malaga and all the other bravely defended Arab forts should be captured by the Spanish.

ON JANUARY 6, 1481, the year that the "Holy War" against the Moslems began, a "Holy Fire" was lighted in Seville and six men and women were burned to death for the good of their souls, so that they need not burn hereafter in the fires of Hell. By the end of the year, 300 had been burned to death, and within the next ten years about 3,000. All had been convicted of being heretics—Christians whose belief was unorthodox, or converts suspected of slipping back into their original Jewish or Moslem religion. The man who passed judgment and stoked the unholy fire was Tómas de Torquemada, a Dominican friar, a thin, sallow, self-righteous man who had been confessor to Isabella when she was a girl. Now he easily convinced the Queen that she could never make Spain a united country if she tolerated any religious differences. All dissenters must be searched out and done away with. To do this, the Inquisition, an ancient tribunal for hunting down heretics, must be revived. His words were so eloquent he persuaded Isabella that what he proposed was the will of God. As for Ferdinand, he looked forward to getting his greedy hands on the wealth and property of the victims. So the Inquisition was re-established. Torquemada was appointed Inquisitor General for all of Spain, and the insane manhunt began.

Labels on illustration: John II, Prince Henry, John II, Alfonso V, AFRICA, GUINEA, CONGO

UNDER THE "PERFECT PRINCE"

YOUNG JOHN II, known as the "Perfect Prince," had now become the King of Portugal. Unlike his father Alfonso, he was tremendously interested in Africa, and devoted to carrying on the work of his great-uncle, Prince Henry. John was but a boy of five in 1460, when Prince Henry the Navigator died. That same year the explorer, Diogo Gomes, returned from the Gambia River. Since then, for twenty years, the actual exploration of Africa had been at a standstill. Though trading ships had been active enough, going out for slaves and gold, no one had been seriously searching for the sea route to India.

In 1481, as soon as John II became King, he renewed the search. First of all he sent out material to build a new fort on the Guinea coast, to be used as a base. For his first explorer, he chose a man whose father and grandfather had been trusted servants in the royal household. The man's name was Diogo Cam.

The fort, called St. George of the Mine, was built about 100 miles beyond the last point on the Guinea coast which Diogo Gomes had reached. Columbus visited the fort a year or two after it was built, going on one of the caravels that stopped at Porto Santo on the way. There he saw an almost endless stream of caravans loaded with gold and silver, trailing in from Timbuktu and other inland places, followed by a long line of pitiful natives, all to be shipped on the waiting caravels to Lisbon. Columbus was in command of two caravels on the return voyage from the new fort on the African gold coast.

Diogo Cam, the explorer, had then sailed from the Guinea fort down the shore of Africa, marking each key point where he landed with a large stone pillar called a Padrao. Each padrao was twice the height of a man, with a cross of lead embedded in it. Carved on one side was the royal coat of arms; on the other, the name of the King, the name of the explorer, and the date of the discovery.

The first padrao, bearing the date 1482, was erected by Diogo Cam 1,000 miles south of the Guinea fort, at the mouth of a mighty river he discovered rushing into the sea. The natives called it the Congo. The land through which it ran was also the Congo, and the great chief of the land was called Manicongo.

Diogo Cam sent four Portuguese up the river to pay their respects to Chief Manicongo while he himself went on to explore the shore farther south. Returning to pick up his four men, he found that they were being held as captives at Manicongo's village.

The explorer therefore seized four Africans, explaining as well as he could to a lesser chief that after fifteen moons he would bring back the four black men in exchange for his four white men, whom he had to assume would still be alive. On shipboard during the voyage the four Negroes were taught to speak some words in Portuguese and to kneel for morning and evening prayers. They were treated as royal guests when they arrived in Lisbon.

The royal welcome that King John gave Diogo Cam, his first explorer, and his reward, were beyond anything a loyal servant could have anticipated. He was given a generous sum of money and raised to the rank of nobleman—Dom Diogo Cam.

Late in the autumn of 1485 the happily successful explorer, Diogo Cam, returned to the Congo taking with him the four equally happy Negroes decked out in splendid Portuguese costumes and carrying a wealth of gifts to their Chief Manicongo. The four Portuguese were found alive and well, and overjoyed at the sight of their companions. The entire village crowded around the four natives to view and touch the fine clothes and hear of the wonders they had seen in the land of Portugal.

Manicongo nodded and smiled and was so happy with his new friend that when Captain Cam was ready to leave for Portugal the Chief sent with him one of his men who had made the first journey and also four younger men, sons of his chief lords. He wanted them instructed in "matters of the Faith," the Portuguese chronicler reported, "so that they might teach it later in their own country." He further begged as a favor that masons and carpenters be sent to build churches like those in Portugal, together with farmers and oxen and also Portuguese women who might teach the natives how to knead bread, for he would be very happy "for love of King John, if everything in the kingdom of the Congo should resemble Portugal."

As a present to King John, the good Manicongo sent the best that his country afforded—ivory and palm-leaf cloth. There was no gold in the Congo.

The last padrao bearing the name of Diogo Cam was left standing at Cape Cross, 700 miles beyond the Congo River. He had sailed 1,400 miles farther than Diogo Gomes, but he was still 900 miles from the end of Africa. The sea route to India was yet to be discovered.

Surely Diogo Cam's welcome and reward would have led Columbus to dream of still greater honors to be his on that great day when he had actually reached India by sailing west. Every year he grew more positive that it could be done.

He had received two encouraging letters from the Italian doctor-astronomer, Toscanelli, who had formerly written to King John's father, King Alfonso:

"To Cristóbal Columbo . . . Greeting," the first letter read. "I observe thy great and noble ambition to pass over where the spices grow. Wherefore in reply to thy letter I send thee the copy of another letter which sometime ago I wrote to a friend of mine, a servant of the most serene King of Portugal before the wars of Castile . . . and I send thee another sea chart like the one which I sent him, wherewith thy demand may be satisfied."

What especially thrilled Columbus was that Toscanelli agreed with Marco Polo about the width of the western ocean. He wrote:

"The course due west from Lisbon will take you in about 5,000 nautical miles to the Chinese province of Manzi . . . there are no great spaces of sea to be passed."

What more did Columbus need before presenting his project to King John? Nothing! He did some more calculation, not to convince himself—there was no need for that—but to prove to King John what a short distance it was from Portugal to India.

Finally the great day dawned. The Italian with the radical idea was ushered into the royal presence. As Columbus knelt before the handsome young king, his hair which had turned completely white must have made him appear much older than thirty-three, only four years older than the King himself. But as he began to speak, his words came tumbling out, charged with life and vigor; his ruddy face was aglow, his blue eyes fairly radiant.

John caught his enthusiasm at once, moved by his eloquence and impressed by his self-confidence. King John had, however, appointed a board of mathematicians to pass on all matters of navigation. He must have their opinion before making any decision.

The mathematicians were not so easily moved by eloquence. They dealt with facts and figures and were stopped cold, and rightly so, by the inaccurate figuring of this would-be explorer.

The earth was round. No scholar questioned that. But it was much farther around the earth than Columbus figured. One would have to sail 10,000—not 5,000—miles from Portugal to the eastern edge of Asia. Such a voyage was impossible. It would mean three months on the open ocean. No sailor had ever been even one month out of sight of land. No, the board did not recommend that King John finance such a costly enterprise, founded simply, as they saw it, "on imagination and such things as Marco Polo's isle of Cipangu (his name for Japan)."

The young enthusiastic King must have sympathized with Columbus in his disappointment. John was definitely curious about what if any unknown islands lay beyond the Azores. Somewhere out in the Atlantic there was supposed to be the island of Antilia, for which seamen had been searching since the days of Prince Henry. John may have wondered what his great-uncle, Prince Henry, would have said or done about this strange proposal. Would he also have sent this man, Christopher Columbus, away?

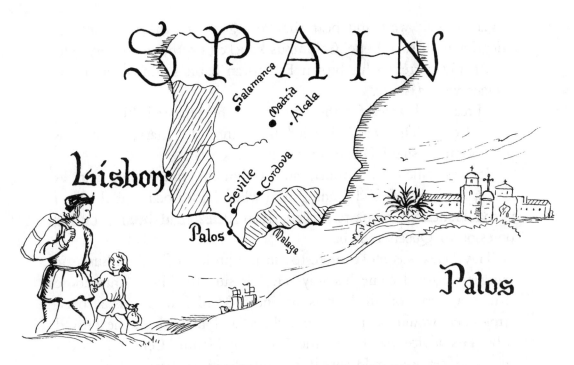

COLUMBUS GOES TO SPAIN

ON A MIDSUMMER DAY IN 1485, Columbus, with a small boy holding his hand, might have been seen trudging up a path from the harbor of Palos in southern Spain, toward a windy gray-green bluff to which clung the low red-tiled buildings of a monastery. The small boy was his five-year-old son Diego, whose mother, Felipa, was now dead and buried in Lisbon. There, too, at home in Lisbon, Uncle Bartholomew was still making maps. The boy Diego did not know why he and his father had to come away. All of a sudden they had hurried aboard a ship, and here they were in this lonesome place, walking up a hill, and he was thirsty.

Columbus had caught sight of the monastery even before the ship came to anchor. There, he thought, he might leave Diego, while he found a way to present his plan to Ferdinand and Isabella. For that one purpose, Columbus had left Portugal and come to Spain. The Spanish sovereigns had no rich gold mines in Africa. Nor were they seeking a way around Africa to India. So why should they not

131

be glad to sail west and beat the Portuguese to the riches of the Orient? Full of such hope, Columbus knocked on the monastery gate.

An old porter in his brown Franciscan habit squinted up at the stranger with a smile.

"Bread and water for the little one?" he repeated. "Indeed yes, and welcome. This way." He led them into the friary, which was to be home to small Diego for the next six years.

It was called La Rabida, and Columbus must have felt, as always, the hand of God guiding him when he learned that the head of the Franciscan monastery, Fray Juan Pérez, had been a former confessor to Queen Isabella.

Fray Pérez was most interested in the project of this enthusiastic stranger who had come his way. He felt sure that Fray Antonio de Marchena, head of all Franciscans near Seville, who was also an astronomer, would be most sympathetic and helpful. So he proved to be. His advice was to see the Count of Medina Celi, who had a merchant fleet and could supply the three or four caravels Columbus needed. But for so unusual an enterprise, the Count felt that he should receive royal permission.

In reply to his request, the Queen ordered Columbus to come to court that she might see the man from Genoa herself.

Isabella was then in Cordova, the main army base, with the four children, Isabel, Juan, Juana and three-year-old Maria, nurses, ladies-in-waiting, and all of the officials and members of the court. Ferdinand was with his generals in the field. As the autumn rains began, he rejoined the family in Cordova and they traveled north to spend the winter in Alcala.

There, on December 16, 1485, Catalina, the last of Isabella's children, was born and named for her mother's English grandmother, Catherine of Lancaster. This little girl was to become a Queen of England, the ill-fated Catherine of Aragon, wife of Henry VIII.

In January, therefore, when Christopher Columbus arrived in Cordova, all he could do was wait until the Queen returned in April.

Cordova

Cordova was a good place to wait, a fascinating old city, rich in the marvelous architecture of the Arabs. Walking through the old mosque with its hundreds of alabaster columns, was like walking through a fabulous forest made of stone. Sight-seeing alone, however, could not fill months of idle hours. Columbus still had time on his hands. Near one of the city gates he found an apothecary shop run by a man from Genoa, a popular meeting place for doctors, astronomers, and various scientists, as well as amateurs listening to their conversations. There he met young Diego de Harana, who one day invited Columbus home with him for dinner. Diego's father, a winepresser by trade, was an intelligent, cultured man. So was his mother. Living with them were two young cousins, orphans, Pedro Enriquez de Harana and his sister Beatriz.

Beatriz had a shy sweet smile for the handsome stranger who

came for dinner, and three years later she was to become the mother of his son Ferdinand.

Pedro de Harana, her brother, was to command one of the ships on Columbus' third voyage to America. Her cousin Diego was to go on the first voyage, which as yet was nothing but a dream and a subject for speculation in the old apothecary shop.

April, 1486, came at last. The royal family returned. Ferdinand went on to join the army for the spring campaign. The Queen and the children took up residence in the Alcazar, which had been the Sultan's palace in the days when the Arabs ruled Spain and their capital city was Cordova. One day in May, Columbus was summoned to an interview.

So it was in Cordova, in the Alcazar, on a day in May, 1486, that Christopher Columbus and Queen Isabella met for the first time, and the written history of America began.

On this May day, as Columbus knelt before her, Isabella saw a man of her own age, thirty-five, of much the same sturdy build and reddish-blond coloring.

This then was the man, the adventurous Italian from Genoa who had the curious idea of sailing westward to the Indies! Isabella listened attentively while he set forth his marvelous idea. She was impressed by the confidence he had in his own ability to cross the sea to India and bring back its treasures. She was especially moved by his fervent desire to carry to those lands the Christian religion. At the same time, practical questions were passing through her mind. Was sailing westward too difficult and costly to be worth the venture? If not, could the royal treasury afford to finance it? She assured Columbus that she would have a committee appointed to study the problems involved in the Enterprise, and arranged for him to live with the royal treasurer.

Very soon Isabella left Cordova, having received word from Ferdinand that the soldiers needed encouragement. She left for the front, taking with her the Infanta Isabel, now her favorite companion, as well as many ladies of the court and a troop of cavaliers and guards. Columbus may have seen them starting out in a splendid cavalcade.

The Queen was riding a chestnut mule, seated on a crimson velvet saddle cushion encrusted with gold, her face shaded by a wide-brimmed black hat. Clattering through Cordova's narrow streets they went, over the stone bridge, through the city gate, and down the road that led southeastward to the district of Jaen.

The mere sight of their Queen was enough to raise the spirits of the soldiers. And when she spoke she made them feel that they were Crusaders in a Holy War, as truly as if they had been trying to recapture Jerusalem.

By late fall Moclin had fallen, as well as many other forts that barred the way to Granada. Ferdinand returned to Cordova where the court was preparing for the annual trek north.

† Salamanca

This winter of 1486 was spent in Salamanca, a university town northwest of Madrid. Columbus accompanied the court, as did the committee who had been studying his Enterprise.

One of the committee members took Columbus to live with him in the Dominican monastery. Columbus was well aware that most of the committee considered his project impractical. But the simple friars of the monastery had faith in him and his sacred mission, as he saw it, and for their faith he was very grateful.

In his search for arguments to present to the skeptical committee, Columbus was now pleased to have found a French author who also thought that the size of Asia was wider and the ocean narrower than Ptolemy admitted. This is what he said:

"The ocean which stretches between Spain . . . and the western edge of India is of no great width . . . and the sea is navigable in a very few days if the wind be fair."

What did the worthy gentlemen of the committee say to that? Did it convince them? It did not. However, it was decided not to make too hasty a report. After all, it was only spring, less than a year since they had begun to deliberate.

So spring had come again, time again to move south. The royal family, the court, the committee, and Columbus all packed up and journeyed back to Cordova, and as usual Ferdinand went south to join the army for the spring campaign.

No one knows what Columbus found to do in that spring of 1487 other than to read and wait—and hope.

 ## Malaga

The spring of 1487 brought the siege of Malaga, the lovely Mediterranean seaport which the Arabs called their "Paradise on Earth." Ferdinand turned upon its walls a constant bombardment, using the most powerful cannon that the munition-makers imported from Germany were able to produce. The Arabs fought desperately, making furious sallies from the fortress against the Spanish troops. In one encounter Ferdinand himself was nearly killed.

When Isabella arrived at camp to stay until Malaga surrendered, the booming of the big guns was almost incessant and the towers of the city all but hidden by the smoke. At her request the firing ceased while a messenger of peace was sent to the Moslem general, offering generous terms if he would surrender. If not, when Malaga was captured, Ferdinand gave warning that he would make slaves of every man, woman, and child still alive in the city.

Hamet Zeli, the proud defender of Malaga, sent back the

Spanish messenger with no reply and threatened death to any coward among his own Arab officers who even dared to utter the word, "surrender." Help was surely on the way, he told them. In that he was both right and wrong. Old El Zagal, "the Bold," was indeed on his way to relieve the city. But the traitor Boabdil was also on the way. His troops attacked the forces of his uncle and prevented them from reaching Malaga to rescue the starving defenders. And so, all hope gone, ammunition exhausted, Hamet Zeli was forced by his officers to open the gates. The Spaniards rushed in and sacked the city. Ferdinand kept his threat to the letter, and then claimed "the blessing of God" for the awful act.

Just a week after the surrender of Malaga, Columbus received a summons to go to the royal encampment and also sufficient funds to make the journey from Cordova. With what a high heart he must have told his skeptical friends in the apothecary shop that the sovereigns had sent for him! How far he must have sailed in imagination on the way to Malaga!

But when he got there, he found no reason to have come. The committee had made no report. The sovereigns had no time to see him. They were too busy preparing to leave for Aragon where Prince Juan, now nine years old, was to be recognized as heir to his father's throne in a formal ceremony.

Columbus had barely a word with them before they left. So what could he do but return to Cordova? There, on top of his blighted hopes, he had to face the ridicule of those skeptics who had known before he went what would happen. Why would the crazy man think that the King and Queen would let him sail off for Asia in the wrong direction?

A year passed. Columbus was still waiting to hear and still holding his faith under all the scorn and ridicule. Isabella may have remembered, but it is likely that Ferdinand had quite forgotten about him, in the tangle of international plots and plans in which he was becoming more and more involved each year.

Le Morte d'Artur

THE RETURN OF "KING ARTHUR"

THE SUMMER OF 1485 when Columbus went to Spain, Henry Tudor returned to England to make himself King. That spring, after waiting around in France for over a year, word came at last that all plans for his return to England had been completed. This time he was to land in Wales.

Men of Wales were ready to take up arms in support of that native son. Henry Tudor's return was even being heralded as the return of King Arthur, whose home had also been in Wales. Welsh bards and minstrels, roaming through the mountains and valleys were singing ballads about their ancient, semi-mythical King and his Knights of the Round Table, adding new verses to the Arthur story as bards had been doing for 1,000 years.

As it happened, just one week before Henry Tudor landed in Wales, the first book in English about King Arthur had been published in London by Sir William Caxton, the printer. It was called

"Morte d'Arthur" and had been written by Sir Thomas Malory while he was in prison during the Wars of the Roses. Malory finished it in 1469. Two years later Henry Tudor, then a boy of fourteen, had fled for refuge to Brittany. Now he was returning, and on August 7, 1485, exactly one week after this book was published, Henry Tudor, of whom the Welsh bards were singing, landed in Milford Haven on the west coast of Wales.

On Monday, August 22nd, two weeks and one day later, Henry Tudor defeated Richard III at the Battle of Bosworth. That day the long line of Plantagenet kings, whose outstanding quality was courage, came to an end. The crown fell from Richard's head, his dead body, naked and bloodied was slung across the back of a horse and taken for burial to the charitable Good Friars of Leicester. In his own city of York, the Mayor and Aldermen recorded that on that day, "King Richard, late mercifully reigning over us was . . . piteously slain and murdered, to the great heaviness of this city."

Men of York could scarcely believe it. Richard, the most experienced and skillful warrior in England had been defeated. They had been slow in sending forces to help him, only because they were so sure the invader had no chance to win.

Henry Tudor himself had been far from confident, never having fought a battle in his life. For two weeks after landing in Wales he had been marching northeast, adding to his forces as he went, but without knowing how to manage the men. He needed generals with experience. He needed the Stanleys. Sir William Stanley, his mother's husband, where was he? Where was Lord Stanley, his brother? Henry had sent both men orders to join him at once. Where were they? Would they never come? Had they deserted him?

The question of where the Stanleys were was also disturbing King Richard. He had written them both—Lord Stanley and Sir William, whom he had once pardoned for treason—to meet him at Nottingham. Lord Stanley had sent the feeble excuse that he was ill. Sir William did not reply. Both, commanding large armies of

their own, were playing it safe. They did not intend to be on the losing side, whichever that might be. Though they favored Henry Tudor, as late as Friday when they met him at Atherstone, they refused to commit themselves.

Sunday, along an ancient Roman side road running east and west, Henry and Richard, with their armies, were traveling steadily toward each other, both men encased in the full armor of medieval knights. Henry's standard and shield bore the red dragon, emblem of the first King of Wales. On King Richard's shield was his personal emblem, the boar. On top of his helmet he wore a golden crown. Above him floated the banners of England and of England's patron saint, St. George, the dragon-slayer.

Monday morning came. On the brow of the hill, on which he was encamped, Richard sat on his white horse quietly scanning the battlefield, his lips set in a thin line. The golden crown on his helmet caught rays of sunlight as he moved his head, even slightly. To his right he saw the army of Sir William Stanley, which he now knew would be used against him. Straight ahead, on a rise of ground, were the forces of Henry Tudor. At his request a man with keener sight than his own located the standard of the red dragon and there, nearby, beneath it, seated on horseback, was Henry.

Richard had made up his mind to take a tremendous risk. Alone, with no more than one hundred volunteers from his own household, he would ride for Henry Tudor, crossing directly in front of the forces of William Stanley, counting on the move being too quick for them to rally. The hour to do it came. He stood in his stirrups and turning, cried to his men, "We ride for Henry Tudor!" With that cry Richard III began the battle of Bosworth.

Closing his visor, he took a battle-ax from one of his squires, spurred his horse, was off down the hill, and across the intervening field. Fighting his way up the other slope, he came so close to Henry that the red dragon struck the ground as his standard bearer parried the blow from Richard's battle-ax.

By then William Stanley's forces had rushed to the scene, overwhelmed, and broken through Richard's small band of men, and reaching the King, pierced through his coat of mail again and again with their swords.

The crown which had fallen from his helmet was picked up by Sir William and placed on the head of the new King, who wasted no time in broadcasting leaflets telling of his victory, announcing that he, Henry Tudor, by grace of God, was now King of England and of France, Prince of Wales and Lord of Ireland.

THE FIRST TUDOR AND HIS ROSE

NEXT IN ORDER of business, the new King of England, Henry VII, having taken the throne by force, set about making his position secure. One of the first things he did after his coronation was to create a standing royal guard, something no King of England had ever had before.

A neat trick by which he gained wealth immediately was to predate the beginning of his reign to two days before the Battle of Bosworth. That way, twenty-eight loyal lords who had defended King Richard could be convicted of treason against "King" Henry and so be beheaded and their property confiscated.

Henry appointed Bishop Morton, who had already served him well and had now been made Archbishop of Canterbury, as Chancellor, or head of the Royal Treasury. The wily Bishop devised a scheme of taxation that came to be known as Morton's Fork, because all subjects rich or poor could be caught on one of its two tines. Those who lived well were made to pay because obviously they had money. Those who did not, it was argued, must be saving their money, and were forced to part with whatever little they had.

Lady Margaret & Queen Elizabeth of York

On January 18, 1486, Henry VII married the Princess Elizabeth, according to the arrangement made by his mother, Lady Margaret, who, in her son's opinion, could do no wrong. Young Queen Elizabeth, who was to live completely in the shadow of her tiny, forceful mother-in-law, fulfilled her duties as a wife, and in the autumn of 1486 bore Henry VII a son of more royal lineage than his own. Henry had arranged that the child should be born at Winchester, the home of Britain's ancient kings, and should be given the famous name of Arthur.

Today in Winchester Castle may be seen a huge round table, decorated at this time with the picture of King Arthur, the names of his knights, and in the center, the new pink Tudor rose, combining the red rose of Lancaster and the white rose of York.

THE YEAR 1488 IN CORDOVA

ON A BRIGHT DAY in the summer of 1488, small round-faced Catalina of Aragon, who was two-and-a-half, dressed in her best brocaded silk dress, stiff with jewels, sat beside her mother, Queen Isabella, at the bull ring in Medina del Campo. For the first time she was seeing a bullfight. First the matadors and the picadors came riding in. Then in came the toreador with his flaming cape. Then came the brave black bull. Men stuck the bull's neck full of colored darts, and the bull lunged at the dancing man with the red cape. His sword flashed. Everybody cried, "Olé Olé." And the black bull was dead.

Next to her mother sat some strange gentlemen who peered at her and smiled at her and called her "Little Princess of Wales."

The strange gentlemen, who were from England, had good reason to smile. They had just made a valuable alliance for their King Henry VII, by arranging a marriage between Arthur, Prince of Wales, who would soon be two, and little Catherine of Aragon. Her dowry of 200,000 crowns would be a tidy sum for the King of England!

144

Ferdinand, for his part, was not too enthusiastic about the alliance with England's new King. In view of their recent history and the reputation of the English for being treacherous people, he was not sure how long Henry VII would last. However, that would be proven before the actual marriage took place. So the bargain was signed and sealed. And little round-faced Catalina was to grow up knowing that when she was old enough she would go to live in England and marry Arthur, the Prince of Wales.

Fernando Colon

In Cordova that same year, 1488, a son was born on August 15th to Beatriz Enriquez de Harana and Christopher Columbus. He was given the name of a saint, which was also that of the King, Fernando, or Ferdinand. This was Ferdinand Columbus, who in the last years of his life was to write the *Historie* of his beloved and illustrious father.

In the year 1488, however, the year of Ferdinand's birth, Christopher Columbus was far from "illustrious." For two years he had been waiting for Isabella's committee to pass on his Enterprise, and no report had been made. Now the sovereigns had cut off his allowance. They seemed to have lost all interest in him. Why should he wait any longer, and starve while he waited?

Why not go back to Portugal? Three years had passed since he had come to Spain. The Portuguese had not yet found the way around the end of Africa to India. They might be ready now to let him prove that he could get to India by sailing west. He decided to go and wrote a letter to King John which reached him at just the right time—just before the exciting news reached Portugal that his ships had rounded the Cape of Good Hope.

Bon Esperañza:

OF HOPE AND DESPAIR

EARLY IN THE YEAR 1488, Bartholomew Dias had discovered the Cape of Good Hope. The sea route to India had been found! But the successful explorer had not yet returned to Portugal when King John received the letter from Columbus.

Bartholomew Dias, a skillful navigator and a most trustworthy man, had sailed from Lisbon in the summer of 1487 to search again for the southern end of Africa and the entrance to the Indian Ocean.

Three months earlier, King John had sent out another explorer, Pero de Covilhao, who was to travel eastward toward India, by way of Egypt, and was also to search for the empire of that mysterious Christian ruler called Prester John, believed to be somewhere in Africa.

Possibly King John was then inclined to send out a third explorer in another direction. Certainly he wrote a most cordial reply to Columbus, calling him his "particular friend" and urging him to come to Portugal immediately.

For some unknown reason, Columbus, as delighted as he must have been with the letter, did not go "immediately." It was late in the year when he left Cordova, and it was December before he set his shabby bags and books down in his brother's shop in Lisbon. And in that very month of December what did Columbus see?

The ships of Bartholomew Dias sailing into the harbor of Lisbon with the great news that the long-sought-for sea route to India had been found!

Columbus was present when Bartholomew Dias made his report describing the voyage to King John.

It had taken about six months to reach the end of Africa which they found 1,400 miles farther south than the last padrao erected by Diogo Cam. They were then in very cold and treacherous waters and had rounded the final cape without knowing it, blown about in such a violent storm that for two weeks the sailors scarcely hoped to survive. But when the storm abated, the shoreline could be seen running east and west instead of north and south. Landing on that southernmost point of Africa, they erected a padrao on the windy but beautiful cape, to be known as the Cape of Good Hope.

Bartholomew Dias was sadly disappointed, however, that having gone so far he could not complete the voyage to India. After sailing on a few miles past the Cape, the officers advised him most strongly to turn back. He did so with such deep regret that he made each man sign a paper that they had made the decision.

One of the officers said that as they were leaving Cape Good Hope behind, Commander Dias stood watching the padrao disappear "with as much sorrow as if he were leaving a son in exile."

Columbus was most impressed by the data and charts which Bartholomew Dias had brought to show the King, particularly as he saw in them added proof of what the French geographer said about the proportion of land and water on the globe. He talked of it to his brother when he returned to the shop. Opening his copy of D'Ailly's geography *Imago Mundi* to the proper page he wrote this note in the margin:

Note: that in December of this year 1488, Bartholomaeus Didacus commander of the three caravels which the King of Portugal had sent out . . . landed in Lisbon. He reported that he had reached a promontory which he called Cabo de Boa Esperanca. He described his voyage and plotted it league by league on a marine chart, in order to place it under the eyes of said King. I was present in all of this.

Closing the book, he waited for his industrious brother Bartholomew to look up from the map on which he was working. It was obvious, they agreed, that since the Portuguese had now discovered their own way to India, King John was not going to be interested in searching for another route. But who would be? What other ruler? What about Henry VII of England? Or possibly Anne of France, who was known to be a collector of maps, and a woman of great intelligence and imagination.

It was finally decided that Bartholomew should go first to England and if Henry VII did not respond, he would go on to Paris to see Anne of France. Since there was still some slight hope that Ferdinand and Isabella might finance the venture, Columbus returned to Spain.

Back in Cordova, Columbus resigned himself to more of the same waiting, praying and hoping for a favorable report from the committee, and to being pointed out and scoffed at as a crackpot clinging to a crazy notion. What else he did, how he got enough to live, is a question. It was a time in his life too miserable for him ever to recall. One more long year finally dragged itself to an end. And at last in 1490 the committee handed in their report and just as the scoffers predicted, it was unfavorable. The sovereigns were advised not "to favor an affair which appeared impossible to any educated person however little learning he might have." They gave the following reasons:

1. A voyage to India would require three years.
2. The western ocean was infinite and perhaps unnavigable.
3. If one reached the other side of the globe he could not get back.
4. There was no land there, because St. Augustine had said that three-fourths of the globe was covered with water.
5. So many centuries after the creation of the world it was not likely that any unknown land of value would be found.

In short, the committee, after due deliberation, considered the project of Columbus, "impossible, vain, and worthy of rejection."

Ferdinand and Isabella, however, told Columbus that he might bring it to their attention later if he cared to, when the war with Granada was over and they had more time to consider it.

At that time, they were also busy with preparations for the wedding of their first daughter, the Infanta Isabel, to Prince Alfonso, son of King John of Portugal, to whom she had been betrothed for eleven years. The Infanta was married by proxy with pomp and ceremony in Seville, after which the bride traveled in state to Lisbon where the marriage was repeated in November, 1490. A few months later young Alfonso was killed in an accident, and a sorrowful young widow returned to her sympathetic parents, who were also distressed that the alliance with Portugal had so suddenly collapsed.

Columbus, meanwhile, was waiting month after month for that possible sometime when the sovereigns might feel free enough to reconsider his Enterprise. Clinging to this thin thread of hope, he read and re-read his books, especially that favorite volume—*The Travels of Marco Polo*—filling the margin of the pages with many notes. He kept studying the map, refiguring the distance Marco Polo traveled across Asia to China, estimating again the distance he him-

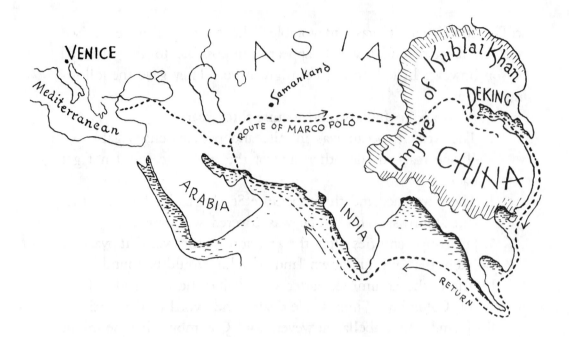

self must sail westward across the ocean to reach the land of the Great Khan. As he did so, he kept building up more and more confidence that it could be done.

This map shows the caravan route followed by Marco Polo to China and also the way he returned home, which was by sea down around the Malay peninsula and India, as far as Persia.

It also shows the empire of the Mongol ruler, Kublai Khan, who had conquered China in 1264 and was the Great Khan whom Marco Polo visited, and whom he called, "The mightiest man who has ever been from Adam our first parent down to the present moment."

Less than one hundred years, however, after the death of the mighty Kublai Khan, the Chinese had overthrown the Mongol rulers and established their own Imperial Chinese Dynasty of Ming. So, although Columbus and all other Europeans still talked about the Great Khan of China, there had been no Khan, great or otherwise, in China for over a century.

On the map: Empire of GENGHIS KHAN · Moscow · SARAI · Samarkand · Andijan · Empire of KUBLAI KHAN 1264 · Grandson of Genghis · Empire of TIMUR 1364 · ARABIA · INDIA · CHINA

BABER, A FUTURE CONQUEROR

THIS IS BABER, the future conqueror of northern India. In 1488, the year that the sea route to India was discovered by the Portuguese, Baber was five years old. In 1526 he was to become the first of those great Moguls who were to rule India for 300 years, until the coming of the British.

Baber had two mighty ancient ancestors. One was Genghis Khan, the first and most famous of the Mongol conquerors, who by 1224 had made himself ruler over a vast area of Asia. The other was Timur, or Tamerlane, who lived a hundred years later, and was half

151

Turk and half Mongol. The capital of his empire was the large and splendid city of Samarkand.

Baber was born in the fertile valley of Fergana in the much smaller town of Andijan, on the caravan trail between Samarkand and China. Caravans coming from China often stopped to rest in the clover meadows just outside the city walls. Drivers could be seen lifting the cargo of silks and jewels from the backs of the long-haired yaks and Mongol ponies that had carried them through the mountains onto horses that would take them on to Samarkand. It was a slow, tedious journey over the mountains and desert, and a dangerous one. In the mountains east of Andijan one winter, a caravan was caught in a narrow pass by the deep snow, and all had frozen to death but two men who had been rescued by Baber's father, Omar Sheik.

It was through his father Omar Sheik that Baber was descended from Timur, and through his mother from Genghis Khan. It was his mother's father who gave him the name of Baber, which was really a nickname meaning "Tiger." When he was just a year old his grandfather, who was the Khan of Stone City, had come riding into Andijan to attend the Mongol ceremony of having the baby boy's head shaved for the first time. The old man had asked what name the baby had been given and was told "Zahir-ud-Din-Muhammad," meaning "Bearer of the Faith of Mohammed."

"Ho ho," he laughed, "that's too long a name for such a little tiger." So from then on Grandfather called the baby boy "Baber," and everyone else did the same.

The year that he was five, Baber was taken by his father Omar Sheik on his first visit to Samarkand. Sultan Ahmed, Baber's uncle, the oldest of his father's brothers, had inherited the ancestral throne in Samarkand. He had invited his three brothers, who were all jealous of one another, to attend a Peace Festival.

As part of the Festival, it had been arranged that Baber should marry Ahmed's small daughter, Ayesha. The five-year-old cousins

did not like each other. Ayesha soon ran away and hid, and Baber
was glad of it. The opinion of these royal children of Asia, however,
mattered no more than that of those royal two-year-olds of Europe,
Catherine of Aragon and Arthur of England, whose betrothal in that
same year was also used to seal a treaty.

Asia's river Syr runs through the beautiful fertile valley of
Fergana. One soft summer day, slim, dark-eyed ten-year-old Baber
sat cross-legged under a shady tree by the river eating a very large,
very juicy, very delicious melon. Not far away his short, fat, amiable
father Omar Sheik was talking with the man who grew the melons
which were known as Lord Timurs. Baber understood why. Nothing
but the very best could be named for that great ancestor of his, whose
palace and tomb he had seen in Samarkand. Baber would never forget what he saw on that visit, especially the Echoing Mosque and
the painting of Lord Timur fighting with the elephants of India.

With a deep sigh of satisfaction, Baber finished the luscious
melon just as his father called to him saying that they would go now
to the pigeon house. He jumped on his horse that had been grazing
nearby, and the man and boy rode off up the trail in the direction
of Akhsi, the oldest, highest fortress in their valley. Baber never
saw his father so blissfully happy as when he was there feeding his
pigeons, the air filled with their fluttering wings as they circled him
from turban to slippers.

The fortress of Akhsi had once been Omar Sheik's home, but
was now deserted except for the pigeons whose house teetered on
the edge of the cliff. The royal family now lived in Andijan where

the dusty streets of the town came right up to the castle walls. Until Baber was six he had lived in the harem with his sister, his mother, and his grandmother, who all loved him dearly, each in her own way. At six he had begun to live in his father's part of the castle and to ride with him through the valley, stopping as they had this morning to sample the fruit and melons.

The valley of Fergana was so rich and fertile that it was the envy of Omar Sheik's older brother, who would take it from him if he could. Omar Sheik did not trust even his oldest brother, the Sultan Ahmed, who had held the Peace Festival.

How would it be, he would sometimes say to Baber, if he, Omar Sheik, should start out one day and conquer Samarkand? Then, as they were riding along, he would go on to imagine great deeds of bravery and daring that he might accomplish, but never would. He was too good-natured and easy-going, Baber knew that. But as to Samarkand, how wonderful it would be to be the Sultan and the ruler of that wonderful city, which he supposed had been built by the great Lord Timur—until he studied history. Then Baber learned, as he told his father, that it had been built 1,600 years earlier by Alexander, a Greek who had also conquered northern India, but had lost it again, just as Lord Timur had.

Omar Sheik knew almost no history, reading little else than the Koran. But he wanted his son Baber to study everything—poetry, music, astronomy, history, mathematics, as well as the teachings of the Prophet. Omar Sheik was not much of a soldier, and was too fat for a horseman, but he was already having a rough old warrior

teach Baber how to ride, how to handle the scimitar and the saber, how to shoot moving objects with the short Turkish bow, and how to hit targets that were behind him, while hanging from his saddle.

Each day Baber studied with his tutor, indoors by the brazier in winter, outside in the orchard garden when the weather was mild. He was quick to learn and helped his smaller half-brothers with arithmetic and algebra, using the same numerals and decimal system that the Arabs had carried into Spain. His books were written in Arabic and Persian, though he spoke a form of Turkish.

Yakub, a clever young Lord, taught Baber to play polo. He also warned him that when he became the Sheik he must find a stronger ruler to protect him for, said he, "If a royal eagle does not fly over you, a black crow will pick your bones!"

The old Judge, most wise and upright of his father's advisors, told Baber that a strong ruler was not enough to rely upon. The only sure protection for any man lay in following the will of Allah.

All those words and warnings Baber was to remember in the fearful days of danger so soon to come upon him.

Old Kasim, master of the household, was first to smell danger in the wind and warn Omar Sheik. The Sultan Ahmed of Samarkand, he said, and the new Khan of Stone City, were seen riding together toward Fergana, grazing their horses ever closer and closer. That meant they planned to invade the valley and attack Andijan. Omar Sheik heard the words but did not heed the meaning and as it happened, never had to face the attack. One afternoon he rode off alone to Akhsi to feed his pigeons, stepped into the pigeon house, and as Baber recorded in his diary:

"The pigeon house fell down the cliff, with its pigeons and with Omar Shaikh, who took his flight to the other world. That month at twelve years of age, I became king of Ferghana."

From that day, the life of the boy King became one long series of hairbreadth escapes. "At first," Baber confessed, "I could not help crying a good deal." But he kept saying his five daily prayers, and kept believing that "God alone could put matters right." Strengthened by that faith, he survived to become years later the ruler of northern India, the first of the Great Moguls.

About the time that Genghis Khan's grandson, Kublai Khan, had conquered China, another grandson, Batu, conquered Russian land along the Volga River. Since then, two hundred years had passed, but the Mongol rulers were still there on the Volga River, still demanding tribute from the Grand Duke of Muscovy, and the Grand Duke, with an exaggerated idea of their power, was still paying it.

Labels on map: NOVGOROD, Moscow, THE OKA RIVER, LITHUANIA, THE VOLGA, Sarai, CASPIAN SEA, BOUNDARY OF THE GOLDEN HORDE, BLACK SEA, CONSTANTINOPLE

IVAN III DEFIES THE MONGOL KHAN

A ND HOW MUCH LONGER do you intend to pay it?" demanded Sophia. "Do you intend to be a slave to those Tatars forever?" This was the Empress of Russia speaking to her husband, Ivan III, who seemed unable to screw up courage enough to throw off the age-old custom of groveling before the Mongol Khans. She

157

called it humiliating and disgraceful, and spoke of the Mongols as Tatars, or Tartars, a scornful name used by Europeans for all nomad tribes living east of the Black Sea.

The Russians also called the nomads along the Volga River the Golden Horde, from the large, golden-yellow pavilions or tents they carried with them on the plains, and which were still to be seen lined up along the Volga outside their city of Sarai.

Just outside Moscow there was a spot on the road where, following the custom of his ancestors, Ivan must go on foot carrying a goblet of mare's milk to meet an emissary of the Khan, or kiss the stirrups of the Khan himself.

At last in 1476, Sophia's prodding bore fruit. When the yearly summons came from the Khan of the Volga to appear before him, Ivan III sent the Khan a hostile reply. And when a second Tatar envoy arrived, he stomped on the Khan's image, which he was expected to revere. The break had been made. What would be the penalty? Four years of uncertainty followed.

Then in 1480, the Khan of the Volga set forth for Moscow, heading a horde of wild riding horsemen, armed with scimitars and short Turkish bows. Horsetail banners flying, they dashed across the windy plains and brought up short on the bank of the Oka River not many miles from Moscow.

Ivan was terror-stricken. Sending Sophia rushing out of the city toward Archangel with their year-old son Basil, he was about to follow when an angry mob blocked his way screaming their grievances.

"You, our Tsar, took our rubles to pay the Khan, and you did not pay him! Now he threatens our lives and you do not protect us!"

Russian generals and soldiers were gathering on the Oka River. That, they said, was where he belonged, there with the army.

The Bishops agreed with the people. "Go and face the Khan," they told him, "for the good of your soul. God will exact payment from you for the blood of your people if you allow it to be shed."

To make sure of his departure, the Metropolitan came from the Cathedral of the Archangel Michael to bless Ivan as a soldier of the cross, and speed him on his way. Bells, large and small, rang and clanged as the hesitant defender finally rode away to join the encampment on the Oka River.

There he found an army of 150,000 men and a golden pavilion waiting for him as rich and elaborate as that of a Mongol Khan. Safely inside the handsome tent, Ivan sat down, but would not even look out across the river for fear of seeing a horde of Mongol horsemen there ready to destroy him. Actually, the far side of the river was peaceful. Horses were grazing, but there was no camp in sight—not one golden pavilion to be seen. The officers urged Ivan to give them orders to move against the enemy, but in vain. Priests came to plead with him after the officers had failed to move him. It was no use. Ivan would not budge. Councillors finally suggested that since he refused to fight he might ask the Khan for a peaceful settlement. That, Ivan agreed to do. The envoys sent to the Khan returned with this answer:

"Let Duke Ivan come in person, kiss the stirrups of the Khan and pay the tribute that he has not paid for years past."

This Ivan would not do. Nor would he move forward. He simply sat. Weeks passed; autumn cold set in. The river began to freeze. Soon the soldiers could have walked across the ice. And at last the Tsar issued the command to move. But not across the river!

Back to Moscow!

And so ended the ridiculous encounter. For some unknown reason, instead of pursuing the retreating Russians, the Tatars also retreated, all the way back to their city on the Volga.

The Khan was later murdered in his sleep and his sons overthrown by a rival, the Tatar Khan of the Crimea.

The Golden Horde along the Volga was no longer a menace. After this absurd "no-battle victory" on the Oka River, no tribute was ever paid by a Russian ruler to a Mongol Khan.

GERMAN ROMAN RUSSIAN

Kings and princes of Europe were now becoming somewhat curious about the mysterious land called Muscovy which lay on the edge of Asia and about Muscovy's Grand Duke, who had begun calling himself Caesar. Ivan III, too, began looking westward beyond his immediate neighbors, Lithuania and Poland, toward the kings and princes of Europe, though even the Roman Emperor seemed to him a feeble creature compared to the mighty Shah of Persia, the powerful Sultan of Turkey, and the Mongol Khans of Asia.

Ivan's first real contact was with Italy. Three years after his new wife had come from Rome, Italian architects were at work in Moscow. It had been Sophia's idea to send for them. Hardly had she set foot in that crude city made of wood, than she began to think of having all the old buildings of the Kremlin replaced with beautiful palaces of stone and marble. Ivan was easily persuaded, because he wanted stronger walls built about the Kremlin.

Some of the old cathedrals also needed rebuilding, but for that Ivan III would not trust an Italian, whose design might be that of a Roman Catholic cathedral. He employed Russians, who knew what a Greek Orthodox Church should be like. That is why, in Moscow, exotic cathedrals with colorful onion-shaped domes stand side by side with marble palaces of classic design.

In 1486, a German named Nicholas Poppel ventured, out of

160

curiosity, as far as Moscow, appeared at the court of Ivan III, and rushed back to Vienna to report what he had seen. The German Emperor, Frederick III, sent Herr Poppel back at once to announce to this reportedly important Duke of Muscovy that he, the Emperor, would be willing to grant the Grand Duke the higher title of "King."

To that condescending offer, Ivan III sent this haughty reply: "We have been emperor of our land since the beginning, and from our earliest forefathers and do hold our commission from God himself even as they." He signed himself Tsar of all Russia. Ivan III, the Grand Duke of Muscovy might call himself Tsar of all Russia, but that was as yet an empty title, for there was no such nation as Russia. It was, however, the firm purpose of the new Tsar that there should be one. He intended to draw all the surrounding steppes and forests into a Russian nation, with Moscow as the heart of it. He had already absorbed ancient Novgorod, adding a vast northern area to his original Muscovy. Now he looked toward Lithuania, and by 1492 was to conquer a large area of that western land and add it to his growing empire. So, in those years just preceding the discovery of the New World, the lands of Russia, as well as those of France, Spain, and England were being welded into a nation.

Only Germany and Italy were to remain as they had been during the Middle Ages, broken up into small independent states.

Germany was more united than Italy. The German princes of state and church acknowledged a sort of loyalty to the Emperor who was elected by them. They sent representatives to his Imperial Diet of Council, and though the Emperor had no political power over them they occasionally voted him a little money.

In Italy there was no unity whatever. All that kept any semblance of peace between the city states was the influence of Lorenzo de Medici. When he should be gone, peace in Italy would also be gone and the golden years of Florence as leader of the Italian Renaissance would have come to an end.

LORENZO, THE MAGNIFICENT

ONE DAY IN THE SPRING of 1489, shortly before his fortieth birthday and three years before his death, Lorenzo the Magnificent was seated at a table in one of the long upper windows of the Medici Palace that looked down on the inner courtyard and Donatello's statue of David. On the dark table that stood at right angles to the window lay an unopened letter, which a few moments before had been delivered by a messenger from Milan.

Also spread before Lorenzo were the pages of an illuminated manuscript, and various small treasures intended for the Medici museum, one a piece of ivory so delicately carved that he had been examining it through a magnifying glass.

After a few moments he laid it aside, reached for the letter from Milan and broke the seal. For a brief second he closed his eyes to endure a sharp pain due to gout from which he suffered extremely. He then unfolded the letter, a mixture of expressions crossing his face as he read it.

The letter was from his friend, Ludovico Sforza, the ruler of Milan, often called Il Moro or "The Moor," due to his complexion which was almost as dark as that of the Moors from North Africa.

Il Moro was writing about Leonardo da Vinci, who was then at his court. Six years ago Sforza had written asking Lorenzo to recommend someone to make an equestrian statue of his father, Francesco Sforza. Lorenzo had unhesitatingly recommended Leonardo da Vinci who then for five years had had a studio in the Medici gardens.

Now Il Moro's patience was exhausted. Leonardo, it seemed, had been making hundreds of sketches and clay models of snorting horses in all possible positions, but was never well enough satisfied to set Father Sforza on the horse and complete the statue. Would Lorenzo recommend another sculptor to finish it?

Lorenzo could well understand Il Moro's impatience. At the same time he appreciated Leonardo's desire for perfection. Taking his quill he quickly scratched a reply saying that he could think of no one better to finish the statue than Leonardo himself.

Sculpture, at this time, was Lorenzo's special interest. He had recently established a school in his gardens where the marvelous collection of ancient Greek and Roman figures would serve as inspiration for the pupils. As teacher, he had engaged a former pupil of his grandfather's famous old sculptor, Donatello.

Ghirlandajo, a well-known painter of Florence, had been asked to select his most promising pupils to be enrolled in the new school.

One of these budding sculptors, a boy of fourteen, had taken a discarded scrap of marble and carved the head of a faun. He was very busy polishing it one morning when, glancing up, he saw the great Lorenzo himself, looking rather amused.

"This faun you are making is old," he said, "yet he has all his teeth. Are not aged men always lacking a tooth or two?"

The boy took his chisel and cleverly chipped out a tooth. Lorenzo, watching, asked his name and that of his father.

"Michelangelo," replied the boy, and gave the name of his father as Ludovico Buonarroti.

"Michelangelo Buonarroti, tell your father when you go home this evening that I wish to speak to him."

Full of excitement at being singled out, Michelangelo delivered the message. His father flew into the same kind of a rage as he had a year ago when the boy had wanted to become a painter. He would go and talk to the great de Medici, because he had to. But give permission for him to make a common stone-cutter out of his son, or ruin him with evil living? That he would never do!

But how could the good man refuse when the Magnificent Lorenzo explained so graciously what his intentions were?

"You have a gifted son," he said, "in your Michelangelo. I am asking him to live here as one of my family to study and become a sculptor. This will give me great pleasure, knowing that one day he will do honor to us all and to Florence."

The charm of the great patron, so unaffected and irresistible, brought a warm response from the boy's father.

"Not Michelangelo alone," said he, "but all of us with our lives and our abilities are at the pleasure of your Magnificence."

And what position, Lorenzo then asked, would the good man desire for himself? Buonarroti replied that as he had never practiced any art or trade, he could think of nothing at the time. Later he asked for a place in the Customs Office that had fallen vacant, feeling "able to fulfill its duties decently."

Lorenzo de Medici had three sons about the age of Michelangelo, who now in 1489 came to live with them as a member of the family.

Pietro

the oldest, was eighteen and handsome, but arrogant and unpleasant, quite unlike his gracious father. He showed no promise for success as a ruler.

Giuliano

the youngest, was ten, a charming little boy whom everyone loved.

Giovanni

the middle boy, who was to become famous as Pope Leo X, was Michelangelo's age. He was a goodnatured, generous boy with a large appetite. He also had a love for everything that was beautiful—music, painting, sculpture, and especially books. His first high office in the church came when he was seven. That year Louis XI, who was then dying, made him an Archbishop of France, being grateful to his father for many favors, especially for sending him the holy monk. At thirteen, through his father's influence with the Pope, Giovanni had been made a Cardinal, the youngest ever to wear the red hat.

Giulio, an eleven-year-old cousin, clever and sharp as a whip, was also part of the family. He was to become Pope Clement VII.

It was soon discovered by the Medici boys that while Michelangelo was very talented, he had a bad disposition. One day he appeared at the dinner table with a broken nose. One of the pupils at the art school later told how it had happened. "We used to go," he said, "to one of the chapels to practice drawing, by copying the paintings, and it was Michelangelo's habit to tease and torment everyone. One day, I got more angry than usual and, clenching my fist, I gave him such a blow on the nose that I felt the bone and cartilage go down like a biscuit beneath my knuckles; and this mark of mine he will carry to the grave."

Carnivals, processions, and festivals! These, Lorenzo put on as always for the amusement of the people. They varied from very beautiful pageants and lovely spectacles to wild drunken revels, obscene and corrupt, like the ancient festivals of Bacchus. But it was said that Lorenzo could make "even corruption seem charming."

Granacci, an older friend of Michelangelo who first encouraged him to study painting, designed floats, chariots, and costumes.

The poet, Poliziano, the boys' tutor, wrote love poems to be sung at the May dances of Tuscany which Lorenzo also revived. These were often danced on the broad piazza in front of the Duomo.

There one day the people of Florence saw and heard something very different but exciting, too, in a terrifying way. A monk in a long, blackhooded robe, with a dark face and burning eyes, strode

across the piazza, mounted the steps of a white marble platform and
began to speak. In a voice tense with emotion he denounced Lorenzo
de Medici and all that he did and stood for.

The name of the monk was Savonarola. He was prior of the
Dominican monastery of San Marco, built by Cosimo de Medici,
grandfather of the man he now consigned to eternal damnation.

"What are these shows, these vile festivals?" cried Savonarola.
"The work of a despot. Why does he put them on? To amuse the people
of Florence so that he may run the government as a tyrant.

"What is that Greek and Roman art which he promoted but
shameless display of naked men and women, idolizing heathen gods?
Is this beauty, I ask you? You women who glory in your ornaments
and your hair. Are you beautiful? No, you are ugly. I tell you.

"Enter the Duomo! Look at the man or woman kneeling there in prayer. There you will see true beauty—the beauty of God shining in his or her face—pure beauty as in the face of an angel."

Lorenzo was disturbed at first. Why should a friar from the monastery which his grandfather had founded, flail out at something of which he knew so little as the government of a state?

What had Florence been before the Medici gained control? A republic, yes, but in name only. Only one-thirtieth of the people had had the right to vote. The strong oppressed the weak. There had been no peace. Yet Savonarola was calling that a time of "freedom." Lorenzo tried to appease the angry monk. He went to mass at San Marco and made rich gifts to the convent. Savonarola scorned them as bribes for him to be silent, saying, "A faithful dog does not stop barking in his master's defense because a bone is thrown to him."

Throngs came to hear the flamboyant preacher denounce evils of which he made them all feel guilty. The huge Duomo was crowded to the doors, when he gave his Lenten sermons, before Easter, 1492.

By the time Lorenzo had given up trying to silence Savonarola. He was too ill—too ill even to attend to the business of government. Leaving that to Pietro, he was moved to the country villa, where both his father and grandfather had also died. Physicians prescribed a mixture of jewels as remedy for the intense pain in his stomach. As he grew worse, he kept regretting that he would not be able to complete his collection of manuscripts.

The condemnation of Savonarola also distressed him. As he was dying he sent for the monk, begging him to hear his last confession. Savonarola came, gave him absolution on three conditions: that he mend his ways if he should recover; that he meet death with courage; and that he have faith in God's mercy.

April 8, 1492, Lorenzo de Medici died, aged forty-three, just two years older than Christopher Columbus who, in October of that same year, was to discover the New World.

Part III

begins in Spain in the year

1492

People who were living when

Boabdil
the last Sultan of Granada
surrendered in January 1492

Ferdinand and **Isabella**
Conquered Granada
Drove the Jews from Spain
Financed Columbus in

1492

Bajazet II
Sultan of Constantinople
welcomed the Jewish exiles.

Martin Behaim
made the first world globe in
Nuremberg Germany 1492

The
Nuremberg Chronicle
the first history of the world
was published in 1492

Pope Alexander VI
(Rodrigo Borgia) divided the
world between Portugal and Spain.

Columbus
reached the New World
on October 12

In 1498
Savonarola
a monk who denounced the Pope was
hanged and burned in Florence.

and some important Events that

Columbus was sailing from Spain

Leonardo da Vinci
designed an airplane,
painted The Last Supper
and was filling Notebooks
with hundreds of ideas.

Vasco da Gama
Portuguese navigator
reached India
in
1497

INDIA

Calicut

Albrecht Dürer
(born 1475) the great German
artist was at home in Nuremberg

A
1493

John Cabot
discovered Newfoundland for
Henry VII of England in 1497

Amerigo Vespucci
sailed once or twice to the new
world, later to be given his name

Erasmus
(born 1466) finished his "Antibarbari"
a book against ignorance and bigotry

Copernicus
(born 1473) had just convinced himself
that the earth moved around the sun!

took place between 1492 and 1500

Sea routes to India:

Australia

Indian Ocean

180°

Tropic of Cancer

Tropic of Capricorn

West East

Pacific Ocean

The Equator

China

Asia

Sunrise route

India

Arab's route

Africa

N.A.

route of Columbus

the Portuguese route

Atlantic Ocean

West East →

0°

S.A.

AFTER THE FALL OF GRANADA

SUMMER had come again to Spain—the hot dusty summer of 1491. Ferdinand and Isabella were laying siege to Granada, the last Moslem stronghold that still remained to be captured. Miles away, forgotten by them, Christopher Columbus, threadbare and travel-weary, plodded slowly up toward the monastery overlooking the little harbor of Palos.

Six years had passed since he had first landed in Palos and trudged up that path, holding the hand of his five-year-old son Diego. Then he had been full of hope. Now he was utterly disgusted. After all those years, he still had no definite answer from the Queen. To wait longer was useless.

His knock on the gate brought a young friar, who shuffled softly off to announce the arrival of a stranger.

Soon Fray Juan Pérez appeared, stopped a puzzled moment, then came striding toward his friend, arms wide open, the knotted cord of his brown habit swinging above his sandalled feet.

"I am here to bid you farewell," said Columbus abruptly. "I am leaving Spain—forever! I have come to call for Diego."

Fray Pérez was dismayed. But he saw that before being questioned his tired friend needed refreshment. Seated comfortably in a shady spot, Fray Pérez then protested against what seemed to him a drastic and over-hasty decision. Surely Columbus could not be leaving Spain! If so, where would he go? Not back to Portugal surely! Where then? To England?

No, said Columbus, to France. His brother Bartholomew had tried England. Finding Henry VII would not risk a penny on that or any venture, he had gone to France. There he was now employed by the King's sister, Madame Anne de Beaujeu, making maps and charts. Columbus felt sure that when he also got to France, either she or the young King, Charles VIII, could be persuaded to finance his voyage to the Indies.

Fray Juan shook his head gravely. He implored Columbus to reconsider, to let him arrange one more audience with the Queen. The war with the Moslems would soon be over, he argued. The sovereigns would then have more time and money to spend on something other than war. Columbus knew this to be true. The siege of Granada which had been going on since early spring must soon end. So he gave in and let Fray Juan write his letter to the Queen.

Isabella was then at Santa Fe, a new city about six miles from Granada, built purposely to serve as headquarters for the Spanish army during the siege. In reply to the friar's letter she sent word for him to come to Santa Fe at once. A mule was soon saddled and he was off, to be followed later by Columbus, in new clothes for which the Queen had sent him money.

From Palos to Santa Fe was one hundred and fifty miles. Jogging along on his mule, Columbus had ample time to think up all the honors, titles, and rewards in money he would now demand, should the Queen decide at last to finance his Enterprise.

Isabella, as usual, gave him no positive answer. Again she turned the plans over to the committee to be reconsidered, and called on the Royal Council to pass on the rewards. Then, before any decision had been reached, the war came to an end. Granada surrendered. Joy broke loose in camp; all else was forgotten in the excitement of that long-awaited event.

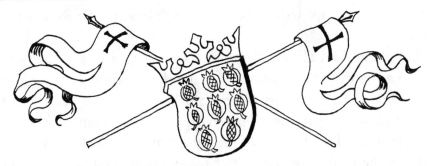

Columbus was in the triumphal procession that set forth on the second day of the new year 1492 to receive the keys of the captured city. Led by Ferdinand and Isabella, the long line of Spaniards with flying banners, waving plumes, and shining helmets rode slowly across the Vega toward the great citadel rising from the valley.

At the same time Boabdil, "the Unlucky," accompanied by a small band of retainers in white robes and turbans, was riding to meet them. Dismounting, bowing low before the Spanish sovereigns, kissing their hands, the last Sultan of Granada handed the keys of his beautiful city to its conquerors. He turned then, remounted his horse, and rode away to the mountains. There it is said he stopped to look back toward the beautiful palace he would never see again—the Alhambra.

"Allah Akbar!" he cried. "Almighty God." And bursting into tears, "There is no conqueror but Allah—No will but the will of Allah."

His mother who was with him, offered no sympathy. "You do well," said she, "to weep like a woman for what you could not defend like a man."

Meanwhile the Spaniards in their triumphal procession, headed by Ferdinand and Isabella, had passed through the gates of Granada and had seen for the first time the amazing Alhambra.

Peter Martyr, for one, was overwhelmed by its beauty. "By the immortal gods," he exclaimed, "there can be but one palace of such beauty in the entire world."

Peter Martyr was an Italian, tutor to the royal children and a great scholar. He was to write the first book about the discovery of Columbus.

Columbus himself was hopeful, now that Granada had surrendered, that he would be allowed to make that discovery. As he hoped, a few days later a summons came from Ferdinand and Isabella. They greeted Columbus graciously when he appeared, told him that they had definitely decided *not* to finance the Enterprise, and bade him farewell. That was the final blow. His bitter disappointment as he rode out of Santa Fe can only be imagined.

Almost at the very hour of his departure, however, Louis Santangel, treasurer for Ferdinand, rushed to Isabella.

"I am astonished," he said, "that Your Highness, who has always shown such resolute spirit, should lack it now. If any other prince should undertake what Columbus offers, it would be of grave damage to your crown and a reproach to Your Highness."

Isabella, moved by his words, thought quickly and had the courage to acknowledge her mistake. She sent a messenger speeding after Columbus to bring him back.

Then she considered the expense of the undertaking.

"I can pledge my jewels, if need be, to raise the money."

Santangel assured her that would not be necessary. Sufficient funds could be made available.

Columbus had gone about four miles down the road when the Queen's messenger caught up with him and presented the royal command to return, which could not be disobeyed.

The Enterprise was accepted immediately, and four months later Columbus had the final document in his hands signed by the King and Queen, and dated April 17, 1492. It read:

"Whereas you, Cristóbal Colon, are setting forth by our command to discover and acquire certain islands and mainland in the ocean sea, it is just and reasonable . . . you be rewarded, therefore it is our will and pleasure that you, the said Cristóbal Colon . . . shall be our Admiral of the said islands and mainland. . . . Viceroy and governor therein and shall be empowered henceforth to call and entitle yourself Don Cristóbal Colon, and your heirs and successors forever may be so entitled and enjoy the offices of the said islands and mainland."

In addition to this agreement, Columbus had a letter written by Ferdinand and Isabella, introducing him to the Great Khan of China. Their letter to this completely unknown ruler, who did not even exist, began with this curious assumption:

"We have heard with joy of your high regard for us and our nation and of your eagerness to receive information concerning our successes. Wherefore we send our noble captain *Christopherus Colon* to you with letters from which you may learn of our health and prosperity.

I, the King   I, the Queen.

So this time it was with a happy farewell that Columbus took leave of Ferdinand and Isabella. In high spirits he departed for the little town of Palos, where he had first landed in Spain and from which he was to leave on his great voyage of discovery.

שְׁמַע יִשְׂרָאֵל

Isaac Abrabanel

EXODUS: 1492

ON MARCH 30, 1492, just two weeks before the agreement with Columbus was considered, a fateful decree had been signed by Ferdinand and Isabella, giving all Jews four months either to be baptized as Christians or to leave Spain. Doctors, lawyers, scholars, top officials at the court, no matter how intellectual or highly skilled—no matter how valuable they were to the kingdom in other ways—were considered a menace simply because of their religion.

This was a Christian kingdom, none but Christians were to live under the Catholic Sovereigns of Spain. No Moslems! No Jews!

Louis Santangel, who had persuaded Isabella to finance the voyage of Columbus, did not have to go, because he was already what was called a Marano, that is, a Jew who had accepted Christianity.

Isaac Abrabanel, however, who had long given Ferdinand valuable assistance in finance, was doomed to exile because he would not renounce his Hebrew faith. Abrabanel and his friend, Abraham Senior, principal collector of taxes for Ferdinand, obtained an audience with the King and Queen to protest the calamity about to befall their people. They offered a large sum of money—30,000 ducats—to revoke the edict. 30,000 golden ducats! Ferdinand's eyes shone, as always, at the mention of money, but he had no time to reply.

At that moment the Inquisitor General, Torquemada, stormed into the royal presence unannounced, and strode up to the King and Queen. Drawing a crucifix out from under his long black gown, he raised it high in his clenched fist, exclaiming:

"Judas Iscariot sold his Master for thirty pieces of silver. Would Your Highnesses sell Him anew for 30,000 ducats of gold? If so, there He is, take Him, barter Him away!" The frantic friar threw the crucifix on the table and strode from the room.

This violent outburst had the desired effect upon Isabella. Ferdinand consoled himself with the thought that many times 30,000 ducats worth of riches and property would be left behind by the exiles, and would be his after they had gone.

So the edict went forth. All Jews must leave the country by August 2, 1492. The port for sailing was the large important harbor of Cadiz. On his way to the small nearby port of Palos, Columbus must have seen hundreds of the pitiful Jewish refugees trailing along the roads. The poorer people, carrying bags, bundles, and small children, leading donkeys heaped with belongings, and hauling carts piled high with household furniture. At Cadiz they were crowded aboard various ships and vessels, chartered by the wealthier Jews, to take them, they knew not where. Where could they go? Where was the country that would take them in?

The nearest place was Portugal, where there were many Jews of great wealth and high position at court. At first the refugees from Spain were allowed to enter. Then John II grew alarmed when 80,000 came pouring across the border, and they were told that after eight months in Portugal they must move on. But where?

North Africa? Some poor souls paid huge sums to shipowners for passage to Africa, only to be thrown overboard, or sold as slaves to the Moors when they reached Morocco.

Isaac Abrabanel, his son, and a group of exiles went to Italy. Others found their way to the Greek islands. Most fortunate were those who landed in Constantinople. The Sultan Bajazet II, a peaceable man, unlike his father Mohammed the Conqueror, welcomed the Jewish exiles from Spain. Many of them were doctors, chemists, bankers, men who would enrich his country with their skills and science. Later, upon hearing Ferdinand of Aragon, who had driven them out of Spain, spoken of as a wise king, he protested.

"A wise king you call that one?" he asked, "One who makes his own country poor, while making mine rich? How for the love of Allah do you call that wisdom?"

THE NINA, THE PINTA, AND THE SANTA MARIA

IT TOOK COLUMBUS ten weeks to procure the ships and enlist sailors for the voyage. The town of Palos, which had been fined by the King and Queen for some misdemeanor, paid its fine by furnishing two of the ships, the Nina and the Pinta, which were caravels. The Santa Maria was a larger, stockier ship known as a carrack. Of the three ships, the Nina proved to be the best, the Pinta was the fastest. The Santa Maria was the flagship, on which Columbus sailed. There were no

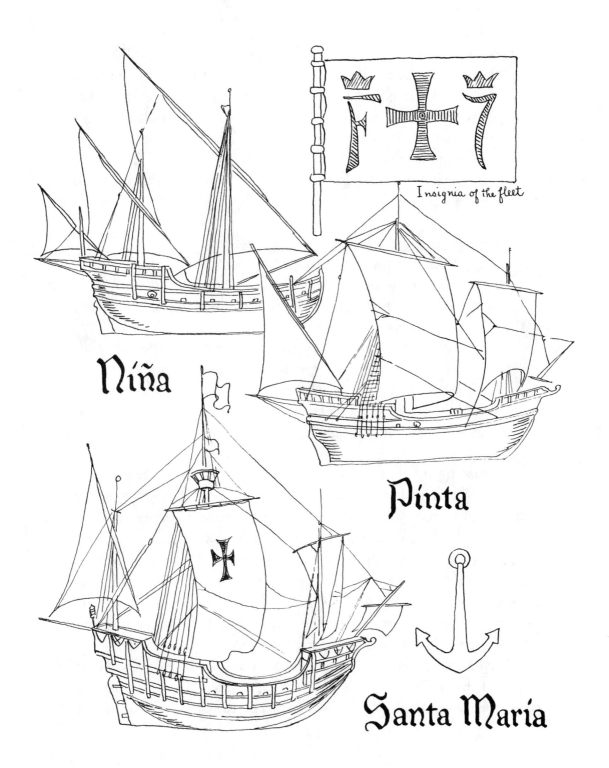

Níña

Insignia of the fleet

Pinta

Santa María

drawings made at that time of the three ships, but it is fairly well known what they looked like. All had large green crosses painted on their sails. Instead of the pointed sails typical of caravels, the Pinta was equipped with square sails like those of the Santa Maria, and the Nina's sails were changed for square ones, when they reached the Canary Islands, as being better fitted for the open ocean. For the three ships, Columbus needed 90 men—24 for the Nina, 26 for the Pinta, and 40 for the Santa Maria.

Each ship had to have three principal officers:
CAPTAIN, to take command and keep order and discipline.
MASTER, who must be a good all-round seaman.
PILOT, in charge of navigation, knowing something of astronomy, and three lesser officers.
BOATSWAIN, who stowed away the cargo and kept the boat tidy.
STEWARD, in charge of water, wine, food, and the galley fire.
GROMET, the ship's boy or apprentice.
Carpenters, caulkers, painters, coopers, cooks, were also needed beside the common seamen—in all, ninety men.

Persuading ninety men to sign up for his peculiar voyage to the Indies was far more difficult for Columbus than procuring ships. In the first place, he was a stranger and a foreigner. Spanish seamen of Palos did not choose to sail under an Italian from Genoa, especially one with such an outlandish idea. If he belonged to one of their good seafaring families, like the Pinzons or the Ninons, they would have had reason to trust him. But who was this Colon? What did they know of him? Nothing, except that he believed he could reach India by sailing west around the world and had persuaded the Queen to let him try.

Maybe the world was round; maybe it wasn't. Nobody had ever proved it. Even if it was round, how then, if you sailed a ship too far down the curve, could you ever sail back up again? As for hunting for more islands in the Atlantic Ocean, that was foolish. Take the Portuguese. After all their searching for that island called Antilia, had they ever found it? No. Nor that other island called Brazil, nor any other islands out beyond the Azores. Arguments such as these went back and forth along the waterfront, until one day it was learned that three Ninons and two Pinzons had agreed to go.

Martin Alonso Pinzon was to be Captain of the Pinta.

Vicente Pinzon was to be Captain of the Nina.

That changed the picture. And in the end, nearly all the crew came from Palos and the nearby villages along the seacoast.

Two were from Cordova, where Columbus went to say goodbye to Beatriz and their little Ferdinand, who was now four. He also left twelve-year-old Diego there in school. Diego de Harana, the cousin who had introduced Columbus to Beatriz, signed up as marshal of the fleet. And Dr. Sanchez, a friend from the old apothecary shop, was to be the surgeon on the Santa Maria.

One other man on the Santa Maria with a uniquely important job, if he should be needed, was Luis de Torres, who could speak Arabic. As that was supposed to be the mother of all languages, including Chinese, he would be the interpreter when Columbus presented his letter to the Grand Khan.

At last the August morning dawned when everything was ready. Food was stored in the hold, barrels of fresh water had been carried on. Each of the ninety men had confessed his sins and received absolution and gone aboard. The anchors were weighed. The Nina, the Pinta, the Santa Maria were off, bound for the Indies. Would they reach their destination?

Would they return loaded with spices and gold? Or would they be swallowed up by horrible monsters of the deep, or sucked down into endless darkness beyond the edge of the sea? Who could say? Surely none among that small cluster of friends and relatives gathered on the shore at Palos to see them off.

183

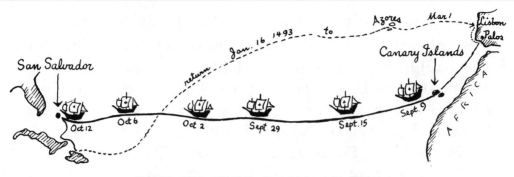

THIRTY-FIVE DAYS AT SEA

THE THREE SHIPS were over a week reaching the Canary Islands, where a month was spent repairing the Pinta's rudder and changing the sails on the Nina. It was September 6th when Columbus started on the actual voyage which was to end 35 days later, on October 12th. Each of those long days at sea had its hours marked by the proper prayers. Shortly after daybreak the gromet on the Santa Maria could be heard singing a prayer to the rising sun:

"Blessed be the light of day
And the Lord of Verite
Blessed be th' immortal soul
And the Lord who keeps it whole
Blessed be the light of day
And he who steals the night away."

The day ended at sunset with the *Salve Regina,* a song to the blessed Virgin, and the words of the ninety-first Psalm.

Then each evening in his cabin, under a swinging lantern, Columbus wrote in his journal all the happenings of that day. Using this journal, Ferdinand later wrote a day-by-day account of the voyage in the book about his father, whom he always spoke of as "the Admiral." These entries are from his book:

Sunday   They completely lost sight of land and many sighed and wept for
Sep. 9   fear that they would not see it again for a long time. The Admiral
         comforted them with great promises of lands and riches. . . . To

184

dispel their fears he decided to reckon less leagues than they actually made . . . that they might not think themselves at so great a distance from Spain, but for himself he kept a secret accurate reckoning.

Sunday Sep. 16   They were surprised to see the surface of the water covered with a great mass of yellowish green weed, which seemed to have been torn away from some island or reef. Many therefore affirmed that they must certainly be near land, especially since they saw a live crab amid those mats of weed.

Tuesday Sep. 18   Martin Alonso Pinzon, who had gone ahead in the Pinta, a very fast sailor, lay to for the Admiral to come up and informed him he had seen a great flight of birds, moving westward; and at sundown he thought he actually saw land to the north covered with darkness and clouds . . . All the ship's people wanted the Admiral to search in that direction, but he would not waste time upon it, because it was not the place where his calculations made him expect to find land. As this was the first voyage of that kind for all the men . . . they did not cease to grumble among themselves. Seeing nothing but water and sky they paid the closest attention to all they observed as was natural for men who had gone a greater distance from land than any had ever done before.

Wednesday Sep. 19   A pelican flew over the Admiral's ship followed by others in the afternoon. This gave him some hope . . . for he reflected that these birds would not have flown far from land.

Thursday Sep. 20   They saw more seaweed than ever before stretching northward as far as they could see . . . It caused them great fright lest the weed grow so thick (as to) hold the ships fast. Another fear was that since the wind was always at their backs they would never have a wind for returning to Spain. The men grew ever more restless and fearful. They met together in the holds of the ships, saying that the Admiral in his mad fantasy proposed to make himself a lord at the cost of their lives. Why then should they work their own ruin by continuing that voyage . . . Others said that they had heard enough gab. If the Admiral would not turn back, they should heave him overboard and report in Spain that he had fallen in accidentally while observing the stars; and no one would question their story. The grumbling, lamenting and plotting went on day after day; and at last the Admiral became aware of their wicked designs. Therefore at times he addressed them with fair words again very passionately as if fearless of death; he threatened punishment to any who hindered the voyage. To bolster up their hopes he reminded them of signs and tokens mentioned above, assuring them they would soon sight land.

Tuesday Sep. 25   At sunset while the Admiral was talking with Pinzon, whose ship had come alongside, Pinzon suddenly cried out, "Land, land, sir. I claim the reward!" And he pointed to a bulk that clearly resembled an island. At this the people felt such joy and relief that they offered thanks to God . . . Next morning they knew that what they had supposed to be land was nothing more than squall clouds which often resemble land.

At sunrise (a week later) a pelican flew over the ship.
Wednesday Oct. 3   Seeing no birds save some pardelas, the men feared that unknowingly they had passed between some islands, The Admiral's people wished to turn off in another direction to look for these lands, but he refused because he feared to lose the fair wind that was carrying him due west along what he believed the most certain route to the Indies. The men were on the point of mutiny, grumbling and plotting against him.

Sunday Oct. 7   At daybreak they saw what appeared to be land lying westward but since it was indistinct, none wished to claim having made the discovery, for fear of losing 10,000 maravedis promised by the Catholic Sovereigns to the first person sighting land. In order to prevent men from crying "Land, Land" at every moment, the Admiral ordered that one who claimed to have seen land

and did not make good his claim in the space of three days would lose the reward.

Monday Oct. 8 There came to the ship twelve vari-colored birds of a kind that sing in the fields, they noted that the air was as fresh and fragrant as April in Seville. But by this time the men's anxiety and desire to sight land had reached such a pitch that no sign of any kind would satisfy them. They did not cease to complain, nor the Admiral to reprove them for their small spirit, telling them that for better or worse they must go through with the enterprise of the Indies on which the Catholic Sovereigns had sent them.

Thursday Oct. 11 ... the flagship's people saw a cane or stick skillfully carved; the Nina's crew saw a thorn branch loaded with red berries that seemed to be freshly cut. These signs and his own reasoning convinced the Admiral that land must be near. That night therefore after they had sung the "Hail Mary," he spoke to the men of the favor that Our Lord had shown them by conducting them so safely ... about two hours before midnight, as the Admiral stood as the sterncastle he saw a light ... but says it was so uncertain a thing that he dared not announce it was land ...

Friday Oct. 12 About two hours after midnight, the Pinta, a speedy sailor that ranged far ahead fired the signal for land! At daybreak, they saw an island ... As soon as they had cast anchor, the Admiral went ashore in an armed boat, displaying the royal standard. The captains of the other two ships did the same. After all had rendered thanks to Our Lord, kneeling on the ground and kissing it with tears of joy for His great favor to them, the Admiral rose and gave this island the name of San Salvador.

And sad to say, Columbus could not resist taking the reward and so planted a seed of resentment in the heart of the Pinta's captain, Martin Alonso Pinzon, that was to bear bitter fruit.

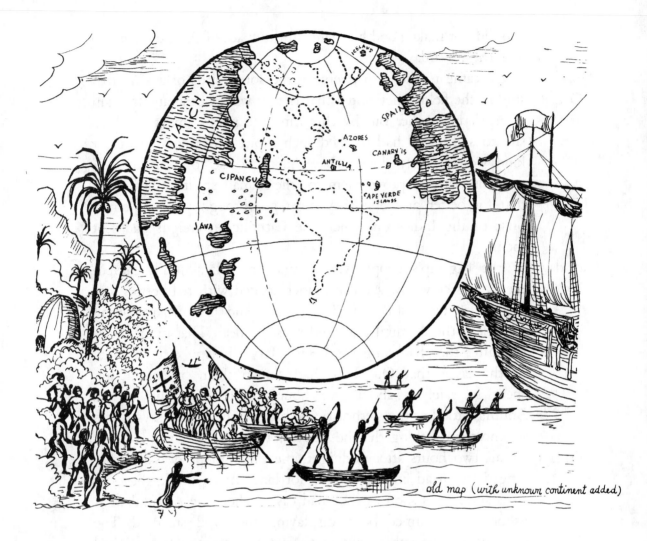

old map (with unknown continent added)

WHERE WERE THEY?

GUANAHANI is what the natives called the island, which Columbus christened San Salvador. Since this island, according to his calculations must be one of the East Indies, he naturally called the natives Indians. Actually these so-called Indians were a gentle peaceful tribe who called themselves Tainos.

At first sight of the ships, they had come running to the shore

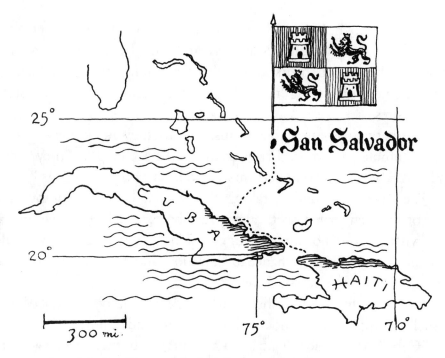

to see what kind of huge bird had flown in from the sea, and what strange people. Men with white skin, what there was to see of it. Their bodies were mostly covered up with cloth, and their faces with bushy hair, almost up to their eyes.

To the Spanish these brown island people looked equally peculiar, quite unlike the natives of Africa, who had black skin and tight curly hair. Though these people had black hair, it was very straight and as coarse as a horse's tail, while their color was similar to that of natives on the Canary Islands. And what was most amazing, all were completely naked, though some had decorated their slim brown bodies with streaks of red and white paint.

They were friendly and happy with the trinkets which Columbus had brought for them, hanging the blue glass beads about their necks "as if they were precious stones of great price."

In return they gave freely of whatever they had. Later when the Spaniards had gone back to the ships, some came swimming out, bringing parrots, skeins of cotton thread, and darts. Others paddled out in boats made of hollowed-out tree trunks, some of which were large enough to hold forty men. All day Saturday, October 13, the Nina, Pinta, and the Santa Maria lay at anchor with seamen rowing ashore in their small boats and Indians paddling back and forth in their dugouts, all trying to make themselves understood by signs and gestures.

The natives repeated the Spanish words they heard very quickly and Columbus noted in his journal that he thought "they could easily be made into good servants as well as good Christians."

The next day, Sunday, taking three small boats, Columbus and some of his men rowed north along the shore, where they saw several small villages, but nothing to suggest Japan, which he knew would be a much larger island than San Salvador, and from all his calculations should lie to the southwest.

By signs and gestures he tried to ask the natives if they knew of such an island. They nodded and smiled and pointed.

"Cuba!" they said. "Cuba!" They stretched their arms wide to suggest an island much larger than their own. Since they pointed in the right direction, it seemed possible that what they called "Cuba" might be "Cipangu," Marco Polo's name for Japan!

The Admiral wrote in his journal that night that he was going from Japan without delay to the mainland of China to present his letter of introduction to the Grand Khan. "All I have to do now is to look for gold and spices."

Monday, the Santa Maria, followed by the Nina and the Pinta, set off for Cuba, with six Indians aboard to act as guides.

They were two weeks on the way, winding in and out among the many smaller islands, each seeming lovelier than the last. Here and there Columbus sent men ashore to look about for gold and spices. They found none, but brought back other items of interest. On one island they saw swinging beds made of coarsely woven cloth, which the natives called "hamacas." These hammocks were so comfortable that the Spaniards later adopted them for use by sailors on shipboard.

Trees and flowers on all the islands were so strangely beautiful, so unlike those in Spain, that Columbus declared that "his eyes never tired of looking at them." But he added, "I believe there are many plants and trees which are worth a lot in Spain for dyes and medicines of spicery, but I do not recognize them, which gives me great grief."

Pepper would have been the greatest find, but any of the spices were so rare in Europe as to be almost as good as gold. Nutmeg, cinnamon, and ginger were weighed in apothecary shops with all the windows closed so that none of the precious powder would blow away.

Although the Spaniards, who had never seen spices growing, would not have recognized them, there was not a man among them who was not certain that he could recognize gold. And gold was what Columbus must find and take back to Spain. That alone would be proof that he had reached Cipangu, where Marco Polo said that temples and palaces were roofed in solid gold.

It was daybreak, October 28th. On the Santa Maria, the gromet had just finished singing his daily prayer to the dawn, as soft and hazy, the nearby shores of Cuba were coming into view. The sun rose high, the sea sparkled, and the three ships with their great square sails dropped anchor in a beautiful bay. Columbus went ashore in the first of several small boats and said he had "never beheld so fair a place." But if this fair place was Japan, why was there no city here? The shore was deserted. Nothing to be seen but a few huts, some palm-fiber fishing nets, and one or two strange-looking yellow dogs that did not bark.

Next morning on another bay to the west, the explorers found a large native village made of tents, pointed like those in a Moorish camp, each with a smoke pipe rising from the point. While the Spaniards searched the village for gold, the six Indian guides whom Columbus had brought from San Salvador talked with the people who were also Tainos. But as yet they had not enough Spanish words to translate what they heard. So it was necessary for all to fall back on signs and gestures.

Touching a chain, a cross, or some other object made of gold, Columbus tried to show that gold was what he wanted to find. The natives, eager to please, nodded and pointed inland, repeating the word "Cubanacan," which was their word for central Cuba.

"Cu-bana-Can!" That sounded to Columbus like "El-Gran-Khan"—the Spanish words meaning the Grand Khan.

It did not seem possible that they were already in or near the Empire of the Grand Khan. Yet when he made gestures indicating a mighty ruler, the Cubans nodded again and again and pointed to the center of their island. This was no mistake, their great chief, or Cacique, did live in Cubanacan.

Columbus was puzzled; instead of being in Japan, was he on the mainland of China? It seemed unlikely. Yet who could say? To be on the safe side, he appointed an embassy of four men to investigate, headed by Luis de Torres, the interpreter, who carried the letter of introduction from Ferdinand and Isabella, and also a royal gift for the Grand Khan.

While they were away, Columbus and the two Pinzon brothers, Martin Alonso and Vicente, did some exploring up the river, eagerly searching for gold, Martin Alonso even more than the others. He found some native peppers. Columbus tasted sweet potatoes, and all three saw cotton growing for the first time. For a short while Martin Alonso mistook something he found for cinnamon, but his vision of making a fortune in spices soon faded away. So far, to his way of thinking, the voyage was a failure. He was a merchant seaman, not an explorer as his brother Vicente was inclined to be. Nor did he care to convert the natives, nor waste his time admiring scenery like this so-called Admiral, Columbus.

The four ambassadors to the Great Khan were back a day earlier than expected, with nothing to report except that they had found a village of palm-leaf huts and a few hundred very friendly natives who, the Spaniards soon discovered, had a most surprising custom.

Men and women drank the smoke of an herb, which they twisted into a roll small enough to stick into one nostril. Then it was lighted and they drew in the smoke. The rolled herbs were called "Tobacos."

The ambassadors, as "men from Heaven," had been shown great honor and hospitality, and in return they had brought back the Cacique and his son to be entertained aboard the Nina or the Pinta. The Santa Maria was then high and dry having her hull cleaned and scraped and being made ready to sail farther on in search of gold. By signs and gestures the natives indicated that to the north of Cuba was an island where gold was so plentiful it could be scooped up on the beach.

When the Santa Maria was afloat again and ready to leave for this island of gold, Columbus repaid the kindness of the Indians by having five friendly young Tainos who came aboard for a final visit, seized and held by force, to be carried off to Spain to be converted.

The wind changed so suddenly after the three ships sailed from Cuba that Columbus gave orders to return. He was obeyed by Vicente Pinzon in the Nina, but the speedy Pinta kept steadily on its way. Martin Alonso was sick of slowing down for the stodgy flagship. He was also fed up with taking orders from that Genoese Admiral who had cheated him out of his reward for being first to see land. He was going to be first to find gold if, at any rate, there was gold to be found.

Columbus was distressed that his senior Captain should have deserted "without his permission or desire," as he wrote that night in his journal, as well as by "many other things he has done and said to me."

The fact remained, however. Martin Alonso Pinzon was gone. And nothing more was to be seen of him or of the speedy Pinto until after the middle of January.

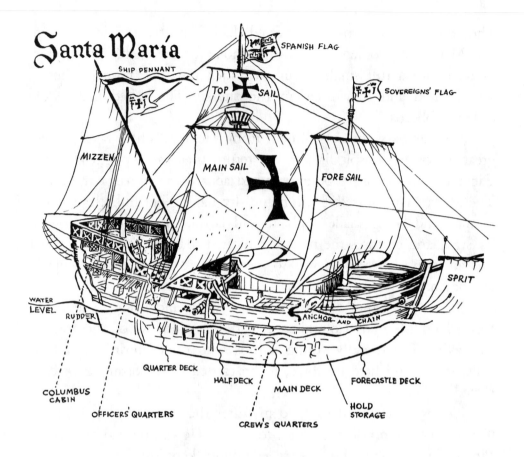

Santa María

SHIP PENNANT

SPANISH FLAG

TOP SAIL

SOVEREIGNS' FLAG

MIZZEN

MAIN SAIL

FORE SAIL

SPRIT

WATER LEVEL

RUDDER

ANCHOR AND CHAIN

COLUMBUS CABIN

QUARTER DECK

HALF DECK

MAIN DECK

FORECASTLE DECK

OFFICERS' QUARTERS

CREW'S QUARTERS

HOLD STORAGE

CHRISTMAS ON HAITI

THE FIRST CHRISTMAS in the New World was celebrated by Columbus and his Spaniards on the island of Haiti. There, the first gold was to be discovered and the first Spanish settlement established. Crossing the Windward passage from Cuba, the two ships, the Nina and the Santa Maria, reached a harbor at the western end of Haiti on December 5th. As this was the eve of the feast of St. Nicholas, Columbus named the harbor Puerto de San Nicolas. Haiti itself seemed to him so similar to Spain that he called

194

it "The Spanish Island," La Isla Española. Hispaniola, the Latin form which Peter Martyr was to use, is still the island's name.

The gentle Tainos whom Columbus had carried with him from their home islands were panic-stricken as they neared the island of Haiti. When the ships anchored and others went ashore, they remained huddled together below deck, shaking with terror for fear of being killed and eaten. They believed that Haiti was the homeland of their enemies, the fierce man-eating Caribs, or Canibas, who often raided their islands. This was a mistake. More of the same gentle Tainos were found to be living on Haiti, but the poor fearful passengers refused to believe it, until one day sailors who had gone ashore captured a very beautiful young girl. They brought her aboard the Santa Maria and she talked to the other Tainos. A lovely beguiling little thing she was, with her slim brown naked body and golden nose plug. Quite delighted with her visit, she hated to leave but went off modestly enveloped in a huge sailor's shirt which Columbus had given her. Her father was a young cacique, who told about an older more powerful cacique, whose name was Guacanagari and who ruled over all the northwest end of Haiti.

Columbus soon sent messengers in a small boat with natives to guide them to Guacanagari's village. They returned full of praise for the old chieftain, who had given them many presents and wished very much to meet their Admiral. Best of all, they brought the great news that there was gold—great quantities of gold—to be found somewhere on this island of Haiti. At that Columbus offered a silent prayer of entreaty, "O Lord, in thy goodness guide me that I may find this gold!"

It was now December 23rd. All agreed that they should spend Christmas with Guacanagari. On Christmas Eve the two ships were sailing slowly toward a large bay from which narrow channels winding through a mangrove swamp led to Guacanagari's village. The sea was quiet, there was little wind. The master of the Santa Maria who was on watch, got so sleepy that he turned the job over to the gromet. The young boy, holding the clumsy tiller, was the only one awake when the ship slid quietly onto a coral reef. He felt the rudder scrape and cried out for help. Columbus woke with a start, rushed to the deck, followed by the guilty master.

"Take one of the boats," Columbus told him. "Get an anchor and cable and try to pull the ship back into deep water."

It might have been possible to ease the Santa Maria gently off the rocks before too much damage was done, if the master had obeyed orders, but he did not. Instead he jumped into the small boat with some of his cronies and pulled away toward the Nina.

Vicente Pinzon, the Nina's loyal captain, refused to take them aboard. He sent them back and also sent his one rowboat to help Columbus. By then it was too late to save the Santa Maria. The coral reef had punched large holes in her wooden hull. It was filling with water, and she had to be abandoned, while Columbus and his crew of forty men crowded onto the little Nina.

Christmas morning, at daybreak, Columbus sent Diego de Harana and another sailor to Guacanagari to ask for help. By the time the sun was high, the cacique had all of his canoes and many of his people at work carrying cargo and gear ashore, while he and his brothers kept careful watch that nothing should be stolen. Columbus, sick at heart, directed operations from the deck of the Nina. From time to time Guacanagari sent one of his relatives to the "weeping Admiral to console him telling him that he must not be troubled or annoyed, that he would give him whatever he had."

The next day, a large canoe was being paddled out to the Nina, bringing Guacanagari himself to meet the Admiral, who presented his guest with a shirt and a pair of gloves and invited him to dinner. The old cacique told the Admiral there was gold, as much gold as he could want, in a part of his island called Cibao.

A day or so later Guacanagari entertained the Admiral on shore at dinner at which he served yams, broiled lobsters, and cassava bread. The neatness with which he ate, washing his hands after the meal and rubbing them with herbs, made Columbus feel that he was dining with a fine gentleman.

Guacanagari spoke to his guest about the Caribs, his fierce enemies, a fearful man-eating tribe, and of their awful bows and arrows. He and his Tainos had no weapons, as the Admiral could see, nothing but darts for spearing fish. Columbus quickly sent to the ship for the strong Turkish bows and put on an exhibition of target shooting. This was followed by some musket shots, even more amazing to the cacique.

What were Carib bows and arrows compared to these deadly weapons? This powerful white man, he told himself, was a friend worth having. For his powerful new friend, Guacanagari now brought forth a gift which he knew would please him. It was a mask which had eyes and ears that were made of *gold!*

That night the thought struck Columbus that his prayer had been answered! It may have been as he was writing in his journal with the mask gleaming in the light of his lantern that he suddenly saw the shipwreck as an act of God, a blessing in disguise. Not only guiding him to the gold, God had also shown him the place to build a fort and what to use—the planks and timbers of the Santa Maria! Once more he was full of hope and spirit, feeling again that he was truly Christopher, "the servant of the Lord."

Morning came. Under his orders the men set to work at once laying out and planning the fort. With the Indians doing all the heavy lifting and hard work, it was completed in a few days. Since the wreck had occurred on Christmas Eve, Columbus called the fort La Navidad, the Nativity.

There was no problem to get forty volunteers to remain in the fort instead of returning to Spain. More than enough clamored to stay and be first to find the gold mine. Diego de Harana was left in command of the forty chosen to stay. The others, more or less envious, bade them farewell and rowed out to the Nina, now ready to leave for home with news of the great discovery.

Columbus intended to sail at top speed for fear that Martin Alonso Pinzon might be on the way. In the speedier Pinta, he could easily reach Spain first and claim all the glory and reward, instead of being punished for "desertion."

Before the Nina had gone far, the lookout on the top mast spotted a ship, and there, by San Fernando, was the Pinta, sailing toward them! Soon Martin Alonso had come aboard, with various unbelievable excuses for his absence. Columbus, inclined to prefer peace at any price, accepted the explanation without argument.

So they set out together, the two ships—the Nina and the Pinta —to make the stormy winter journey home across the Atlantic, leaving behind the old Santa Maria, converted into Fort La Navidad.

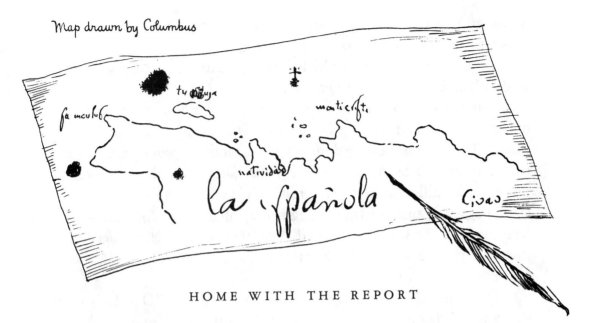

HOME WITH THE REPORT

THE FIRST THREE WEEKS at sea were fair enough. Then the storm broke, raising mountainous green waves that broke upon the deck of the Nina in torrents. The ship rolled and pitched in such a dreadful manner it seemed that it might break in two at any moment. Columbus was desperate. He sat in his cabin struggling to write, an ink horn clutched in one hand, his quill in the other. Above him, the lantern swung madly from the beam; the table tipped at dizzy angles. He was trying to write a short record of the voyage that might survive. Wrapped in wax paper, sealed in a barrel, and cast into the sea, it might be washed ashore somewhere. Otherwise, if the Nina went down, all would be lost. No one in Spain would ever know that the Enterprise had been a success, unless the Pinta reached home. But then Martin Alonso Pinzon might take all the credit. That, too, was a dreadful thought. This short true account might be found and save his name from disgrace, if he went down with the ship. It was his only hope.

Another day, when the storm was so bad that it seemed as though nothing but a miracle could save them, the sailors got down on their knees and swore to heaven above that if they survived they would go in a procession to the first shrine of the Virgin they found anywhere "and offer prayers of thanksgiving."

At last the sky cleared. On Friday, February 15th, they sighted land. What land was it? Where could they be?

Columbus, who was an expert navigator, said it must be one of the Azores. And so it proved to be—the small island of Santa Maria. The Azores belonged to Portugal, and he would not have landed there in a Spanish ship except that after what they had been through, the sailors had to have rest.

The people of the island thought it a miracle that the Spaniards had survived. Never, they vowed, had they seen such a dreadful storm. A good place for the Nina to anchor, they pointed out, was in the bay about a mile or so from the village.

The name of their village was Anjos, short for "Our Lady of the Angels," because, as they explained, a fisherman long ago had seen Our Lady surrounded by angels standing on a rock—there where they had built their chapel. A chapel to the Virgin! Here then was the place and time for the sailors to fulfil their vow.

Columbus sent ten men ashore in the Nina's one small boat. They were to return and let the others go. Several hours passed with no sign of them. While saying their prayers, clad only in their shirts, which was the proper way for penitents, the men had been seized and marched off to the village prison.

Soon a boatload of armed men rowed out to the caravel, bringing the Captain of the island. He demanded that Columbus show his credentials. Sharp words passed between them. In the end the Portuguese Captain could not prove that Columbus had been trespassing on the coast of Guinea, or any other Portuguese possession. So he allowed the ten penitents to return to the ship and as soon as the weather permitted, Columbus sailed for Spain. But again the weather changed. The wind whirled about and blew the ship completely off its course. In the early morning of March 4th, after the worst of all nights, Columbus recognized the rock at the entrance to the harbor of Lisbon. Again, though it was Portugal, he had to enter with his Spanish ship and anchor there until it was safe to venture out and sail on to Palos.

Moored nearby was a large Portuguese man-of-war. Very soon the master, who happened to be Bartholomew Dias, appeared on board the Nina and told Columbus that the Captain wished to see him. When Columbus, as Admiral of Spain, refused to go to the Portuguese Captain, the Captain came himself, "in great state with drums trumpets and pipes" to welcome the new Admiral of the Ocean Sea "making a great celebration of it."

A few days later a letter came from King John II inviting his former friend, now an Admiral, to visit him. Taking with him several of his Indians, parrots, samples of gold, and so forth, Columbus set out on muleback for the monastery thirty miles beyond Lisbon where the King was staying at the time because of the plague that was raging in the city.

As he rode along, Columbus was looking forward with smug satisfaction to showing King John how wrong he had been in refusing to finance his voyage. At the same time he was somewhat worried that he might be prevented from leaving Portugal, since his discovery had been made for a rival nation.

King John, however, received him cordially, with the honor due to his new rank, and seemed sincerely pleased that his voyage had been successful. So Columbus wrote in his journal.

The Portuguese chronicler took a different view of the meeting. As he saw it, Columbus was boastful, raised above his station. The King was irritated, only pretending to be pleased, and said that the islands Columbus had discovered belonged to Portugal since they lay within the boundaries of Guinea. On this Columbus begged to differ. He had been ordered by the sovereigns, Ferdinand and Isabella, to go to no part of Guinea and he had obeyed. King John dismissed the matter graciously, saying that he was sure that all could be satisfactorily arranged.

His courtiers were not so easily pacified. They crowded around the King, when Columbus was out of sight, and urged that the boastful creature be assassinated. It could be done discreetly and an end put to this Spanish Enterprise.

King John not only waved aside the evil suggestion, but continued to show Columbus every courtesy. He did so, even though he believed that what Columbus had discovered must be Antilia, for which the Portuguese had been searching so long. One morning he asked the Indians to make a map of their islands using some dried beans. This only confirmed his belief that he, alas, had let that long-sought-for treasure slip through his fingers.

Despite the King's kindness, Columbus was not truly at ease until he was again on the Nina, sailing safely away from Portugal.

At high tide on the 15th of March he entered the harbor of Palos, which he had left exactly ten months and two weeks before. He had already sent a letter from Lisbon to Ferdinand and Isabella describing his Voyage of Discovery.

Before that, as Columbus had feared, they had also heard from Martin Alonso Pinzon. The Pinta had escaped the cyclone and had reached Spain first, but was not yet in the harbor of Palos. Pinzon's calculations had been wrong and he landed north of Portugal. From there he sent word to Ferdinand and Isabella, who were then at Barcelona, asking permission to come to court and give them a report of the discovery. They replied that they chose to hear the report from the Admiral himself.

The Pinta followed the Nina into Palos on the same day with the same tide. Martin Alonso Pinzon was rowed ashore and without a word to Columbus went immediately to his country home near Palos. The Admiral and the Captain never saw each other again.

But the Pinzon family never ceased to make trouble with endless lawsuits that continued long after Columbus was dead.

ADMIRAL OF THE OCEAN SEA

Now came days of triumph—the most glorious days in the life of Christopher Columbus. It was at Eastertime in Seville, where he was spending Holy Week, that he received a letter from Ferdinand and Isabella, summoning him to Barcelona. His heart leaped as he saw it addressed to: Don Cristobal Colon, Admiral of the Ocean Sea, Vice Roy and Governor of the Islands that he hath discovered in the Indies. There, following the Spanish form of his name, were all the titles they had promised him: Admiral—Governor —Vice Roy!

Riches, too, as well as honors were to be his, for he was promised one-tenth of all the gold and spices to be found in those islands.

It also added to his happiness, that they spoke of his voyage as a service to the Lord. For to him, the purpose of his Enterprise had been not merely to gain riches and honor, but to serve the Lord like his beloved saint, the giant Christopher.

That was shown in the way he signed his letter replying to that of the King and Queen. For the first time he used this cryptic arrangement of letters that from now on was to be his signature:

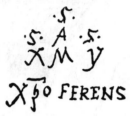

Although Columbus never revealed the secret meaning, the last line is clearly the name Christopher—the Greek letters xno, meaning Christ, and Ferens, the Latin word for bearing.

The first four letters are believed to stand for the Latin words:

SERVUS	SUM	ALTISSIMI	SALVATORIS—meaning
Servant	am I	of the most high	Savior.

The third line is uncertain, except for X meaning Christ.

After Easter Sunday in Seville, the new Admiral prepared to leave for Barcelona. Having purchased beautiful and costly garments and most elegant traveling equipment, Columbus set forth proudly, riding in high style, accompanied by his servants.

His fame preceded him, and the journey across Spain from Seville to Barcelona became one continuous reception, with the mayor and council of every town turning out to do him homage, and people flocking to see the marvelous man who had crossed the great ocean and returned alive. They stared at the red-brown Indians, at the colored birds, called parrots, at the gold ornaments and "many other things never before seen or heard of in Spain."

On the second or third day Columbus, in all his glory, was

204

crossing the stone bridge and entering the familiar streets of Cordova. What a thrill to be returning so proudly to that city where he had suffered so much poverty and humiliation! What a sweet revenge to see those people who had scoffed at "crazy Columbus" have to eat their words! What a joy to sweep Diego and Ferdinand up into his arms and see them glory in their famous father, while Beatriz stood back quietly smiling in the shadows.

At Barcelona all the court turned out to welcome the hero, including the royal children. Don Juan, the Infante, now a charming, delicate-looking young prince of fifteen, whom everyone adored, was seated with his royal parents in the throne room of the Alcazar when they received the Admiral. As Columbus knelt to kiss their hands, Ferdinand and Isabella rose from their thrones and a singular honor, bade him be seated with them while they questioned him about the voyage. The Queen now suggested that Columbus' two sons, Diego and Ferdinand, who were to inherit the titles and rights of their father should be brought to court to act as pages to Don Juan. Nor were the two brothers of Columbus forgotten. They were also made Spanish noblemen—Don Bartholomew and Don Diego, the younger brother, still in Italy. To this new noble family the sovereigns granted a coat of arms, which as a special honor was to have on it the golden castle of Castile and the purple lion of Leon.

Peter Martyr, the scholar and tutor to the royal children, was soon spreading word of the Admiral's wonderful discovery. He talked at length with Columbus and was planning to write a book about what he was the first person to call the "New World." But by "New World" he did not mean a new continent, but merely newly discovered islands off the coast of Asia. That there might be a continent lying between Europe and Asia had not yet entered anyone's mind, not even that of a scholar such as Peter Martyr.

Nor was any such continent shown on a new globe just completed in the German city of Nuremberg and advertised by the proud city fathers as a great novelty, completely up to date.

MARTIN BEHAIM'S ''EARTH APPLE''

MARTIN BEHAIM'S "EARTH APPLE," as he called it, made in 1492, is the oldest globe of the world now in existence. It was undertaken at the request of the worthy members of the town Council of the imperial German city of Nuremberg. Inasmuch as the world was known to be round, they held it should be shown in such fashion, rather than on a flat map.

Upon due consideration, they elected the "worshipful and honorable D. Martin Behaim, Knight" for the task, since he had spent some time in Portugal, the center of exploration, and was skilled in the art of cosmography.

The globe, when finished, was about 29 inches in diameter, made of pasteboard, covered with parchment carefully cut in sections to fit smoothly. It was then beautifully painted and decorated with flags, ships, whales, and signs of the zodiac.

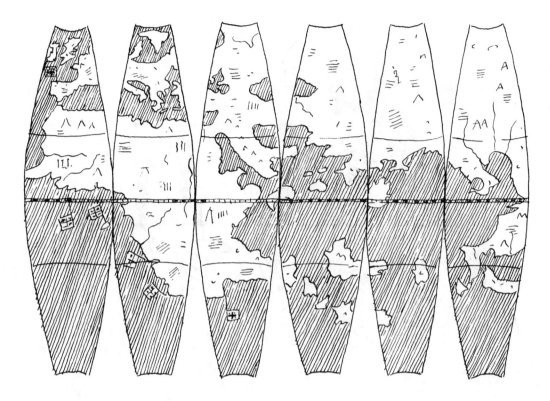

The Councilmen were well pleased and vowed that it would bring honor and enjoyment to the city of Nuremberg. And, they were confident, it embodied all the latest information. They gave the authorities that had been consulted:

"Be it known that on this Apple here present is laid out the whole world according to its length and breadth as described by Ptolemy . . . and (also) from what the Knight Marco Polo of Venice caused to be written down in 1250 . . . (added to this) The Serene King John of Portugal has caused to be visited in his vessels that part to the south not yet known to Ptolemy. . . . Towards the west the Sea Ocean has likewise been navigated farther . . . Far off places towards midnight such as Iceland, Norway and Russia are likewise now known to us and visited annually by ships, wherefore let none doubt the simple arrangement of the world and that every part may be reached in ships as here seen."

THE FLAMBOYANT BORGIAS

IN ROME in August, 1492, just before Columbus sailed, Cardinal Rodrigo Borgia, a Spaniard of immense wealth and no scruples, had become Pope Alexander VI.

Borgia was a man of sixty years, with the most charming manners but complete lack of morals. He had gone to Rome in his early twenties and been made a Cardinal by his doting old uncle, Pope Calixtus III. The young Cardinal's charm and magnetism for women were irresistible and his conduct was scandalous. His behavior had not improved with the passing years. Now, at sixty, he made no effort to conceal the fact that he had broken his vows and that he was the father of five children, all of whom he adored.

208

Lucrezia, who was twelve, with long hair like spun gold and the eyes of an angel, was the idol of her father.

Caesar, his second son, was eighteen, handsome, tall, and so very strong that he could slice off the head of a bull with a single blow of his sword. The bullfight was his favorite sport and that of his father, the Pope. The old Roman Colosseum, then in ruins, was turned into the Plaza del Toros, the bull ring of the Spanish Pope. There young Caesar Borgia often entered the ring as the toreador. Once, it was said, as the bull became mad, having gored the horse of the picador and tossed the rider to his death, Caesar rushed in, pierced the bull in the neck, and killed it.

"Ole! Ole!" shouted the crowd as the great animal staggered, swayed and fell to the ground.

"Ole! Ole! Ole!" shouted the Pope in his resonant voice, cheering on his own torero for having vanquished the black bull. Bowing to the right and left, Caesar gracefully accepted the plaudits of the crowd, while Lucrezia threw down upon him a shower of yellow roses.

Alexander VI, filled with pride and love of his children, now began to arrange marriages for them that would be of use to him as ruler of the Papal State. The husband he settled on for Lucrezia was a relative of Ludovico Sforza of Milan. For his older son, Juan, who was twenty, he had arranged a Spanish marriage with a young cousin of Ferdinand of Aragon. The wedding ceremony took place in August, 1493, in Barcelona, at the court of Ferdinand and Isabella.

Columbus was not there to witness the ceremony, for by August he was already on his way back to the seaport of Cadiz from which he was to leave on his second voyage to the New World.

The letter which Columbus had sent on from Lisbon, describing his Voyage of Discovery, was soon being printed with imaginary illustrations and widely circulated. A handwritten copy had been sent at once to Pope Alexander with an appeal from Ferdinand and Isabella that he verify their ownership of the islands which Columbus had discovered. They had had word that King John was already equipping a fleet to be sent to these islands, claiming that they belonged to Portugal.

Happily for them, the Pope was a Borgia—and a loyal Spaniard. On May 4, 1493, Alexander VI obligingly issued a Papal Bull in which he declared that all lands Columbus had discovered belonged to the sovereigns of Castile, provided the lands had never been in the possession of any other Christian prince.

Even before the Papal Bull had reached Barcelona, the Portuguese ambassador was there claiming that these lands had indeed been in the possession of another Christian prince—namely, his own prince—King John of Portugal. In 1481 it had been decreed by a previous Pope that all lands south of the Canary Islands and west of Guinea should belong to Portugal. The islands which Columbus had discovered lay west of Guinea.

West, yes, the Spaniards agreed, but too far west! Here was a map, they pointed out, on which a line had been drawn running north and south. The Pope had decreed that all land west of that line should belong to Spain.

West of Guinea meant west of Guinea, no matter how far west, argued the Portuguese. Something more unfair to the Portuguese was written into that decree by the Spanish Pope. The eastern route to India down around the coast of Africa, which Portuguese explorers had been working forty years to discover, and which Pope Nicholas

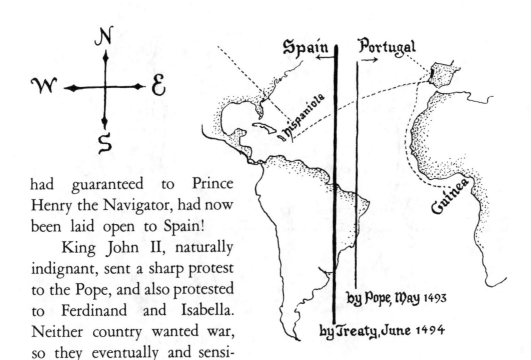

had guaranteed to Prince Henry the Navigator, had now been laid open to Spain!

King John II, naturally indignant, sent a sharp protest to the Pope, and also protested to Ferdinand and Isabella. Neither country wanted war, so they eventually and sensibly worked out a compromise. The north-south dividing line was moved 270 leagues farther west. All discoveries made east of the line, even in Spanish ships, were to belong to Portugal; all west, even though made in Portuguese ships, were to belong to Spain.

And so, having divided the world between them, Portugal and Spain were about to reach and tap untold riches in the ancient east and the unknown west.

Europe was on the very threshold of a wonderful new age. But no one seemed to see it. People in general had no hope for the future. The whole structure of society seemed to be falling apart. The Church, which had united Christendom for 1,000 years, had grown worldly and corrupt. The eastern empire had fallen to the Turks. The end of the world could not be far away—before many years would come the rising of the dead and the awful Day of Judgment. This prophecy of doom was to be found in the great book of history published that year 1493 in the German City of Nuremberg—the first illustrated history of the world ever to be printed.

211

THE NUREMBERG CHRONICLE

THIS DANCE OF DEATH is an illustration from the famous world history, published in Nuremberg in 1493, first in Latin and then in German. It was a huge volume, with pages over 18 inches long and 12 inches wide, of which there were 327; it weighed 14 pounds. The author, Dr. Hartman Schedel, described it as "A book of Chronicles from the Creation of the World even unto the troubles of our own time." For novelty it rivaled the Earth Apple of his friend Martin Behaim, made the year before. The "good reader" was told in the introduction that:

"The great Good Fortune of the Ages had dawned on us today . . . Nothing like this has hitherto appeared to increase and heighten the Delight of men of Learning and Everyone who has any Education at all. The new book of Chronicles with its Pictures of Famous men and Cities has just been printed at the Expense of Generous Citizens of Nuremberg . . . Do not let this book escape you."

Michael Wohlgemut and Wilhelm Pleydenwurff, two well-known artists, made the illustrations, which were turned by skilled artisans into woodcuts for printing. Printer and publisher of this gigantic book which had 1,800 woodcuts was Anton Koberger, owner of what was then the largest printing plant in the world.

Upon opening this chronicle, the "good reader" found the history of the world to be divided into seven parts, beginning with the Creation and ending with the Last Judgment. Part Six, from the birth of Jesus to the end of the world, took up 162 pages, over half of the book. To this, the author explained he had added a few blank pages, enough for whatever few events might take place between this year 1493 and the end of the world.

"And so," he says in conclusion, "we have now journeyed to the goal of our own time, For this is the fifty-third year of the reign of the most glorious Emperor Frederick III and the seventh of his illustrious son King Maximilian and the first of the pontificate of Pope Alexander VI."

Albrecht Dürer of Nuremberg, the great German artist of the Renaissance was twenty-two and traveling abroad for study when the *Chronicle* was published. Anton Koberger, the printer, had been godfather at the christening of Albrecht, the son of his good friend and neighbor, the goldsmith. As soon as the boy was old enough he had been apprenticed by his father to the artist, Michael Wohlgemut. Young Albrecht, like young Leonardo da Vinci, soon outstripped his teacher. He was also strikingly handsome; this is a self-portrait made when he was fourteen.

Imperator Maximilianus

THE HOUSE OF HAPSBURG

THE "MOST GLORIOUS" Emperor Frederick III died in August, 1493. For the past seven years he had been ineffectual as a ruler. Living in retirement, he had passed his time musing on the past and future greatness of his country, Austria, and of his family, the House of Hapsburg.

One day, to his delight, using the five vowels of the alphabet in order, he evolved a sentence that expressed the supremacy of Austria, both in Latin and in German, and from then on this motto appeared in all of his books.

A	E	I	O	U
Austriae	est	imperator	orbi	universo
Alles	Erde	ist	Oesterreich	unterthan

214

AUSTRIA IS RULER OF THE UNIVERSE, are the Latin words. ALL THE EARTH IS SUBJECT TO AUSTRIA, is the German translation.

How much of the earth actually would be subject to his great-grandson could not have been imagined by anyone in 1493, when Frederick III died and his "illustrious son" Maximilian succeeded to the ancient title of Holy Roman Emperor.

Always the exact opposite of his listless father, the new Emperor Maximilian, was as boyish and likable and full of life at thirty-four as he had been at eighteen, when he dashed in like a white knight to rescue and marry Mary of Burgundy.

He was still the white knight, ready for romance and adventure. He always had a great scheme in his mind, which he was sure would turn out right, happy if it did, never downhearted if it did not. He just went off hunting in the Tyrol mountains and forgot about it.

Two years before he became emperor, one of his fine schemes that miscarried was designed against France. This was a plan to get hold of Brittany by marrying the Duchess Anne, much as he had gotten hold of Burgundy by marrying the Duchess Mary.

The Duke of Brittany had then died, leaving as his heir a thirteen-year-old daughter Anne, a rather plain, but very intelligent girl with a decided mind of her own. She loved Brittany and did not propose to let her Brittany become part of France. So for protection she accepted Maximilian's proposal of marriage. At that time Maximilian was far away in the neighborhood of Vienna fighting against Hungary. He sent a proxy to Brittany and he and Anne were married at long distance. The plain determined girl of thirteen and her dashing bridegroom were never to meet.

Madame Anne of France saw to that. She did not propose to stand by and see Brittany slip away to Austria. This was her last year as regent for her brother Charles VIII. Nothing could have delighted their old father more than this last act of hers, which was to annex Brittany and complete the unity of France.

There was only one way she could see to accomplish this. Charles VIII must marry Anne of Brittany, and do it quickly, before Maximilian should have time to get there to claim his bride. True, Charles was already married to Margaret of Austria, who had been Queen of France for eight years and was now eleven. Madame Anne loved Margaret and was sorry that she must suffer for the rash act of her father Maximilian. But private feelings could never be allowed to interfere with affairs of state.

The welfare of France demanded that Charles VIII should marry Anne. Brittany would fight desperately against this union, and her cities would have to be taken by force. So Charles was sent off at the head of an army to capture the cities one after another. When the last one fell, Anne of Brittany was given her choice—either to go to Maximilian and lose Brittany entirely, or to marry Charles and keep Brittany as long as she lived. Caring more for Brittany than anything else in the world, Anne accepted the lesser of the two evils.

They were married on December 6, 1491, Anne of Brittany and Charles VIII of France.

Maximilian had been robbed of his wife. His young daughter Margaret had been robbed of her husband and her crown.

Margaret was heartsick. When Charles came to say goodbye, as he was leaving for Brittany, she had been suspicious that he might not be coming back to her. Even though he reassured her, she was haunted by fear. Madame de Segré tried her best to comfort her.

"Do not weep, my sweet," she told her. "You are the daughter of a great King, your brother Philip is a great prince. You may not have this king, but you will have another—do not weep, my darling."

Soon, too soon, Margaret's clothes were being packed and she was leaving Amboise to make room for Queen Anne. But she was not yet allowed to leave France, because Charles VIII did not want to give back the French duchies which Margaret had brought as her dowry. It was two years before he was persuaded to give them back to her

father Maximilian and Margaret could go home to Flanders. Her escort was Charles of Angoulême. He had married Louise of Savoy, who now had a baby daughter, named Marguerite.

It was then June, 1493. Ten years had passed since the three-year-old Margaret had been handed over by representatives from Ghent. Now a lovely girl of thirteen, she was being handed back.

Madame la Grande, who was waiting for her at Cambrai, still looked surprisingly young and beautiful, and was delighted to see what a charming girl her little namesake had become. She was so poised and yet so natural in her manner, and so brave as she was saying farewell to each of the dear friends from France who had come this far with her. To each one she gave a parting gift, with a sad smile, but no sign of tears until she reached Madame de Segré. As she handed the gift to this dearest one, whom she would never see again, she could not bear it. Tears rolled down her face.

Margaret went with Madame la Grande to her residence which was at Malines, a small quiet town in the Flemish countryside, on the banks of a small river. There again, as the Archduchess of Austria, Margaret would await a further assignment by her father Maximilian —the next marriage that he thought would be of advantage to the House of Hapsburg.

In addition to Margaret there was also her brother, fifteen-year-old Philip, a spoiled, good-looking boy known as Philip "the Handsome." For Philip their father the Emperor must likewise arrange a marriage calculated to enhance the wealth and power of the Hapsburgs.

Philip, who was the Duke of Burgundy as well as the Archduke of Austria, had now become the ruler of the Netherlands, to the great joy of the people of Flanders. Philip was their "natural ruler," son of their Duchess Mary—not a foreigner foisted on them like his German father. Philip spoke only French and Flemish, not a word of German, even though as heir to the throne of Austria, he might one day be the next German emperor. The boy's whole education, in fact, had been sketchy and haphazard.

That suited Philip. Why worry about an education when he was happy without one and everyone liked him? He was glad to be the Duke, but to struggle over the government—that was boring business. To hunt, to wrestle, to joust, to sing, to dine late and dance till dawn with the rosiest girls at court—those were the hearty pleasures that filled the life of the active, lazy-minded, good-looking, selfish Philip of Hapsburg. This was the prize awaiting the lucky or unlucky princess his father the Emperor Maximilian was to select for him.

ERASMUS OF ROTTERDAM

THE YEAR that Margaret came home from France, a young poet who was to become the most esteemed scholar, not only in Maximilian's empire, but in all of Europe, arrived at the court in Brussels. He was called Erasmus.

Recently ordained a priest, he came as secretary to the Bishop of Cambrai. The Bishop was the most mighty churchman at the court of Burgundy, as it was still called, even though it had actually become the court of Hapsburg.

Erasmus was delighted to be there, relieved beyond words to be freed from the confines of that awful Augustinian monastery of Steyn. There he had been for five endless years, his freedom to think so restricted he could barely endure it. He had been forced to enter the monastery by his guardian, Peter Winckel, the schoolmaster of Gouda,

219

a mean, narrow-minded tyrant, in whose care he and his brother had been left after both his mother and father had died of the plague.

Gouda was a small cheese-making town about twelve miles from Rotterdam, in the section of the Netherlands known as Holland where Erasmus had been born. His early life might have been quite different had his father lived. He was a priest and a Greek and Latin scholar who had worked in Italy making copies of classic authors. School-master Winckel had no sympathy with those pagan authors—that newfangled classical learning. Ancient medieval textbooks were good enough for him and for his pupils.

In the monastery the teaching was equally medieval. The un-tutored monks cared not at all for Virgil, Horace, Cicero, or any of the classical poets and writers who so delighted the young Erasmus. He put his despair into this verse:

"Though I had mouths as many as the stars that sparkle in the silent firmament on quiet nights

Or as many as the roses that the gentle breeze of Spring scatters on the ground

I could not complain enough of all the evils which now oppress the sacred art of poetry . . ."

Erasmus wrote his poem in Latin, which he had mastered so thoroughly that he used it entirely, instead of his native Dutch, both in speaking and writing. It was his fluency in Latin that had gained him his appointment as secretary to the Bishop of Cambrai. Latin was the all-important language, spoken and used in every country of Europe. It was the language of the Church, of the courts of law, of all international relations. Latin was the language in which books were written, university courses were conducted, and scholars and scientists exchanged their ideas. All public men needed secretaries who could write their letters and papers in Latin with elegance and style. The Bishop of Cambrai had been looking for some time for a secretary who would handle such matters efficiently and intelligently to travel with him to Rome, where he hoped to be made a Cardinal.

This did not come off, to the great disappointment of Erasmus, who found life too much of a merry-go-round in Brussels, following the Bishop from church to court, from town house to country house. And where, complained Erasmus, "In such a bustle and clamor about me, do you think I can find leisure for the work of the Muses?"

Every spare moment he did have was put to use. In a monastery near Brussels, he found the works of St. Augustine and became so absorbed in them as to amaze the monks.

Near Bergen op Zoom, the Bishop had a country house. Here Erasmus squeezed in some hours of writing, and finished a book which he had begun in the monastery at Steyn.

It was called *Antibarbari—Against Barbarism.* Many years later he was to autograph a copy for Ferdinand Columbus.

The book was in the form of a conversation. A small group of friends meet in a garden house outside of a town to enjoy a simple meal and to talk about things of the mind, especially poetry and Latin literature. They quote St. Augustine and St. Jerome and others to prove that one can be a devout Christian and still appreciate the truth and beauty of Greek and Roman thought. War is solemnly declared against those ignorant people who deny this. Those barbarians in the dark forests of ignorance and superstition endanger civilization.

Antibarbari might well be the title of all the books Erasmus was ever to write. All of his life he was to fight against superstition and prejudice as being utter barbarism and folly.

Since the Bishop would not be going to Rome, Erasmus thought the next best thing for him would be to study for a degree in Theology at the University of Paris, the best and oldest one north of Italy. He got the consent of the Bishop, and a small allowance to live on. And in the late summer of 1495 Erasmus departed for Paris, as delighted to be free and leaving Brussels as he had been to leave the monastery at Steyn.

MARTIN LUTHER, SCHOOLBOY

THE NORTH GERMAN MINING TOWN of Mansfeld was deep in winter—the winter of 1493. Snow was falling in large, soft flakes outside the window of the common school. Inside, a sturdy peasant boy of ten, supposed to be listening to Latin conjugation and declensions, was watching the snow pile up on the window sill. He was thinking how deep and soft it would be when they walked around that night singing Christmas carols, when he heard his name called.

"Martin Luther!" He jumped up. He had heard his name, but not the verb he was to conjugate, so he stood there like a "Dumkopf" which he was not. Martin was a bright boy, and he liked Latin well enough, but this had been a bad week. Now he was in for fifteen beatings with the birch rod from the master. Some of the marks against him were for speaking German. No one in the school room was to be caught speaking anything but Latin, even by mistake. If he did he had to wear a donkey mask to show what a stupid ass he was, until the next careless fellow was caught.

Latin was most important. If you wanted to be somebody in this world, you must know Latin. So his father had told Martin from such time as he was big enough to listen. That his son should be a lawyer was the wish of Martin's father.

He, Hans Luther, had had no such chance as he was giving his son. When he came from the farm to Eisleben he was so poor a boy he had had to go to work in the iron mines. Greta had brought but a meager wedding dowry, so they had lived in a small dark house near St. Peter's Church. There their first son had been born on St. Martin's Day, November 11, 1483.

Martin did not remember his birthplace, because the next year father Hans moved to Mansfeld where there was a chance to go into business for himself. He leased a small furnace for smelting ore from the Count of Mansfeld, and he did so well that he was soon operating three. Hans Luther prospered through hard work, and also, as he never forgot, with the help of St. Anne, the miners' patron saint. Every night of his life he knelt by the bedside of his boy while they prayed to St. Anne.

In 1491, Hans Luther had been elected one of the four members of the town council. The family had a comfortable house with a fine porcelain stove, but no luxuries. Greta went as always to the forest to bring back bundles of firewood on her back. And she ruled her children with the same iron hand she had always known. She taught Martin the Ten Commandments for him to obey, and expected him to do it. One day she beat him until the blood came for stealing a nut. Once his father whipped him so badly that he ran away. But deep inside Martin knew that they were doing their best to make a good boy of him and a respected citizen. He often heard his mother singing a little ditty:

> "If folk don't like you and me
> The fault with us is like to be."

Martin loved music—psalms, hymns, and best of all the "Ave Maria." He sang at school. He sang at vespers and at masses and in all holyday processions, and also at funerals, for which he was paid. Once he got three groschen for singing in a funeral procession of a man who everyone said had died a good death. That man had studied a book telling him just what to do so that the devils would not get his soul. He was going straight to Heaven because he had bought so many indulgences that he did not have to stop off in Purgatory, that half-way place between heaven and hell.

One day Martin had actually seen a devil depart out of a man. Devils were terrible things. They caused diseases like the plague and bewitched people and made them crazy. Small devils, or sprites, his mother said, turned milk sour and stole eggs, and kept butter from churning. On top of a high mountain there was a lake full of captive demons. If anyone threw a stone in the water, it would set them free and they would send storms and floods over the whole region. The worst of all devils were those that nabbed a person when he was dead. Martin had seen awful pictures of devils dragging the damned right out of their graves down into the jaws of the horrible monsters and raging fires of hell.

Christ was the Judge. He sat on a rainbow or a cloud, separating those who were damned for their sins from the few who were to be saved and led by angels into heaven.

Sometimes even though he prayed hard before he went to bed, Martin could not sleep for worrying that a devil might get him during the night. Sometimes the moonlight and the branches in the wind made shadows on his wall that looked like dancing devils. He kept his eyes on them as long as he could keep them open.

Next morning he woke up happy and hungry for breakfast, the devils gone with the sun. Soon he was trudging off to school, a sturdy, healthy peasant boy, with no idea in his head that the new Emperor Maximilian would ever hear of him, Martin Luther, much less the Holy Father of the Church in Rome.

ADMIRAL COLUMBUS SAILS AGAIN

WHAT A DAY that was in the harbor of Cadiz—September 25, 1493! Trumpets blaring, drums beating, crowds laughing and shouting—seventeen ships and a thousand men leaving with Admiral Columbus for the land of gold! What a glorious day for the two boys, Ferdinand and Diego, who had come to see their famous father going out to be the Governor of Hispaniola. There they stood on a parapet of the castle overlooking the harbor, five-year-

225

old Ferdinand with his red-gold hair blowing in the breeze, beside his darker, taller brother Diego, who was thirteen. Leaning on the white stone wall, they could see everything—all the small boats coming and going.

In the last busy hours before sailing, twenty horses had been taken aboard. There were no horses in that strange part of the world which their father had discovered, not even any mules.

Sails on all seventeen ships were spread to the wind, bright banners flying from every mast and spar. A cannon boomed and they were off, like a flock of huge birds. One ship had made the voyage before, the Nina, which had brought their father home. Many more men than the ships would hold had wanted to make the voyage, and were disappointed and envious of those who were going.

Uncle Diego had come from Genoa to go. He was a nice, gentle man who wore plain clothes like a monk or a priest.

Uncle Bartholomew did not get to Cadiz in time, as he was in France, which was very far away. Ferdinand had never seen Uncle Bartholomew, but Diego remembered him. He had had a map shop when they lived in Lisbon. When Uncle Bartholomew came, he was going to take them to court to meet the King and Queen and become pages to the Infante Don Juan, which was something to look forward to. Till then they were to be home at school in Cordova.

One day, early in the new year, Uncle Bartholomew appeared. He was so brisk and business-like anyone could see he would have been at Cadiz in time to sail, if their father's letter had reached him. Actually it was the King of France, he said, Charles VIII, who had told him about their father's first voyage and its great success. King Charles had also given him 100 crowns to pay for his journey to Spain. Now they must be up and off, he and the boys, to Valladolid to meet the King and Queen. At court they found that nothing had yet been heard from their father, or the fort at La Navidad, made from the Santa Maria.

It was early March, when a Captain Torres arrived from Hispaniola with news that the Fort La Navidad was gone. They had found it burned to the ground. All forty men left there had been murdered by an Indian chief who was an enemy of their friend, Guacanagari. However, a new fort had been built, Fort Isabella, which was nearer to the gold mines, nearer, that is, to where they expected to find the mines. The Admiral had sent out fifteen or twenty men to search for gold in the mountains of Cibao, the central part of the island, but so far the only gold found had been nuggets taken from the mountain streams. Torres had brought some samples, about 30,000 ducats worth, to show the Queen. The Admiral had hoped to have more to send, but could not wait. Three or four hundred men were seriously ill at Fort Isabella and he was desperately in need of medicine and supplies.

Isabella and Ferdinand sent three caravels back at once with supplies, and wrote a letter to Columbus expressing their high regard for him. Bartholomew, who was now called "El Adelantado," the Leader, was given command of the three caravels. Every mile of the long voyage across the Atlantic, he was looking forward to being once more with his now-famous older brother whom he had not seen since they parted in Lisbon, six years ago.

Columbus was not there when Bartholomew reached Isabella. His brother Diego was in charge of the fort. The Admiral had been gone two months on an exploring trip to Cuba, Diego explained. Before he went he had appointed Margarit, a Spanish officer, as commander-in-chief of the island, and had sent Hojeda, another officer, with four hundred men off to a small, newly-built fort near the future gold mines in Cibao. Then Columbus had taken the Nina and two other ships and sixty men and sailed for Cuba.

As soon as he was gone, things went from bad to worse. Margarit did nothing to control the men. He let them go roving all over the island, extorting gold from the Indians, abusing them, stealing their women, and stirring up so much resentment that Diego feared that the Indians might attack and burn down this fort, full of men too weak to be moved.

Very soon Bartholomew saw the haughty Spaniard, Margarit, who had been left in command of the island. Marching arrogantly into Isabella one day, he seized the three ships which Bartholomew had brought and sailed for Spain, taking with him a crowd of malcontents like himself, intending no doubt to make a most unfavorable report to the King and Queen.

What a relief to both brothers—Diego and Bartholomew—to look out one morning and see the sails of the Admiral's ships coming in toward the island. Hardly was the Nina at anchor than Bartholomew was in a small boat being rowed out to it and climbing aboard.

Columbus was so ill he could barely speak. He had to be carried ashore. He was both ill in body and low in spirit.

The question of Cuba had still not been answered to his satisfaction. The men had made him turn back too soon. Although he had never heard of so large an island, and had made the men sign an oath that it was part of the mainland, how could he be sure?

And here at Isabella, he was again faced with hundreds of ill, discontented, unruly men who gave him no rest. Some relief came when four more caravels arrived with medicine and supplies. But then there was the worry of what to send back in the four empty ships. What could it be? It must be something of value or the sovereigns would believe what Margarit was sure to say—that Hispaniola was worthless. But what? There was as yet no great amount of gold. What else was there to send but—slaves? Nothing. Slaves, then, it had to be.

So men were sent out with hounds and horses, to round up 1,500 Indians and herd them into the fort. There, 500 of the "best males and females" were selected and loaded on the four caravels bound for the slave market in Seville. Diego Columbus went back on one of the ships so that he might go to court and try to correct the report of Margarit.

Columbus and Bartholomew, with the help of Hojeda, spent the summer subduing the Indians of the island.

The caciques were forced to submit to the rule of Spain, and obliged to pay a tax to their new rulers of far more in gold dust and nuggets than the poor Indians could possibly sift from the sand of the streams working day and night.

In the fall an officer sent by the Queen arrived at the fort obviously sent to check on Margarit's report. Columbus now decided to go back himself and make his own report. While he was gone, Bartholomew was to choose a better site and after building a new fort, abandon this hole of sickness and misery.

Many who had been so eager to come with Columbus, were now frantically anxious to go home. So many crowded onto the two small ships he was taking that they almost starved to death on the way. There were 225 Spaniards and 30 Indians on the Nina and the India, each supposed to carry about 25. Halfway over, the rations had to be reduced to six ounces of cassava bread and one cup of water a day. So it was a pitiful crew of bony men, with skin as yellow as saffron, who reached the end of the voyage and dragged themselves ashore at Cadiz, the harbor from which they had sailed almost three years before with such high hope.

Columbus betook himself quietly to Seville, to the home of his friend Bernaldez, chaplain to the Archbishop. His friend was very glad to see the many curious and beautiful articles made by the Tainos, which Columbus had brought, and to see that they were made of genuine gold, not a baser metal, as a goldsmith of Seville was telling everyone. All kinds of bad rumors were being circulated. To avoid being insulted on the street, Columbus seldom went out except to attend mass, and then he wore the coarse brown habit of a Franciscan friar. Perhaps he felt he was being made to suffer for the sin of pride, which he had formerly taken in wearing the elegant costumes of an Admiral.

An invitation from the sovereigns, who were at Burgos, came in about a month and he set out, anxious to make his report and to assure his two boys that all the bad things they must have heard of their father were not true. As the poor man expected, his enemies had done their work. Many at court turned their backs on him. Ferdinand and Isabella, however, received him most graciously. They listened with interest to all he had to say. They agreed that he should have what he asked for—eight ships, two to be sent to Hispaniola and six to be used by him in further exploration. But they did nothing more. They had not lost their trust in him. They simply had other things to think about.

Ferdinand, as always, deep in international affairs, had become involved in a war against France, his perpetual enemy. Pope Alexander VI had called for his help against Charles VIII who in 1494 had invaded Italy.

THE TRAGEDY OF ITALY

THE INVASION of Italy by Charles VIII was the opening of a tragedy lasting almost 400 years, during which France, Spain, and Austria turned Italy into a bloody battleground. Hardly was Lorenzo de Medici gone than peace, too, was gone. Angry Italian voices everywhere were crying out, begging for help to destroy one another. Quite forgetful of his father's maxims for peace, Charles accepted the invitation of Ludovico Sforza. The tragic drama therefore opens in Milan.

SCENE I MILAN A room in the Palace.

Ludovico Sforza, a dark man with olive skin, elegantly dressed, his long fingers loaded with rings, is talking with his attractive young wife, Beatrice. She is wearing a lovely mesh cap edged with pearls for Leonardo da Vinci had been painting her portrait. Beatrice is worried about the future of their young son because, although Ludovico Sforza had been ruler of Milan for thirteen years, he does not have the legal right to rule. He does not hold the title of Duke. Nor did his father, Francesco Sforza, hold the title of Duke, for the reason that he had married into the Visconti family which held the title and had seized the power when the old Duke of Visconti died, leaving no heir. Il Moro agrees with Beatrice that he should be called Duke. The one person that can give him the title is German Emperor Maximilian. So he composes a letter to Maximilian offering his niece, Bianca Sforza, to him in marriage and also 400,000 ducats, in exchange for being made Duke of Milan.

from a sketch by Leonardo

SCENE II MILAN The courtyard of the Palace.

The time is March, 1494, the day after the wedding by proxy of Bianca and Maximilian, also celebrated by the unveiling of the statue of her grandfather, Francesco Sforza, on horseback, which Leonardo da Vinci had finally finished. As the scene opens, Leonardo stands alone, gazing up at the statue considering, since this is only a plaster model, how to have it cast in bronze. Il Moro, now Duke of Milan, enters, exchanges a few words with Leonardo who hastens away, leaving Il Moro to pace back and forth in deep concern. Now he is worried that he may be deposed by the King of Naples, because even though he has the title of Duke, he still has not the right to be ruling Milan.

During the past thirteen years he has been only acting as Regent for his young nephew. Having ruled well, being a very capable man, he does not wish, now that his nephew has come of age, to hand over power to him. The nephew, being an idle, luxury-loving, no-account fellow, does not want it. But his young wife does. And Ludovico fears that she will call upon her father for help. And her father is the King of Naples!

Il Moro suddenly comes to a decision, goes into the palace to write a letter to the King of France.

SCENE III FRANCE The Castle of Amboise.

Charles VIII, now twenty-four, still small, big-headed, and bandy-legged, is pondering over the letter that has just come from Milan. Ludovico Sforza promises him free passage through northern Italy plus 200,000 ducats, if he will come, attack the King of Naples, and capture his throne. This is very tempting because the French have an ancient claim to the throne of Naples. However, the King of Naples is a Spaniard, a relative of Ferdinand of Aragon, whom Charles does not wish to stir up. He is also a good friend of the Spanish Pope, Alexander VI. On the other hand, there is an Italian, Cardinal Rovere, a warlike man who hates the Pope. The monk Savonarola, too, has been writing Charles to come and rid Italy of that "vile Father of the Church," as well as to free Florence from the wicked Medici. Now Charles decides to accept Il Moro's invitation.

Louis of Orleans, his brother-in-law, enters the room. As an older man, an experienced soldier, he advises Charles to take a force of 40,000 men. He himself will go along as far as Milan. Louis has reasons of his own for taking a look at the Duchy of Milan—very special reasons to be revealed later.

SCENE IV ASTI A room at the Inn.

It is a stifling day in early August, 1494. French soldiers are milling about. Charles VIII walks in, dressed in uniform. With him is Louis of Orleans, who acts and talks as if this town of Asti belonged to him. The Duke of Milan is announced. He enters, tall, dark, handsome, elegant in dress and manner. He meets the King of France for the first time, and also Louis of Orleans, which is an unpleasant surprise. The Duke says that his young wife has come with him to meet the French visitors, and is at the castle, where Leonardo da Vinci is preparing entertainment for them. The elegant Sforza then departs, mopping his brow and casting an uneasy glance at Louis of Orleans for good reason.

The town of Asti does belong to Louis of Orleans. He had inherited it from his grandmother, a Visconti of Milan—the original Visconti family from whom Francesco Sforza had seized the duchy. What does Louis of Orleans think? That Milan is rightfully his? He says he is going no farther. Charles will proceed on to Naples alone. The sooner they both go the better for Il Moro, who is already beginning to wonder what he has let himself in for.

SCENE V FLORENCE From Piazza to Palace.

November 9, 1494. The Signoria, or Council, has just adjourned; the hall is buzzing with excitement. Outside on the piazza can be heard angry voices of the crowd crying, "Down with the Medici!" and calling Pietro a traitor and a coward.

Pietro de Medici had handed over to the King of France all

the border forts which protected Florence. Without consulting the Council, as his father Lorenzo would have done, Pietro met the French King at Pisa, got panicky at sight of the huge French army, and gave Charles VIII free passage through Florence on the way to Naples. The Signoria have just passed a decree banishing the Medici, offering 4,000 florins for the head of Pietro, 2,000 florins each for the heads of Giovanni and Giuliano.

"Down with the Medici," the people scream. "Down with the Medici!" They rush to the Medici Palace. Mobs of people, turned loose to plunder and destroy, go tramping through the beautiful halls and gardens. Treasures that took fifty years to collect are being carted off; precious objects ruthlessly smashed.

The Medici brothers have fled for their lives.

SCENE VI ROME The Papal Apartment.

Pope Alexander VI, rather portly and short of breath, is waiting to receive Charles VIII. He has returned to the Vatican, from the Castel Angelo, a fortress on the Tiber River, where he took refuge when Charles reached Rome and was welcomed by the Pope's enemies, the chief one being Cardinal Rovere. The Pope had already sent an appeal for help to the Sultan of Turkey, warning him that after Naples, the French King planned to attack Constantinople. He then sent a cautious message to Charles, and is now waiting for him. Knowing that the Pope had sent an appeal to the Sultan, Charles is fearful that he may also appeal to Ferdinand of Aragon, who might well invade France while he is gone.

Caesar Borgia, the Pope's son, is now introduced. It is arranged that he, the big handsome bullfighter, shall go with little Charles to Naples as a hostage.

SCENE VII NAPLES The King's Palace.

The King of Naples has gone. He has given over the city, kingdom, and palace to the French, without any resistance, and departed. Charles VIII is blissfully enjoying the palace, the view of the blue bay and Mount Vesuvius, the gaiety and music, all the joys of Naples—most of all, the luscious dark-eyed, red-lipped Neapolitan beauties. He is so enraptured that he has not even noticed that his hostage is gone—that Caesar Borgia has escaped and returned to Rome!

EXIT CHARLES

Pope Alexander's courage is instantly renewed at the sight of his son Caesar. With characteristic vigor he bounces back into action and organizes a League to drive the French out of Italy. Those who join him are Ferdinand of Aragon, the Emperor Maximilian, the Doge of Venice, and one more—the Duke of Milan, Ludovico Sforza. After having felt Louis of Orleans breathing down his neck, Sforza has grown more and more remorseful for having invited Charles VIII to Italy.

Whereas Charles VIII, seeing no ally left in Italy except Savonarola, who had refused to be associated with the "vile" Pope, knows that the wise thing for him to do is to get out and go home to France as fast as possible, which he does.

The King of Naples returns.

The invasion accomplished nothing for the French, but it marked a turning point in history. It showed the Kings of Europe how weak and divided Italy was, and how easily it could be invaded and conquered, and made them all—French, German, and Spanish—eager to try.

FINALE

In addition to joining the pact against France, the Emperor Maximilian, and Ferdinand of Aragon make a private treaty to be sealed by a double wedding of their sons and daughters. The Infante Juan is betrothed to Margaret of Austria; the Infanta Juana is to marry Philip the Handsome.

JUANA AND PHILIP

QUEEN ISABELLA spent the summer of 1496 assembling a
large fleet for the purpose of exchanging the two brides—
to carry Juana to Philip the Handsome in Flanders, and to
bring back Margaret of Austria to the Infante Don Juan. On the
morning of August 22nd, 120 top-heavy ships with huge square sails
and high poop decks were creaking and rocking in the Spanish harbor
of Laredo. On board were 20,000 people to accompany the Infanta
Juana. Ladies-in-waiting—all chosen from noble families of the bluest
blood—chaplains, stewards, clerks, and countless lesser members made
up the royal retinue.

In the last precious moments before parting, Isabella was standing beside her daughter on the deck of the royal ship, only a word or two breaking their silence.

Juana was a strange child. Of her five, Isabella understood her least—this tense silent girl with her dark, mysterious, almond-shaped eyes. She watched the others who had come to see her off.

There was Juan, so friendly and gracious in his gentle manner who would soon be welcoming his own bride.

And Isabel, twenty-six, the young widow, who might soon be going back to Portugal, since the new King Manuel wished to marry her.

Maria, always so even-tempered, was the only one so far whose marriage had not yet been arranged.

Catalina, who was eleven, had been promised for nine years to Arthur, the Crown Prince of England.

Ferdinand, who had arranged all these weddings, was not there to bid his daughter Juana farewell. He was still in Barcelona, occupied with manipulations against the French.

The Queen was sad to see Juana leave and also worried about the autumn storms on the English Channel. She had already written King Henry VII for his hospitality, fearing the ships bearing the Infanta might have to take refuge in one of the English ports. Her fears were justified.

The Spanish vessels were caught in a bad storm as they entered the English Channel. Two went down in a roaring wind that tossed them about and drove all the others into the English harbor of Portland. After some time the sailors ventured forth again, and finally landed on the sandy banks of Zeeland at Middleburg. Juana had to be carried ashore, seasick and ill with a frightful cold. The handsome Philip was not there to meet his bride, which was just as well considering her swollen eyes and runny nose. Juana was in Antwerp, still in bed with her cold, when her new family came to welcome her. There was Margaret, Philip's sister, so charming and gay and easy to know, and the beautiful young grandmother, who was called Madame la Grande.

A courier had been sent for Philip, who was then in Austria. October 20th was the date set for the wedding which was to take place in Lille. Actually it took place the night before, because that evening with much clatter of hooves in the courtyard Philip arrived, much too impatient to wait. One look at that handsome young man and Juana was madly in love with him. So they were married that night, and their passionate, tumultous tragic life together began. Next day, the Bishop of Cambrai—the patron of Erasmus—performed the formal church ceremony, after which in celebration, the jolly burghers danced so hard and long back and forth across the town bridge that it collapsed into the river.

Juana's long-repressed spirit burst all bounds, pouring itself out in adoration of her young husband, but making her so jealous and possessive that his own ardor shortly began to cool. He loved her, to be sure, but he had also loved many other girls and he had no idea of changing his ways because of her jealousy. Juana was grieved to find his love not so deep as her own, and soon began to look and act unhappy. She appeared almost miserable at Margaret's wedding to her brother Juan, which took place by proxy early in November.

Margaret, wearing a gold crown, was radiant. At sixteen, five years after losing the King of France, she was being married, as dear Madame de Segré had then predicted, to another royal prince, the Infante Juan of Castile and Aragon.

Early in January, her brother Philip escorted her to Middleburg where the Spanish fleet was still waiting to take her to the bridegroom she had not yet seen. The Spanish sailors had grown impatient to be off, even though it was winter and the return voyage would surely be a stormy one. It proved to be far worse than the first. This time the battered ships were blown into the English harbor of Southampton. Margaret received a letter from Henry VII inviting her to stay as long

239

as she wished. The ships set out again as soon as possible, everyone on board being impatient to reach Spain and have the agony over. In the Bay of Biscay, however, the storm became so terrific that no one expected to reach any port alive. But even on the worst day, facing death, Margaret kept her sense of humor. She wrote this little epitaph, had it rolled in wax and fastened to her wrist with a few gold pieces for her burial.

> Ci -gist Margot la gente demoiselle
> Qu-eut deux maris mais si mourut pucelle.
> Here lies Margot, the gentle maiden
> Who had two husbands but died a virgin.

Queen Isabella, waiting at Burgos, was again extremely worried about the fate of the fleet. She sent for Columbus who was still at court, and asked his opinion as an expert navigator. Did he, or did he not, believe that the ships from the Netherlands would arrive safely? Columubus assured her that they would, which was most consoling to her, and most fortunate for him, since his prediction proved to be true.

On March 8, 1497, the ships were washed ashore at the port of Santander. Ferdinand and Don Juan were there to meet the bride and escort her to Burgos. Margaret, riding between them on horseback, charming both with her natural manner, must have been struck by the contrast between father and son.. On the one hand she saw a shrewd, worldly man; on the other a poetic-looking lad of eighteen, pale and slender, with narrow face and large, dark, almost melancholy eyes.

In the City Hall of Burgos, hung with richly colored tapestries for her formal reception, Margaret met and knelt before the real ruler of Spain, Queen Isabella. In a few days the older woman and the girl, who were much alike in their outlook and ability, became fast friends.

Juan and Margaret, sharing love of poetry and music, and complementing each other in temperament, were soon happily in love.

Although Margaret did not speak Spanish, there was no language barrier for, being well educated, they both spoke Latin.

On April 3, 1497, the marriage ceremony was performed in the Cathedral at Burgos by the Archbishop of Toledo. Among the guests who were there to admire the young couple was Christopher Columbus. Three weeks later, as a result of the Admiral's happy prediction about Margaret's safe arrival, the sovereigns issued the first definite orders for a fleet to be prepared for him. It would, however, take a full year of preparation before Columbus could start on his third voyage to the New World.

His sons, Diego and Ferdinand, meanwhile, as pages to the bridegroom, were enjoying a succession of splendid entertainments given for Don Juan and Donna Margharita following their wedding in Toledo. Margaret sparkled and responded gaily to the festivities which were held in various cities, but Don Juan, who was very delicate, soon became exhausted. The circles under his eyes grew deeper and darker as the strenuous pace continued.

On the first of October, 1497, word reached Ferdinand and Isabella that, in the midst of the festivities at Salamanca, Juan had been taken desperately ill. Ferdinand left at once, but Juan was dying when he reached his bedside. He was only nineteen.

Margaret could not believe it. In a few months their baby would be born. And Juan would never see it.

Isabella bore the tragic news with courage.

"The Lord giveth and the Lord taketh away," she said simply. And after a pause she could add, "Blessed be the name of the Lord."

All the land was in lamentation and mourning. Black banners floated over every tower and gateway. Rich and poor went about in the sackcloth of mourning. Diego and Ferdinand, all in black, were now taken as pages at her own court, by Queen Isabella.

Life must go on, even though her son and heir to the throne was gone. There was the comforting hope that Juan's child might be a boy to take the place of his young father. Margaret passionately shared that hope, but unhappily her baby, a little girl, was born dead.

What now? Where was she to go now? What a strange thing her life was—fortune—misfortune—fortune—misfortune. "But I still have hope," she thought.

"From my childhood, I have had hope,
And wish that I may always have it."

Soon a letter came from England that gave Margaret something to do that she enjoyed and made her feel at least useful. It was a letter to Queen Isabella from the Spanish ambassador in London regarding Catalina, whom the English always called the "Princess of Wales." The letter read:

"Queen Elizabeth and also the mother of Henry VII wish that the Princess of Wales should always speak French with the Princess Margot, who is now in Spain . . . to learn the language and be able to talk it, as they, the Queens do not understand Latin much less Spanish . . ."

One year after Juan's death, tragedy struck again.

Queen Isabella lost her daughter Isabel who, after Juan's death, had been heir to the throne. Isabel, who had been married about a year to King Manuel, the King of Portugal, lost her life in giving birth to a son, Miguel, who was now heir to the thrones of Castile and Aragon, as well as Portugal.

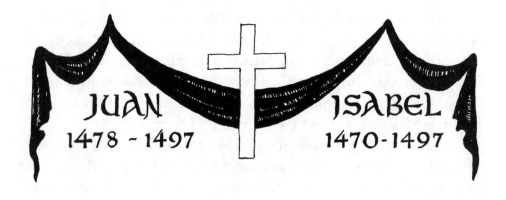

JUAN
1478 - 1497

ISABEL
1470 - 1497

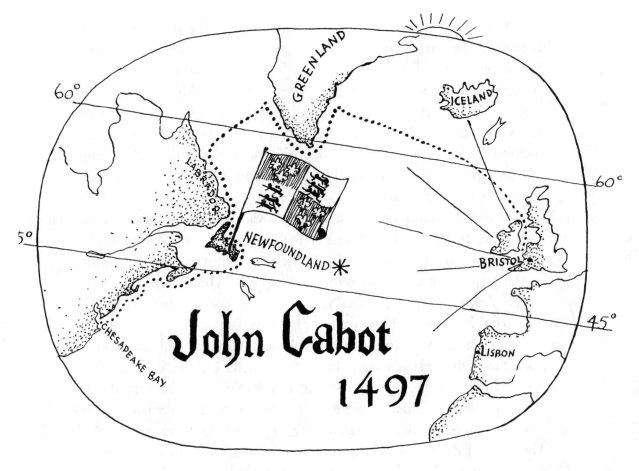

John Cabot 1497

JOHN CABOT AND HENRY VII

IT WAS IN THE SUMMER of 1497 while Columbus was preparing for his third voyage that Giovanni Caboto, who had also been born in Genoa, and had also thought of reaching India by going west, sailed for Henry VII. Although the miserly King of England had not risked a precious penny on the venture, he was to gain by it a foothold in a large part of North America. The merchants of Bristol, England, who financed the voyage of their fellow townsman, called him John Cabot. He had come to England from Venice where, he told them, from the time he was old enough, he had sailed on Venetian ships through the eastern Mediterranean.

243

How the spices which they picked up at the various ports got there from the land where they originated always puzzled him. Some, he learned, came from China by a long overland route that led through Samarkand to the Caspian Sea. Once in Mecca, the Holy City of the Moslems, he had seen spices brought in by camel caravan across the Arabian desert. Most of the spices to be had in the great market of Alexandria were picked up in India in the port of Calicut and brought by boat up the Red Sea to Suez and there taken by camels to the Egyptian port. All these ways were slow and costly.

How much cheaper and simpler it would be if the goods from China and India could be brought to Europe all the way by water. Why not bring them across the western ocean, stopping at islands on the way? He had seen many maps in Venice which showed islands in the Atlantic called Antilia and Brazil. If these could be found they would serve as stepping stones across the ocean.

The merchant seamen of Bristol became interested in Cabot's plan. Since they carried on a brisk trade with Iceland carrying fish from there to Portugal, they too had heard of Antilia and Brazil and thought that they must be somewhere southwest of Greenland. They were sending ships out to search for them until the summer of 1493. Then one of their pilots, returning from Lisbon, brought word that an Italian named Colombo or Colon, sailing for Queen Isabella, had already reached the Indies, or an island off the coast of China!

John Cabot and the Bristol merchants quickly decided to forget about stepping stones and push on directly for the mainland. For this they had to obtain permission from the King. After much delay a paper came stating that Henry VII gave to his:

"well-beloved John Cabot, citizen of Venice, and sonnes of said John . . . leave and power, upon their own proper costs and charge to seek out . . . whatsoever isles . . . of the heathen and infidels, which before this time have been unknown to all Christians . . ." One-fifth of the net gains was to go to the King.

On May 2, 1497, John Cabot, with eighteen seamen, sailed from Bristol in a tiny ship, the Mathew. He steered north between Britain and Ireland toward Iceland. Then he turned west by south and after fifty-two days at sea reached the northern edge of Cape Breton Island. There he had the royal banner of England unfurled and took possession of the country in the name of Henry VII.

By August 6th the Mathew was back in Bristol Harbor. From there John Cabot hastened to London to make his report to King Henry VII, from whom he received a miserly ten pounds for having "found the new isle," and later a pension of twenty pounds.

In December, 1497, Ludovico Sforza, Duke of Milan, received a letter from his ambassador in London, about Cabot's discovery.

"Most illustrious and most Excellent Lord:

"Perhaps amidst so many occupations of your Excellency it will not be unwelcome to learn his Majesty here has acquired a portion of Asia without a stroke of his sword.

"In this Kingdom there is a lower-class Venetian named Zoanne Cabato, of fine mind, very expert in navigation, who seeing that the most serene Kings, first of Portugal then of Spain, have occupied unknown islands, meditated the achievement of a similar acquisition for his Majesty aforesaid... having obtained royal grants ... he set out from Bristol, and having passed Ireland and wandered about considerably, at length he fell in with terra firma, where he set up the royal standard and came back again. The said Master Zoanne, being a foreigner and a poor man would not be believed if the crew, who are nearly all English and from Bristol, did not testify that what he says is true.

"This master Zoanne has a drawing of the world on a map also on a solid globe which he has made, and shows the point he reached on the country of Asia. But Master Zoanne has set his mind on something greater, for he expects to go from that place already occupied, constantly hugging the shore until he is opposite an island called by him Cipangu, . . . where he thinks grow all the spices of the world and also the precious stones . . .

"And he speaks of it in such a way that . . . I too believe him. And what is more his Majesty here who is wise and not lavish like-wise puts some faith in him. . . . And it is said that in the Spring his Majesty will fit out some ships and they will proceed to form a colony, by means of which they hope to make London a greater depot for spices than Alexandria.

Your excellency's most humble servant, Raimundus."

In May of 1498, John Cabot again left Bristol, this time with five ships and three hundred men. Earlier in the spring he had visited Lisbon and Seville to secure services of men who had sailed with Cam or Dias or better still, with Columbus. At Lisbon he met a Portuguese sailor named Llavrador, who had visited Greenland. So in the spring of 1498 after leaving Bristol, John Cabot sailed to Greenland and called it the land of Llavrador. He followed north along the east coast of Greenland until the crews refused to go farther. Turning about he went down around the end and up the west coast until icebergs blocked the way.

Crossing the strait, he then followed south along the coast of the North American continent, almost to what is now Chesapeake Bay. He was looking for Cipangu—Japan. By that time supplies were so low he had to give up hope of finding Japan until his next voyage.

John Cabot never made another voyage. No one knows when or where he died. Some say only four ships returned safely to Bristol in 1498, and that the one on which John Cabot sailed was missing.

For fifty years or more the English were to give little thought to what John Cabot had found for them. And his capable but egotis-tical son, Sebastian, who later in the service of Spain, always implied with sad lack of loyalty that he, not his father, was truly the great voyager.

MANUEL I

from an old print

VASCO DA GAMA REACHES INDIA

Dom MANUEL, the Fortunate, King of Portugal, held an
official audience in January, 1497, and appointed as Admiral
of the India fleet a tall, glittering young cavalier and nobleman about his own age, named Vasco da Gama. The Portuguese
were now convinced that whatever country Columbus had discovered
it was *not* India. They would renew their attempt to reach India by
their own route. Nine years had passed since Bartholomew Dias had
rounded the Cape of Good Hope. By July, 1497, three new ships
had been built and equipped for the voyage.

In the harbor of Lisbon, where the Tagus River meets the

BERRIO

ocean, stood a small chapel built by Prince Henry the Navigator and dedicated to Our Lady of Bethlehem. All the night before sailing, Vasco da Gama was there praying with the other officers and the monks from the nearby monastery. As the light of dawn came through the small windows, the mass ended, the bells of the chapel and monastery rang. A procession emerged from the chapel, led by the vicar, followed by priests and monks chanting. Then came the Admiral and one hundred officers, each carrying a lighted candle. Lastly, the men of the crew, who had been waiting outside with friends and relatives, knelt to be given absolution, and joined the procession to the beach. There the women—wives and mothers in black mantillas—were weeping bitterly.

Three brand-new ships, the St. Gabriel, St. Raphael, and the Berrio, were to make the voyage. Soon the anchors were weighed; their great square sails, marked with bright red crosses, caught the brisk morning breeze, and they were off.

This was the great adventure for Portugal. This voyage was to crown with success the seventy-five years of trial and error which had cost so much gold and the lives of so many men. Now at last the dreams of Prince Henry the Navigator, the efforts of his grand-nephew John II, the Perfect Prince, were to be realized under John's cousin, King Manuel, the Fortunate.

Vasco da Gama

At dawn on July 8, 1497, the day of sailing, Dom Manuel called his father confessor and before a number of witnesses made a solemn vow. In place of the small chapel at the harbor he vowed to erect, if the voyage were a success, a splendid new cloister and chapel in memory of Prince Henry and dedicated to Our Lady of Bethlehem.

The voyage began quietly. On July 26th the ships reached the Cape Verde Islands, stopped eight days for water and food, fresh meat and vegetables. They then turned eastward, sailed along the Guinea coast from which they swung far out toward the undiscovered coast of Brazil, then back again east and southeast until, on November

1st they came in sight of Africa again. Three weeks later they rounded the Cape of Good Hope and anchored in Mossel Bay, where Bartholomew Dias had landed nine years before and been obliged to turn back.

The men had then been on shipboard four months without proper food. Many of them were ill and dying of scurvy. Their gums had become sore, their noses bled, their skin turned greenish-yellow and ulcerated, their bodies swelled up with water, and they died in agony. In early January, the ships entered the mouth of the Zambesi River and those who were well enough began digging graves for the thirty men who had died. The crew was heartened to know that they had now gone the greater part of the distance.

By early March they reached Mozambique. They had then passed out of the lands occupied by simple Negro tribes, into an area of Africa controlled by the Moslems—Arabs whose culture was wholly equal to that of the Portuguese. There in the harbor they saw Arab freighters returning from India. The Arab ships, or dhows, were made of planks sewn together with fibers, and had sails made of palm matting. That such frail ships could make the voyage was encouraging to the Portuguese. The four Arab dhows in the harbor were loaded with gold and silver, pearls and rubies, and spices—cloves, pepper, nutmeg, and ginger. For centuries, since 500 B.C., the Arabs had controlled this trade with India, carrying products from the Far East to Alexandria in Egypt where the ships from Venice and Genoa picked them up in exchange for goods from Europe. The Portuguese threatened this monopoly. At first the Sheik of Mozambique had supposed that they were also Moslems, and Vasco da

Gama, who wanted two pilots to guide him to India, let him continue to think so. When it was discovered that they were Christians, no one in the harbor would even give them water. So Da Gama turned the bombards on his ships toward land and fired stone balls at Mozambique's flimsy wooden fort for three hours. Two days later, he had all the water they needed, and sailed north up the coast to Mombasa, the finest harbor on the East African shore.

News of the coming of these hated foreigners had preceded them to Mombasa and they had difficulty fighting off a night attack. But with good luck they escaped to the high seas and sailed north to Malindi. The Sheik of Malindi, they were happy to discover, was an enemy of the Sheik of Mombasa, and he gave Da Gama a pilot to guide the Portuguese ships across the Indian Ocean, a very skillful pilot about sixty years of age.

Ahmad ibn Majid was his name. He wore a green turban, which was a sign that he was a Hadji, one who had made the holy pilgrimage to Mecca. He had Vasco da Gama wait until the monsoons began to blow. Then the sails bearing their great red crosses were bellied out by the southern wind and the ships of Dom Manuel of Portugal were off on the last lap of their voyage. They were crossing the Indian Ocean!

After the twenty-third day, the brown-faced pilot in his green turban, pointed out over the blue water, saying, "Here is the land to which you desired to go. We have arrived. We are just to the north of Calicut."

At sunset, in the pink and green Indian evening of May 20, 1498, the Portuguese reached the teeming docks of Calicut. The sea route to India was open!

As they entered the harbor, many fishermen in small boats came close to inspect these three strange ships, with red crosses on their sails. Then the fishermen hurried ashore to carry the news of the foreigners' arrival to the Rajah of Cannanore. The Rajah called his soothsayers, who reminded him of an ancient prophecy which said:

251

"One day all India will be ruled by white men from a distant land, whose king will do great harm to those who are not his friends."

Vasco da Gama had studied carefully all the information on India, collected by King John. He knew that Calicut was the most important town on the whole of the Malabar coast.

The Rajah who ruled Calicut was called Zamorin, "Lord of the Sea," and the Arab merchants of Calicut held great power in his kingdom. Some owned fifty or sixty ships, sailing back and forth with the monsoons to Africa. The Rajah's main wealth came from the money the Arab merchants paid for his protection.

As soon as the three ships were anchored in the harbor, Vasco da Gama sent a messenger ashore to scout cautiously about. A messenger was also sent to the Zamorin to announce that Vasco da Gama, Captain General of the fleet, had come bearing a message from the King of Portugal to be delivered with his own hand. The Zamorin replied with a formal message of welcome and granted him an interview.

On May 28th, an hour before sunset, Vasco da Gama, elegantly attired in brown satin coat, white satin breeches, blue velvet tunic, and cap with a white plume, was entering the royal palace of the Zamorin, accompanied by twelve of his officers. They had traveled all day to get there, carried in palanquins borne by relays of six men, along the road to the city. The way had been lined with men, women, and children, curious to see the foreigners.

The first place they visited in the city was a Hindu temple. Being completely ignorant of the Hindu religion, the Portuguese thought it was a Christian church, even though they were mildly surprised to see some of the saints shown with four or five arms.

Each officer carried a present for the Zamorin, pieces of scarlet material, a gilded mirror, fifty silk caps, and fifty gilded cases containing Flemish knives. These were sent in ahead to the Zamorin who was amazed and scornful of them. That King must be poor indeed to send such modest gifts as these.

"The poorest mechant from Mecca," sneered one of his Arab councillors, "would give more."

One of the Portuguese kept a diary of this journey to India in which he described this first meeting between East and West.

"The Zamorin was found seated in a vast hall under a white canopy, reclining on a green divan covered with rich silks. He was a dark brown color, and was naked to the waist, from which a white garment reached to his knees. On his left arm he wore an armband, richly set with precious stones. A diamond the size of a thumb hung from the central bangle. About his neck, the king wore a double string of pearls, which reached to his waist, each pearl the size of a hazelnut. Above this was a thin round golden chain, with a heart shaped pendant surrounded by large pearls and covered with a mass of rubies; in the middle of it was a green stone as large as a bean (an emerald). This precious stone, the diamond in the armband and a pearl fastened to the Zamorin's hair belonged to the ancient treasure of the Kings of Calicut. Close to the King stood a little boy. He carried a red shield decorated in gold and a short sword. On the other side a page had a copious golden basin, into which the King would spit his betel. Next to his chair there stood a high Brahman who from time to time would hand the King a green leaf enveloping

253

other objects, and the King would chew at it continuously and then spit it into the basin and start on a fresh one."

The King made not the slightest motion as Vasco da Gama entered, except to nod to the Brahman who took Da Gama's hand and led him to his master. Gama joined his hands in the Indian manner which he had observed, and made a profound obeisance. The Zamorin bowed ever so slightly, touched Da Gama's hand with the tip of his fingers and bade him be seated on the dais below his couch. Gama remained standing, and addressed him through his interpreter.

"Most powerful sire, most powerful ruler of India, the great King of Portugal, my master, has heard of your greatness, the fame of which girdles the earth, and is desirous of making a treaty of friendship with you as a brother. He has therefore sent his ships with wares of his own country to dispose of in yours and desires to acquire especially pepper and spices which are not found in Portugal."

The interpreter hesitated to repeat the King's answer.

"You say you come from a great King, yet the gifts you have brought me from your King are of trifling value."

Vasco da Gama replied to this with a lie. The three ships were but a small part of the great fleet sent by the King of Portugal. He said that others bearing great gifts had been wrecked in a storm. The King would send goods of such value as to buy everything in the markets of Calicut. He then kissed the letter from Dom Manuel and presented it to the Zamorin, who pressed it against his breast as a sign of love and promised a further audience.

On leaving, Da Gama took away gifts from the Zamorin worth a thousand times more than the modest gifts he had brought.

Plotting against the intruder, the Arab merchants meanwhile had bribed the head officer of the Zamorin to seize and hold Vasco da Gama. Da Gama told him that if he did not set him free, all the ships in the harbor of Calicut would be sunk and the whole city destroyed. This "insolent threat" was reported to the Zamorin at once with the advice that the Portuguese be put to death.

The great Brahman intervened.

"My lord, do not do that," he said, "You have no reason for it. The stranger has so far done no harm."

Vasco da Gama felt fortunate in having escaped death and in being allowed to load his ships with spices before he departed. The real riches of the Orient, he learned, lay still farther east in what were called the Spice Islands or Moluccas, but he dared not undertake the voyage with his depleted crew. The journey home was slow, with more dreadful scurvy. Soon half of his men were dead. Without enough sailors left to man the three ships, the St. Raphael had to be abandoned.

It was late in the summer of 1499, two years after they had started, that the weatherbeaten St. Gabriel and the Berrio were again anchored in the harbor of Lisbon.

King Manuel received Vasco da Gama with great ceremony in the presence of the whole court, and made him Admiral of the Sea of India. The King also fulfilled his vow to replace the small chapel where Da Gama and his men had prayed the night before their great voyage, with one in memory of Prince Henry.

Maria, who followed her sister Isabel as wife of Dom Manuel, was there in 1500 to see the cornerstone laid. The Brothers of St. Jeronimo were charged with the obligation "to offer their prayers for the soul of Prince Henry, founder of the original chapel, and of the monarch and his successors."

A gold coin was struck to commemorate the voyage which had opened the sea route to India. For nearly 400 years, until the opening of the Suez Canal, this way opened by Portugal was to be the route from Europe to the Far East.

255

TO TRINIDAD AND SANTO DOMINGO

O N MAY 30, 1498, Columbus started on his third voyage. Neither he nor anyone else in Europe knew that just ten days earlier, on May 20th, Vasco da Gama had landed in Calicut and the Portuguese had reached India. It was known, however, that the King of Portugal believed that a mainland existed south of the islands which Columbus had discovered, and might soon be searching for it. The Admiral's purpose on this voyage was to find whether that mainland did exist, and if so, whether it lay west of the dividing line and could therefore be claimed for Spain.

Columbus was far from well, suffering severely from arthritis, as he left Seville for the port of embarkation at the mouth of the river.

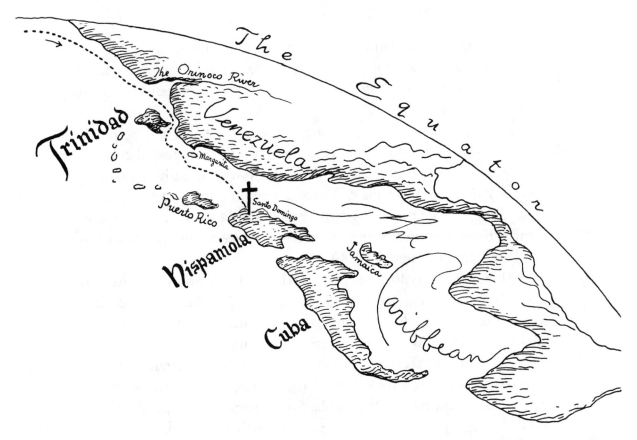

"I departed," he wrote, "in the name of the Most Holy Trinity from the town of San Lucar very wearied. I had hoped to rest there, but my pain had doubled. I navigated to the island of Madeira, and from there . . . to the Canary Islands, where I departed with one ship and two caravels . . . I sent the other ships on the direct course to the island of Espanola [to take supplies for the new fort which Bartholomew had built] having reached the islands of Cape Verde, I sailed to the southward 480 miles. There the wind failed me and I came into great heat, so intense that I believed that the ships and people would be burned. The heat lasted for eight days. And it pleased Our Lord at the end of these eight days to give me a favorable wind and I steered westward. On Tuesday, July 31, at midday land appeared to us. A sailor went up to the maintop to look out and to the westward saw three mountains near to one another. We repeated the Salve Regina and other prayers and we all gave many thanks to Our Lord."

This, then, was Trinidad! Columbus had vowed to name the first island he reached for the Trinity. What could be more suitable than that this island, blessed with the three peaks, should be given that Holy Name!

Passing through a narrow strait which he called the Serpent's Mouth (Boca de la Sierpe) he entered the Gulf and crossed to what he thought was another island, but which was actually a point of the mainland, the peninsula of Paria. There on Sunday, a little to the west along the southern coast of the peninsula, men from the ship went ashore, the first Spaniards ever to set foot on the American continent. It was August 5, 1498.

After searching for the end of the "island," they reported to Columbus at evening when they returned to the ship that they had found four rivers feeding streams of fresh water into the Gulf. What could this mean? What four rivers could they be?

Columbus was exhausted, too tired to think, certainly too ill to carry on with the exploration at this time. Also, he felt he should get to Bartholomew in Hispaniola. So he turned about, and left the Gulf through the narrow strait to the north of Trinidad which he called the Mouth of the Dragons (Bocas del Dragon), and sailed on to the west.

When they had sailed west farther than the depth of the Gulf and still found no end to the "island," it dawned on Columbus that what they had found had not been an island—but a continent! The night of August 15th he wrote in his journal:

"I believe that this is a very great continent which until today had been unknown. And reason aids me greatly because of that so great river and fresh water sea."

But what continent was it? Where and how did it fit into the geography of the world, as it was then known? Where in the world had he heard of four rivers before? It came to him—in Genesis! Did it not say, "And a river went out of Eden to water the garden and from thence it was parted and became four"?

This then must be Paradise on Earth—the continent on which was located the Garden of Eden!

Surely, this was the place to form the next settlement, later, after he had been to Hispaniola. Now he was desperate to get to the fort where he could rest and relieve the pain in his eyes. Never, he said, had his "eyes been so injured nor did they run blood and cause so much pain as now."

Santo Domingo, the new fort that Bartholomew had built, was named for the patron saint of their father. It had a fine harbor, and was far better, Columbus saw, in every way than the old fort of Isabella. But the behavior of the men had grown worse and there was no chance for him to rest. The Chief Justice, whom he had appointed to act during his absence, had led a rebellion against Bartholomew and he and his men were now roaming the island.

Columbus sent his flagship home at once with two letters to Ferdinand and Isabella, one describing "a very great continent" which he had found, including maps and charts. The other asked that they send a new Chief Justice to the island. Both letters had unexpected consequences.

Almost as soon as the ship sailed, the Chief Justice who had rebelled offered to make peace, though on humiliating terms. Columbus was so exhausted and so eager for peace that he accepted the offer. That was barely settled when he heard that the former rebel, Hojeda, who had gone back to Spain, had now returned and landed somewhere on the island. Men were sent to locate the invader but Hojeda escaped, sailed away to the Bahama Islands where he loaded up with slaves and returned to Spain with a description of what he had discovered. For Hojeda had now become an explorer, one of the many, eager for glory and gold, who were already following in the wake of Columbus. After Columbus' flagship had returned to Spain with his letter announcing the new continent, Hojeda had managed to get hold of the Admiral's charts, and also to obtain a license to make a voyage of exploration to this "Garden of Eden."

259

Hojeda had discovered rich pearl fisheries near the island which Columbus had named Margarita (for Margaret of Austria) and then passed on by, in his haste to get to Santo Domingo, missing the valuable pearls.

Following along the mainland, Hojeda had given the first European name to a country in South America. The natives whom he saw lived in huts built on piles out into the water which reminded him of Venice. So he called the country, "Little Venice," or Venezuela.

In the summer of 1500 came the crowning disaster for Columbus. The new Chief Justice he had asked for arrived. In answer to his letter, the sovereigns had appointed an officer named Bobadilla, who was not only overly endowed with Spanish pride, but happened to arrive at a most inopportune time. Columbus, who was usually weak in discipline, had been driven to desperation and had just hanged seven Spanish rebels. As soon as Bobadilla's ship entered the harbor and he saw those seven dead bodies dangling from the gallows, his proud Spanish blood boiled. He strode ashore to settle with that dastardly Italian. As Viceroy he took immediate possession of the fort and began issuing orders right and left. He threw Columbus in jail, loaded him with chains; did the same to Bartholomew and Diego; and sent all three back for trial on the first ship leaving Santo Domingo for Spain.

"As soon as they put to sea the skipper, who had come to know Bobadilla's malice, offered to remove his chains, but the Admiral refused. He had been placed in chains in the Sovereign's name, he said, and would wear them until the Sovereign ordered them removed, for he was resolved to keep those chains as a memorial of how well he had been rewarded for his many services ... and that he wanted them buried with his bones ..." This is what Ferdinand Columbus later wrote in his book.

A VOICE OF THE MIDDLE AGES IS SILENCED

IN FLORENCE, after months of upheaval following the banishment of the Medicis, the monk Savonarola, through a series of political sermons, had made himself the chief power in government. He formed a Grand Council of over 1,000 members to take the place of the Signoria, or Council of Eight, elected to support the Medici.

Savonarola had steadfastly refused to join Pope Alexander's League against France. Rather than become an ally of that "vile Father of the Church," he preferred to rely on the friendship of the French King. The Pope, annoyed by Savonarola's lack of cooperation and his hostility, demanded that the people of Florence either silence the stubborn monk, or banish him.

The Pope's words fell on deaf ears. The people of Florence could hear nothing but the voice of Savonarola. They were completely under his spell. Convinced of their sin, filled with remorse and a frenzy of repentance, they went to extremes in renouncing all worldly pleasure. Young men became monks and priests, young women discarded all aids to beauty designed to make themselves attractive to men.

Botticelli, who had painted gods and goddesses of Greek mythology to celebrate the triumphs of the Medici, now painted only religious themes inspired by the sermons of Savonarola.

Life in Florence became as drab and somber as its gray stone walls. No longer were the narrow streets gay with colorful processions. No more chariots, no more dancers, no more singers making merry as in the ancient festivals of Bacchus. Carnival time of 1497 presented a strange and different scene.

Across the Piazza of the Palazzo Vecchio came frenzied people, their arms full of carnival masks and masquerade costumes, wigs and tinsel finery to be thrown in a huge pile of worldly "Vanities" and burned. Playing cards, dice, false curls, pots of rouge, perfumes, mirrors, and jewelry of all kinds were wildly tossed away. Paintings and portraits, statues and piles of books were also heaped up to feed the flames. Crowds filled the square and also the balcony of the Palazzo as the fire was lighted. The clanging of the bronze bell in the tower, and the monks' chanting of the *Te Deum* mingled with the cracking flames. The "Vanities" were reduced to a pile of ashes. The frenzy also burned itself out in the somber days that followed.

Savonarola, spurred on to further reform by his success in Florence, now raised his voice against the graver evils of Rome, crying out against the sins of the priesthood and the corruption of the Church.

"Thou ribald Church," cried Savonarola. "Thou art shameless. A monster of abomination. Once anointed priests called their sons nephews; now they speak of their sons. O prostitute Church, thou hast displayed thy foulness to the whole world and stinkest unto Heaven."

Savonarola realized that such tirades aimed at Pope Alexander VI would bring excommunication. But let it come, he said, if need be. He would welcome it. "Let it come quickly, O Lord. Let me be persecuted. I beg this grace, O Lord. Let me give my blood for thee!"

His fervent prayer for martyrdom did not go unanswered.

The righteous monk might cry out against the sins of the people but not those of the priests and the Pope. In castigating Rome his preaching had gone beyond the proper limits. Even in Florence reaction set in. Days were too joyless and drab to be endured any longer. The Signoria, enemies of Savonarola, regained control of the government. They forbade him to preach any longer in the Cathedral or the churches of Florence.

On May 13, 1497, Pope Alexander VI excommunicated Savonarola but offered to rescind the decree if the friar would come to Rome, and if Florence would join the League against France. Savonarola not only refused, he wrote to the Kings of Europe begging them to call a General Council and reform the Church. The Lord, he said, had commanded him to do so. He was a prophet speaking for the Lord saying, "Cleanse my Church!"

A prophet of the Lord, indeed! That was too much for the rival order of Franciscans. They denounced the Dominicans and their friar, calling him a false prophet and a heretic. They challenged Savonarola to a medieval trial by fire in the Piazza, in which the truth of the conflicting views were to be proved by seeing whether he or the Franciscan could walk unhurt through the flames.

A huge crowd of spectators gathered for the spectacle and went away in a rage of disappointment when the show did not come off. This was due to a long argument between the two orders. But the crowd turned against Savonarola as if he alone were to blame—as if by cowardice he had proved himself guilty.

Two days later, at the Dominican monastery of San Marco, Savonarola was presented with a summons to appear before the Signoria and give himself up. The friars would not let him go. When troops came to take him they defended him bravely with swords and clubs, until Savonarola bade them lay down their arms. Standing by the altar, he calmly waited to be taken. In the evening with another loyal friar, he was led off to the Palazzo, while mobs laughed and jeered and spat at them. The two monks were put into cells, and tortured day after day, in the approved manner of the Inquisition. Messengers from the Pope kept urging the Signoria to wring a confession out of Savonarola that would give reason for putting him to death. After three terrible ordeals by torture, the exhausted monk signed whatever they asked him to confess—that he had lied—that he had not been divinely inspired—that he had urged foreign powers to call a Council and depose the Pope. On those grounds Savonarola was condemned to death.

On May 23, 1498, Savonarola and two other Dominicans in long white robes were led from the cells of the Palazzo Vecchio to the same spot in the Piazza where the "Vanities" had been burned the year before. There the people of Florence watched while the man who had been their idol was hanged to death and his body burned to ashes. The ashes were thrown into the Arno River for fear that they might later be recognized and revered as those of a saint. But no later Pope was ever to award the crowning glory of sainthood to this critic of the Church who spoke up at a time when his warning should have been heeded. It was too late now to avoid disaster.

MICHELANGELO GOES TO ROME

THE SUMMER Savonarola was killed, young Michelangelo was in Rome, beginning work on this famous statue of the Pieta. This is how he happened to leave Florence, as told by the painter Vasari. One day when the young sculptor had finished modeling a sleeping cupid, his patron saw it and said: "If you were to treat it artificially so as to make it look as though it had been dug up, I would send it to Rome; it would be taken as an antique and you would be able to sell it at a far higher price."

Michelangelo followed the suggestion and the Cupid was sent to Rome. There a dealer bought it for 30 ducats and resold it as an antique for 200 ducats to a certain Cardinal. The Cardinal began to suspect that it was not old, but might have been made in Florence and sent a gentlemen there to see if he could discover who had made it. When he got to Florence . . .

"This gentleman pretended to be on the lookout for a sculptor capable of executing certain works in Rome. After visiting several he was addressed to Michelangelo. When he saw the young artist he begged him to show some proof of his ability; whereupon Michelangelo took a pen and drew a hand with such grace that the gentleman was stupified. Afterwards he asked if he had ever worked in marble and Michelangelo said yes, and when he mentioned among other things a Cupid of such height and such an attitude, the man knew he had found the right person. He promised Michelangelo, if he would come with him to Rome, to get the difference in price made up and to introduce him to his patron. Michelangelo went with him and lodged in his house near the palace of the Cardinal."

There was considerable argument with the original dealer who had purchased the Cupid, trying to recover the money. Just what ensued is confusing, but in the end the Sleeping Cupid became the possession of Caesar Borgia.

In the summer of 1498, the young unknown sculptor signed a contract that was to make him famous. The Abbot of St. Denys agreed with Master Michelangelo, sculptor of Florence...

"To wit that the said master shall make a Pieta of marble at his own cost; that is to say a Virgin Mary clothed with the dead Christ in her arms of the size of a proper man, for the price of 450 ducats of the Papal mint within one year from the day of the commencement of the work."

The Pieta, when finished, was set up in the chapel of old St. Peter's Basilica. One day Michelangelo happened to overhear some people from northern Italy stop to admire it, saying that they believed it to be the work of a certain sculptor of Milan. Michelangelo slipped in later and engraved his name on the belt of the Madonna. It is the only piece of his work that he ever signed.

In the fall of the year 1498, a couple of months after Michelangelo began work on his Pieta, Caesar Borgia, the owner of the Sleeping Cupid, was sent by his father, Pope Alexander VI, with an important message for the new King of France. It included an invitation to invade Italy!

266

Lentree du roi

ENTER LOUIS XII

OPE ALEXANDER'S INVITATION to the French King to invade Italy, just three years after he had driven out the French army with such gusto, came about in this way. Upon his return to France, Charles VIII had brought workmen from Naples and had begun remodeling the old medieval fortress of Amboise, adding Italian terraces and gardens.

He did not live to enjoy them. One April afternoon as he and Queen Anne were on their way to a tennis match in the old moat,

267

Charles hit his head on a low beam, swayed, regained his balance, straightened his velvet cap, and then fell unconscious. A servant dropped a mattress onto the terrace and the King died there at midnight, April 8, 1498. He was twenty-seven.

Louis of Orleans then became King of France, Louis XII. He was thirty-six, but had lived at such a fast pace that he looked and acted like a much older man.

Francis, the four-year-old son of the late Count of Angoulême, now stepped up into Louis' former place as heir to the throne. His young mother, Louise of Savoy, was almost beside herself with joy. As soon as the news reached her, she was on her way to Rheims for the coronation, taking her precious four-year-old so that all the court could see and admire the future Francis I. Small Francis, who was the pet of his sister Marguerite and the idol of his mother, took admiration as a matter of course and knew how to charm everyone at court who stopped to admire him.

What a King he would make! thought Louise, sure now that he would be King. What could prevent it? Louis XII had no son. He and Jeanne, Charles's sister, who was a cripple, had been married many years and had had no children.

That was quite true. Louis XII had no son, but he had a plan to correct that lack, which soon came as a shock to Louise of Savoy, and also to Anne of Brittany, the young widow of Charles VIII. What the King proposed to do was to marry Anne, in the hope of having a son to inherit the throne. But there were difficulties in the way.

In the first place, Anne did not want to marry him. She had her heart set on going back to Brittany and had already shipped home her silver and furniture. Louis overcame that difficulty by offering to give her as a wedding present two towns that she wanted very much to own. She consented to accept him along with the towns, and become his queen—provided, of course, he was allowed to divorce Jeanne and remarry. For that he needed a dispensation from Rome.

Louis sent a messenger off at once to Pope Alexander VI with the request, wondering what the oily Spaniard would ask for in return. While he was waiting to hear, he thought it sensible to keep an eye on the present heir to the crown and his pretty but scheming mother. Louise of Savoy and little Francis were invited to spend the summer at his castle in Chinon. They became good friends that summer, the present and future Kings. Francis loved to ride on big Louis' knee and listen to tales of heroes and knights and what a fine thing it was to be general, a really great general—like Julius Caesar, for example, who had once conquered Italy and France and almost the whole world!

Summer passed and with October the ambassador from Rome arrived in Chinon with the answer from the Pope that Louis had been waiting for. To Francis the envoy might have been Julius Caesar himself, he was so haughty and so handsome, all in silks and jewels and shining silver. Everyone from the Court and Church hurried out to meet him; abbots and monks bowed almost to the ground because this soldier was the son of the Pope, a mighty prince whose name was Caesar Borgia. He carried a silver sword engraved with scenes from the wars of Julius Caesar and the motto "Either Caesar or no-body." Perhaps he, too, was going back to cross the Rubicon like Julius Caesar and conquer all of Italy!

Now, with the Papal permission in hand, all proceeded promptly. Anne of Brittany married Louis and became Queen of France for the second time. Little Francis and his mother, fuming with jealousy, were sent off to live in the Castle of Amboise. Caesar Borgia was given a French title and a French wife. And in the summer of 1499, Louis XII, with Caesar and a splendid French army, was on his way to Italy to fulfill his bargain with the Pope.

Pope Alexander had long wanted to recapture certain cities in central Italy that had broken away from the Papal State, but he could not do so alone. In exchange, therefore, for allowing Louis to be divorced and remarried, he had proposed that the French King invade

Italy, help Caesar capture the independent cities, and at the same time take Milan for himself.

Milan was precisely what Louis XII had had in mind ever since he had come to Asti with Charles VIII and had there met Ludovico Sforza. He had even assumed the title, "Duke of Milan," at his coronation. Nothing could please him more than to be setting forth for Italy, to be crossing the border, and approaching the city he considered rightfully his. On October 6th, accompanied by Caesar Borgia, Louis XII, King of France, rode gloriously into Milan with no difficulty whatsoever.

Ludovico Sforza was gone. In great alarm, as the French approached, the Duke had hastened off to Switzerland to look for the Emperor Maximilian, hoping for his help, hoping also to hire an army of Swiss mercenaries, with which to return and drive out the French. The citizens of Milan offered no resistance. The people merely stood and watched as Louis XII and the handsome Caesar rode into the city, followed by the splendid French soldiers trooping by in perfect order.

The palace was deserted. There was no sign of the Sforzas as Louis entered the courtyard, only the statue of Francesco Sforza standing there in the twilight. So on that first night Louis XII slept peacefully in Milan, the city from which his grandmother, Valentina Visconti, had gone to marry the first Duke of Orleans.

Two weeks later a messenger from Chinon arrived with news for Louis XII—that he had a newborn daughter named Claude. A daughter! The King's disappointment could have been equalled only by the joy of one small boy's mother.

Louise of Savoy had fairly held her breath for fear Queen Anne's baby might be a boy. Mais non! Thanks be to Heaven. Her darling Francis was still safe as heir to the throne of France!

270

The statue of Francesco Sforza, Louis XII knew, was the work of Leonardo da Vinci, who had designed the evening's entertainment for Il Moro when they met at Asti. Since then, he was told, Leonardo had made a wonderful painting in the Dominican monastery of Santa Maria della Gracie. The King found the friars proud and happy to show him their most beautiful possession. The painting covered one end of the long room where they took their meals.

There it was—on the far wall—a painting of the Last Supper. Christ and his twelve disciples were shown at the very moment when the Master had said that one of them would betray him. Each one—Peter, John, Matthew, Judas, and the others—was to be seen reacting in his own way to the shocking words. Yet all the figures and gestures blended together into a beautiful pattern.

Louis XII was so deeply moved by the painting that he planned to have it taken down and shipped to France. He even had the frame made for it before he found that it was painted directly on the wall and could not be removed.

It had taken the artist over two years to paint it, the friars said, he had to be doing so many other things for Il Moro at the same time. Often they had seen him rush into the room, mount the scaffold, make a stroke or two with his brush, and be off again. Sometimes he would stand half a day, looking at the painting without raising his brush, just thinking.

Sometimes he would reach in his pocket, draw out a notebook, and write down something that occurred to him or make a little sketch. He always seemed to be writing in this notebook. But his writing, what they happened to see of it, was impossible to read. He held his pen in his left hand and wrote from right to left, making his words appear as if reflected in a mirror.

Those now-famous notebooks of Leonardo da Vinci, when later deciphered, were to prove him to be the most versatile man of the Renaissance, probably the most truly creative man that ever lived.

Leonardo

from a self portrait

LEONARDO

ABOUT THE TIME that he had finished painting the "Last Supper," Leonardo had met a Franciscan friar by the name of Luca Pacioli, and they had become fast friends. Fra Pacioli was a noted mathematician, whose book on geometry Leonardo had already discovered before meeting the author.

At that time, it seemed that the statue of Francesco Sforza might soon be cast in bronze, and Pacioli was helping Leonardo figure out the necessary measurements. Now, however, with the French in Milan and Ludovico gone, there was no hope of its being cast. Pacioli was writing a new book for which Leonardo was working on the illustrations.

The book was called *Divine Proportions.*

In it Pacioli explained how all forms in the universe follow the same law of proportion. Everything made by men that is truly beauti-

ful also has the same divine proportions, that can be checked mathematically. To Leonardo this was a most fascinating thought— that truth and beauty had a basis in the science of numbers—that the same rhythm, the same balance, ran through the entire universe, from the stars and planets down to a fern frond or a snail shell.

Fra Pacioli was not surprised at Leonardo's interest. Looking through the Notebooks, which he found fascinating, he saw that the painter was always probing below the surface, wanting to know the reason for what he saw. There were many sketches of the human figure in which the proportions had been carefully noted, such as:

"The foot is as long as the whole head of a man."

"Every man at three years is half the full height he will become." Other sketches showed how the human joints and muscles worked and also compared them to those of other animals, as:

"The walking of a man is always like that of animals with four legs—that is, if he puts forward his right foot, he puts forward his left arm at the same time and vice versa."

There were also drawings of the interior organs, for which Leonardo said he had dissected more than ten bodies. He wrote that it would be better for you to watch an anatomist at work than go by these drawings, for "even if you had a love for such things . . . you might be deterred by fear of living the night hours in company of those corpses, quartered, flayed and horrible to see."

Such things, Pacioli knew, would never deter his friend Leonardo from finding out what he wanted to know. He had gathered material enough for a hundred books that he intended to write but had been hindered, he said, "simply for want of time," and by the amount there was to learn. "Kindly nature," he wrote, "sees to it that you may find something to learn everywhere in the world."

Birds fascinated Leonardo, the wings especially. Studying why and how they were able to fly, he made the following note:

"A bird is an instrument working according to a mathematical law, which instrument it is within the power of man to reproduce with all its movements."

He invented a parachute and worked out a form of helicopter or flying machine, making a note to: "Remember that your flying machine must imitate no other wing than that of a bat, because the web is what gives strength to the wings."

His notes about the earth and sun and formation of the universe show how far ahead Leonardo da Vinci was of his day and age. He wrote:

"The earth is a star much like the moon."

"The earth is not the center of the sun's orbit, nor at the center of the universe. Anyone standing on the moon when it and the sun are both beneath us, would see our earth just as we see the moon and the earth would light it as it lights us."

Louis XII left for France about the end of October. Leonardo and Fra Pacioli stayed on in Milan another two months. Although Milan was very peaceful under the French governor who had been

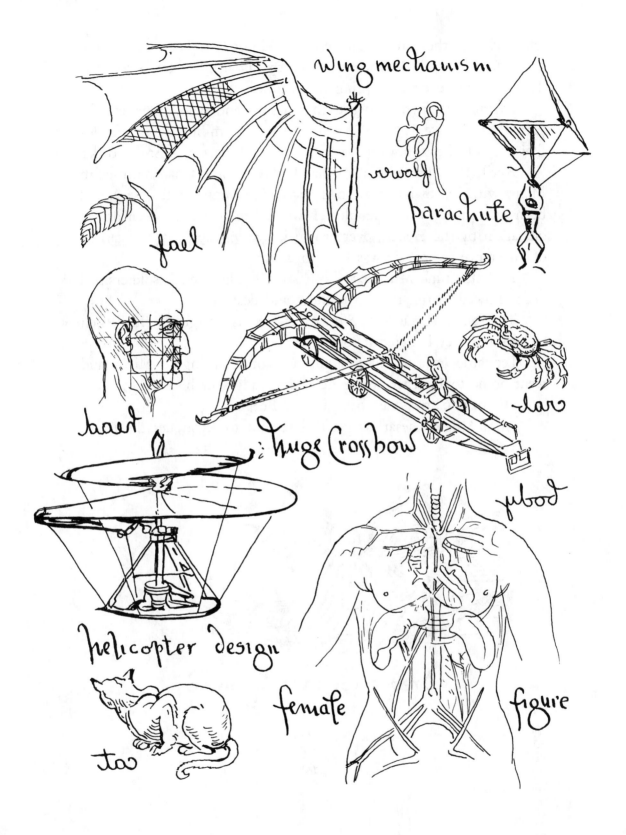

Wing mechanism

vvwalf

parachute

fael

baart

Huge Crossbow

dlav

helicopter design

jubod

female figure

tao

left in charge, they knew that peace could not last. The storm would break as soon as Il Moro returned with his army of Swiss soldiers. There would be bitter fighting to recapture the city.

So the two friends packed their books and belongings and departed for Venice, where Leonardo acted as military engineer for that city, which was always in need of better defense against the Turks.

April, 1500, brought word that Ludovico Sforza had returned to Milan with his Swiss army, had successfully entered that city, and been welcomed by the people. However, he had then been driven out again by the French, overthrown in battle, captured, and carried off to France (where he was later to die in prison).

And this time Milan had been sacked. The French soldiers had been allowed to run riot, to plunder and destroy.

The statue of Francesco Sforza was used as a target by the French archers and they battered it to pieces.

Leonardo gave up all thought now of returning to Milan, and went home to Florence where he had already sent his savings.

His next patron was to be Caesar Borgia.

From Milan, Caesar Borgia had set out to reconquer the Papal

a dredge for marsh mud

States, either for his father's benefit, or to make them into a kingdom of his own. No one was ever quite sure which his final intentions were. Inside of two months he was extremely successful, subduing the feudal lords, by trickery, bribery, or cruelty, as well as force. His campaign was then cut short when the French troops mutinied because he could not pay them. So he hastened to Rome to get more money from his father.

January, 1500, opened a Jubilee year in the Holy City. Thousands of pilgrims were flocking into Rome. Their offerings replenished the papal treasury and supplied Caesar with all he needed to finance another campaign.

While in Rome the bullfighter took time to give an exhibition of his prowess in St. Peter's Square, and to murder the second husband of his golden-haired sister. Her adoring father then sent Lucrezia as a bride to the Duke of Ferrara, to whom she made a faithful and almost perfect wife, freed at last from the evil influence of her father and brother.

From then until 1503, Caesar Borgia was in the Romagna, consolidating his conquests, improving the country, and actually giving it the best government it had had in hundreds of years.

Leonardo da Vinci was with him for more than a year, as chief engineer, designing all kinds of equipment, planning roads, harbors and canals, making detailed maps of the countryside.

In the summer of 1503, Caesar was back in Rome, to gather more troops. Both he and his father were stricken with malaria. Pope Alexander VI died. In October his old rival, Cardinal Rovere, was elected Pope Julius II. Without his father's support, and with the Borgia's worst enemy on the Papal throne, Caesar's plans collapsed.

He fled to the King of Naples, who had him arrested and eventually sent him as a prisoner to Spain.

So ended the rule of the turbulent, flamboyant Spanish family who played such a violent role in the history of Italy.

COPERNICUS

COPERNICUS

ONE OF THE VISITORS to Rome in 1500, the year of the Jubilee, was a young Polish student, Mikolaj Kopernik, or in Latin, Nicolaus Copernicus. He was about the age of Caesar Borgia, but while the Pope's son was bullfighting in St. Peter's Square, Copernicus was giving lectures on the stars and planets and suggesting the motion of the earth.

Nicolaus had been studying astronomy, mathematics, and physics at the University of Bologna for the past four years. There, one of the teachers had criticized the system of Ptolemy which put the earth in the center of the universe. He urged his students to go back to the ancient Greek astronomers, who in the fifth century before Christ, doubted that the earth stood still.

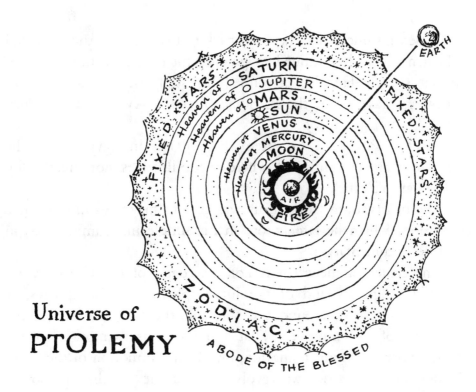

Universe of
PTOLEMY

Copernicus would like to have continued his studies in Bologna but his leave of absence was over and he had to go back to his home in Poland and resume his duties as canon on the staff of the Cathedral at Frauenburg. His uncle, the Prince-Bishop of Ermeland, had been sympathetic when Nicolaus had not liked the old-fashioned studies at the University of Cracow and had made it possible for him to go to Italy. And again in 1500 when his nephew returned, the kindly Bishop was persuaded to let him return to Italy, but this time to take up the study of medicine and law, which seemed more practical than astronomy. This time Nicolaus went to study in Ferrara, and so was there when golden-haired Lucrezia arrived to marry the Duke. Two years later, in 1503, Copernicus received his degree in law and returned to Poland to live as secretary and physician to his uncle, the Bishop, in his castle in Heilsberg. There he worked out the mathematics of his theory about the movement of the planets.

279

When his uncle died, he went back to his duties at the Cathedral in Frauenberg and continued to practice medicine, treating the poor without charge. He also continued his study of the heavens, but Frauenberg was so near the Baltic Sea that the sky was often hidden in clouds of mist and fog.

"I envy Ptolemy," he often said, "living in Egypt where the skies are more cheerful and where the Nile does not breathe fog as does our Vistula."

The observations Copernicus was able to make led him to these conclusions which he later wrote in his simple unassuming way, in a "Little Commentary":

> The center of the earth is not the center of the Universe, but only of gravity and of the lunar sphere. All the spheres, or planets, revolve around the sun and therefore the sun is the center of the universe. What appears to us as motions of the sun arise not from its motion, but from the motion of the earth, our sphere... (for) we revolve around the sun like any other planet.

This was not printed during his lifetime, but he sent out a few manuscript copies. Other astronomers who saw it paid little attention. It was an amusing theory, but it could not be proved.

The necessary instruments were lacking. Copernicus could see no more planets than Ptolemy could, 1,300 years ago in Egypt. Only seven planets could be seen with the naked eye. There was no telescope. It would be 100 years before this was developed by Galileo, who would then be able to test and prove the theory of Copernicus.

Meantime the average-minded man would believe, as did Martin Luther, who was to say in 1530 regarding Copernicus:

"People give ear to an upstart astrologer who strives to show that the earth revolves, not the heavens or the firmament, the sun and the moon. This fool wishes to reverse the entire scheme of astronomy ... but sacred scripture tells us that Joshua commanded the sun to stand still, not the earth...."

Part IV

begins in Granada in the year

1500

People who were living when

Ferdinand
went on his father's last voyage ending Nov. 1504

Admiral of the Ocean Sea
Columbus
died in Valladolid on May 22, 1506

Queen Isabella
died in Medina November 26, 1504

Juana
became Queen; her four year old Charles, the heir.

Thomas More
wrote his book describing an imaginary state, "Utopia"

Erasmus
Erasmus was Europe's most celebrated scholar.

The PRINCE
Machiavelli
of Florence wrote the since famous book "The Prince"

Michelangelo
began to paint the ceiling of the Sistine Chapel in 1508

(born 1497)
Holbein
to be Henry VIII's court painter, met his first patron, Erasmus

Raphael (born 1483)
was painting his "Stanzas" in the Vatican for Pope Julius II.

and some important Events that

Columbus made his final voyage

Charles I
became King of Spain 1516
and was crowned
Charles V
Emperor of Germany 1520

Henry VIII
became King of England 1509
Catherine of Aragon, his queen

Francis I
(born 1494) became the
King of France in 1515

Pope Leo X
excommunicated
Martin Luther; had
his books burned

"Here I stand"
Martinus Luther

Charles V
issued an Edict
against Luther at
the Diet of Worms

1521

HISPANIOLA
Santa Domingo

1509 to 1523
Diego Columbus
lived in Hispaniola as
the Governor. His son was
created Duke of Veragua.

1519
Magellan
sailed for Charles V on what would
be the first voyage around the world

Ferdinand Columbus
went with Charles V to his
coronation, returning with
new books for his library.

took place between 1500 and 1522

Isabella

Ferdinand

Mary

Maximilian

Juana

Philip

Charles

AN HEIR IS BORN

FEBRUARY 24, 1500. The Eve of St. Matthias. Joy broke loose in
the Netherlands on that frosty winter night as word spread from
the palace at Ghent that a son had been born to the Archduke
Philip and the Duchess Juana. Two years earlier the birth of his sister
Eleanor had caused no such outburst of joy, and her christening had
been a pale affair compared to the celebration for this newborn boy
who was heir to the duchy.

The whole city of Ghent, the surrounding countryside, and
neighboring towns turned out and joined in a spectacular parade.
There were bells, bonfires, minstrels, and mummers and as it grew
dark, fireworks from the tower of St. Nicholas lit up the sky. Philip

and Juana watched them from a balcony of the palace while the burghers danced all night in the streets in noisy celebration.

The religious ceremony took place before midday, in the Church of St. John. A wooden platform five feet high had been built from the palace to the Church, spanned by thirty-nine triumphal arches and lighted by ten thousand torches. Houses along the way which belonged to prosperous merchants and proud city fathers were draped with crimson and purple velvet, each window filled with faces as the christening procession passed by.

Hundreds of high dignitaries led the way, all carrying lighted torches—Knights of the Golden Fleece, members of the law courts, deans of the trade guilds, followed by a few high nobles, each one bearing a christening vessel made of gold. Then came the baby prince in a very long lace gown, carried by Madame la Grande, who had also held Philip at his christening—a far handsomer baby than this odd-looking little one.

At the church door, four bishops and nine abbots in their high miters, richly embroidered capes and stoles, were waiting to lead the way to the baptismal font. There, standing between Madame la Grande and Philip, was a young widow in deep mourning—Margaret. She had returned from Spain just in time to act as godmother for this newest member of the Hapsburg family—first grandson of the Emperor Maximilian.

Charles was the name that had been chosen for him, the name of his great-grandfather Charles the Bold, the last native Duke of Burgundy to rule over the Netherlands.

This newly-christened Charles also bore the name of the first Holy Roman Emperor, Charlemagne, and twenty years later was to become the Emperor Charles. He was to be not only the most powerful ruler in Europe, but also the richest. As grandson of Ferdinand and Isabella he was to become King of Spain, heir to all that immense wealth of the New World made available by the discovery of Christopher Columbus.

WAITING IN GRANADA

For Isabella, far away in Granada, it was a sad thought that her crown and throne would eventually go to this little grandson born on the Eve of St. Matthias. Although he was Juana's son, the Queen thought of him as a Hapsburg and a foreigner. Little Michael, her other grandson, the frail baby Portuguese prince, Isabel's son, died the summer after Charles was born.

"And so the lot falls" said Isabella, quietly accepting what happened, in the faith that since it had been allowed to happen, it must be the will of God.

Diego and Ferdinand Columbus, serving as pages to the Queen, found the year 1500 one of misery and humiliation, being continually pointed out and scoffed at as sons of the no-good Admiral who had reduced Spanish gentlemen to poverty. Granada was full of discontented adventurers who had come back from Hispaniola, cursing Columbus. Ferdinand was to write of them in his book, saying:

"I remember that when I was in Granada at the time of the death of Prince Michael, more than fifty of these shameless wretches (who claimed they had not been paid for many years past) bought a quantity of grapes and sat down to eat them in the court of the Alhambra loudly proclaiming that their Highnesses and the Admiral had reduced them to that pitiful state by withholding their pay, adding many other insolent remarks. They were so shameless that if the Catholic King rode out they would crowd about him shouting, Pay, pay. And if my brother and I who were pages to the Queen happened by, they followed us crying, "There go the sons of the Admiral of the Mosquitoes, of him who discovered lands of vanity and illusion, the grave and ruin of Castilian gentlemen, adding so many other insults that we took care not to pass before them."

All summer and fall through months of scorn and ridicule the boys held fast to the belief that what these "shameless wretches" said could not possibly be true. But in November came the awful news that their father had been brought home in chains like a common criminal. He was then in Seville, staying at the monastery with his friend, Fray Gaspar Gorricio, but still a prisoner.

As soon as the Catholic Sovereigns heard from Columbus and learned of his plight, they sent orders that he should be set at liberty at once, and come to court, sending him 2,000 ducats.

Just before Christmas the boys saw their father, and also their two uncles who had come with the Admiral to Granada. The three brothers presented themselves at once to the sovereigns in the famous Audience Hall of the Alhambra.

Ferdinand and Isabella accepted the Admiral's apologies and explanations. They assured him that his imprisonment by Bobadilla had not been according to their wishes or command. They promised that all his property which Bobadilla had confiscated would be restored to him. Nothing, however, was said about where, when, or if he should make another voyage. At that time, Columbus may not have felt well enough to care. But after resting in the Alhambra's sunny courts and gardens for several weeks and being fully recuperated, he began to grow restless with the old longing to be on shipboard again. He saw himself starting out on what he truly believed would be the greatest voyage of his life. Still not one word was mentioned by the sovereigns about his making any other voyage.

To be sure, they were very busy. As Columbus wrote Fray Gaspar, they always seemed to have other things on their minds that shoved the matter most important to him into the background. The Queen was occupied with affairs of state, to which she devoted herself unceasingly, day after day. Ferdinand, as usual, was busy with foreign affairs.

Recent news from England was disturbing. Henry VII, it was said, now planned to have his son Arthur, Prince of Wales, marry Juan's young widow, Margaret of Austria, instead of Catalina. Twelve years ago, when Henry VII had been insecure on his throne, he had been glad enough to make a marriage alliance with Ferdinand. Now he evidently intended to slip out of it for a more valuable alliance with the Emperor Maximilian.

Ferdinand, a past master himself at slipping through loopholes in a contract, had no idea of letting old Henry play that trick on him. Catalina, who was now fifteen, must be made ready and shipped off without delay on her wedding journey to England.

Columbus was encouraged enough by this prospect to write Fray Gaspar that he hoped "after the Lady Princess departed in the name of the Lord" something would be done about his voyage to the Indies. But there were still two years of waiting ahead before he could start that fourth voyage, one on which he hoped not only to reach the Indies, but to sail on around the world!

FRIENDS IN ENGLAND

THE HAWTHORN was in blossom in England; bushes and trees were thick with foliage. It was spring, a radiant April morning of 1499.

Across the river from London two men were walking along a country road near Greenwich, deep in conversation. They were speaking in Latin, each listening with relish to the other's words. The older man was Erasmus; his companion was young Thomas More. They were on their way to Eltham Palace, where the royal children were living, all except Arthur, the Prince of Wales, who was now thir-

290

teen. He had his own court at Ludlow Castle on the border of Wales.

Erasmus had come to England as the guest of a pupil he had been teaching in Paris, young Lord Mountjoy, whose country house lay just behind the two men around a bend in the road. Erasmus had been delighted to leave Paris and come to England. The University of Paris, alas, had proved to be far from what he had anticipated when he went there from Brussels. The dormitory was a filthy place with foul food, spoiled eggs, and squalid bedrooms full of fleas.

And the teaching of theology was absurd. Serious discussions were carried on as to whether God could turn himself into an ox or an ass, if he chose to, or if John the Baptist's head, after being cut off, could have been in more than one place at the same time!

Becoming mentally as well as physically ill, Erasmus had left. To make a living, then, he had begun taking pupils, hoping to save enough money to go to Italy. Meanwhile, by happy chance, Lord Mountjoy had invited him to come to England.

And so here he was! And delighted to be here—delighted to be walking down the road with this charming young Englishman who could converse in perfect Latin, had a love and knowledge of classical literature, and such a rare sense of humor.

Thomas More, then an attorney of twenty-one, was soon to be admitted to the bar; he was later to be knighted and still later to be beheaded by Henry VIII, now the eight-year-old Prince of York, whom he was taking his new friend Erasmus to visit.

The young Tudors and their household were assembled in the hall to greet their guests when they reached the palace. In the center of the group, acting as host, stood young Henry, who looked like an over-sized cherub, with very fat round cheeks, blue eyes, pink and white skin, and a head of golden curls. On one side stood his sister Margaret, who was ten, and on the other a pretty, lively three-year-old, whose name was Marie.

Thomas More saluted the Prince and then presented him with

"some writing or other." Erasmus felt embarrassed, having nothing to offer, but later sent a poem on England dedicated to Henry.

In October Erasmus was at Oxford. There he attended lectures on the meaning of the Bible that were so stimulating to him, so worthwhile, that he determined to make the serious study of the Bible the object of his life. The lecturer was a brilliant young priest by the name of John Colet, who was also a student of Plato. Colet urged Erasmus to teach the meaning of the Old Testament at Oxford.

"Ah no, my dear Colet, no. How should I teach that which I have not learned? You cannot get water from a stone."

The first requirement, Erasmus felt, was to learn Greek in order to read the original text from which St. Jerome had made the Latin translation then in use. Erasmus knew well how many errors can arise in any translation and that even St. Jerome might have made some mistakes. So, to prepare himself for what was to be his life's work, he was determined to learn Greek.

This he began to do shortly after his return to Paris, which was in December. At the time he also began to compile a book of Latin quotations that was to make him famous. For this the King of England was indirectly responsible. According to an old law, re-enacted by Henry VII who had an eye out for every penny, no English gold or silver could be taken from the country. At Dover, before Erasmus boarded the ship to cross the Channel, he was stripped of all he had by the customs officers.

"And so," said he, "I was shipwrecked before I went to sea. Returning to Paris a poor man, I resolved to publish something as quickly as possible" to bring in some money.

Unfortunately, he was immediately laid low by an attack of fever, but while he was recovering, he re-read his favorite authors. As he came upon so many wonderful quotations it occurred to him that he might make a collection of them. "Why, in Plato alone," he exclaimed, "proverbs are scattered thick as little stars!" What could be more useful for a gentleman with the average smattering of Latin than a handy little book of these adages or proverbs that he could draw on in making speeches or writing letters?

Adagia, Familiar Quotations from the Classics, was the title of this handbook which appeared in 1500, dedicated to his former pupil, Lord Mountjoy. There were 800 quotations in this first edition, which was such an enormous success that even those who had not seen or read it, knew the name of the now-famous author.

The serious study of Greek was also going along with furious intensity. In March, 1500, Erasmus wrote a friend that "Greek is nearly killing me, but I have no time and no money to buy books or take a master. By lucky chance I got some Greek books which I am stealthily copying day and night. . . . I am determined that it is better to learn later than to be without knowledge which it is of utmost importance to possess. . . . Afterwards (I shall) devote myself entirely to the sacred learning after which my soul has been hankering for a long time. I am in fairly good health, so I shall have to strain every nerve this year."

By fall of 1502, Erasmus declared that he could properly write all he wanted to in Greek.

By that time, never happy to stay too long in one place, the restless author left Paris and went traveling about the Netherlands for a while, visiting various friends and patrons.

Doodles by
Erasmus Ro
from the Margin of a Manuscript

MARTIN LUTHER BECOMES A MONK

HANS AND GRETA LUTHER watched their son Martin leave for the University of Erfurt with honest pride in their hearts. He had been home after graduation and was now going back for more study to become a lawyer. Hans had presented him with a fine law book called *Juris,* and in honor of the educated man he had now become, no longer addressed his son with the familiar "du," but with "Ihr," the polite German form of "you" used for people of higher station.

It was a sultry day in July, 1505. Soon after Martin left, storm clouds began to gather. Martin's law book was well wrapped, Greta knew, and would not get wet if the storm came. Hans had seen to that. Both looked forward to the proud day when Martin should have become a lawyer, able to provide for them in their old age.

294

That night, as always, Hans Luther knelt to give thanks for such a good son to St. Anne, the saint of miners. Meanwhile that good son of his had seen St. Anne in a vision and made a vow to her that would destroy his father's hopes.

Trudging along the road, Martin Luther had been struck by lightning and thrown to the ground. All about him in the blinding light he saw leering friends writhing, dancing, and just about to seize and drag him down into the hideous fires of hell, when there, too, above him he saw an angel of light!

"St. Anne!" he cried, "Help me. Help me. Save my life and I vow to you I will become a monk."

After that fearful vision Martin was eager and ready to take the surest way he knew to salvation, which was to become a monk and devote his life to prayer. Just two weeks later, Martin Luther, ready to start a new life, had presented himself and been accepted as a novice in the Augustinian monastery.

Periods of prayer came seven times a day, beginning between one and two in the morning when the monks were awakened by the ringing of the cloister bell. They rose, dressed, and at the second bell went to the church, knelt before the high altar. Day ended as did every period of prayer with the chanting of the *Salve Regina.*

At the end of one year, Martin Luther, confident that this was the right life for him, took the final vows and thus became Brother Martin, an Augustinian monk.

Then came the day when he was to say his first mass, a very special occasion which proud parents of the young priests usually attended. All these months Martin Luther had not seen his father, who had been violently opposed to his son's decision to enter the monastery. Martin was overjoyed when the disappointed man accepted the invitation to be present at the mass. Bent on making a good appearance, Hans Luther rode into Erfurt with a company of twenty horsemen, and donated quite a substantial sum to the monastery.

The great day for Martin began as usual with the cloister bells. At the proper hour he took his place before the altar and began the words of the mass. Suddenly he was terror-stricken as he heard himself addressing, "the living, the true, the eternal God." It was as if again he had been struck by a bolt of lightning.

"Who am I," he thought, "that I should lift mine eyes or raise my voice to the eternal God? I, a miserable little pygmy—I who am dust and ashes and full of sin."

He barely held himself at the altar to complete the service; then he hurried to the table where his father was seated with the guests and brothers. Desperately in need of some word of encouragement, Martin turned to him.

"Dear father, why were you so contrary to my becoming a monk? Are you not satisfied now?"

Hans Luther had been doing his best to control himself, but he now grew red in the face, and his eyes blazed.

"You learned scholar, you," he blurted out. "Have you never read in the Bible that you should honor your father and your mother? You have left me and your mother to look after ourselves in our old age!"

"But father," replied Luther, "I can do you more good by my prayers than if I had stayed in the world."

He reminded his father of the voice from heaven which he had heard, and the angel of light which he had seen.

"God grant," replied old Hans Luther, "that it was an angel, not an apparition of the devil, that you heard and saw."

Already shaken from his experience at the altar, Luther was struck with horror at his father's suggestion that it might have been the devil. For it could have been! The devil could easily disguise himself as an angel of light. What if he had been deceived? All the more reason, that he, miserable sinner that he was, should go to the limit in fasting, prayers, vigils, or whatever else he could do to save his soul from eternal damnation.

BETWEEN TWO ROYAL LIONS

B Y THE SUMMER OF 1501, Ferdinand of Aragon had six ships ready and waiting in the harbor of Laredo to take his youngest daughter to England, and Catalina, soon to be known as Catherine, was saying a last sad farewell to her mother in Granada. Isabella could not put into words how deeply she regretted being unable to go with Catalina to the border, as she had with Isabel and Juana. Even a year ago when Maria had gone to Portugal to marry her sister Isabel's former husband, King Manuel, Isabella had gone with her as far as Santa Fe. But now problems had arisen that made it necessary for her to remain with the government in Granada.

Catherine, very like her mother, understood without question that a Queen's duty to her country came first. She herself was being sent to England to be of service to Spain, and also to her husband's country when she should become its Queen. Every night she prayed most earnestly that she might not fail.

She hoped that her looks would meet with King Henry's approval; he had insisted that all the Spanish girls who were to come with her as ladies-in-waiting should be beautiful. Sixty people from home were to remain as members of his household in England.

Five years ago, when Juana had gone to be married in the Netherlands, a fleet of 120 ships had sailed from the harbor of Laredo. There were only six ships waiting for Catherine, but she understood her father's reason for that. He considered the King of England a far less important person than the Emperor Maximilian.

On August 25th, four days after sailing, the six ships struck a storm and were driven back into the harbor for repairs. Before they were ready to start out again, an English pilot arrived, sent by the King to look for the Spanish princess and see if Ferdinand was playing some kind of trick on him.

Henry VII would be suspicious until he saw with his own eyes that no queer-looking girl was being shoved off on him as the future Queen of England. Just as soon as he heard that the Spanish fleet had reached the English harbor of Plymouth, he set out with his council and several hundred guards for Lambeth where the formal reception was to be held. Too impatient to wait for that, the King rode on to the house of the Bishop of Bath, where Catherine was spending the night. He was told that according to Spanish custom, a bride could not be seen until the wedding morning.

"Nonsense," replied the King, "I'll speak with her now, even though she be gone to bed."

Catherine was not in bed, but in an adjoining room adjusting her veil and shawl to meet His Majesty. As he entered, she made a deep curtsy. The King kissed her hand, which he noticed was very small and white. And her forehead was white. And her cheeks were as pink, her eyes as blue, her hair as blonde as if she had been an English girl. A suitable bride, indeed, for his son Arthur!

He made a most courteous remark, to which she made an equally courteous reply, and neither understood the other. The King spoke no Spanish and for the moment all the French that Catherine had learned from Margaret of Austria slipped her mind.

An hour or so later they met again at the formal reception and this time Prince Arthur was with his father. Like her brother Juan, Arthur was very slight and delicate, which made him look even younger than fifteen.

Conversation was carried on this time through two interpreters. An English Bishop translated what the King and Prince said into Latin, which another Bishop translated into Spanish. Catherine could have replied directly in Latin, but would not be so discourteous as to show that she had more learning than the King and Prince. That evening after supper, minstrels played and sang for entertainment. Then Catherine and one of her ladies danced the dances of Spain, one stately and slow, the other gay and lively with whirling skirts and castenets. Prince Arthur hung back, but pushed into it by his father, did an English dance with his aunt. Next day the company left for London where elaborate preparations were under way for the wedding. The King spared no expense, since not he but the city of London and the nobility were to pay for it.

St. Paul's Cathedral was the scene of the wedding. There, ready to greet his brother's bride and be her escort, was Henry, his round cherub face beaming, his golden curls brushed and glistening, and his sturdy body encased in shining white satin. A big boy for ten, he was stouter by far than Arthur and almost as tall. He made a bow, offered his right hand to Catherine, and then conducted her solemnly down the long nave to the altar.

After the wedding the court journeyed to Windsor Castle. There an argument immediately arose as to whether Catherine should go with Arthur when he went to his own court at Ludlow Castle on the border of Wales, or whether they should live apart for a while until Arthur was stronger and did not cough so much. The Spanish ambassadors, remembering the tragic death of Juan after his early marriage, would have favored having Catherine remain at Windsor, but they were not consulted. It was decided that when the Prince left, Catherine should go with him.

The young couple, starting out before Christmas, spent the holiday in Ludlow Castle, which was a cold and gloomy place. The ceiling and walls of the great hall were black with smoke from the vast open hearths, which did not keep the place warm. For entertainment, wild Welsh bards strummed their harps in the firelight and sang dirge-like ballads of the death of King Arthur.

All winter Catherine, used to the sunny warmth of Granada, bravely endured the cold like a good soldier. But in March both she and Arthur were stricken with some mysterious disease.

On April 2, 1502, Arthur was dead, and Catherine was still too desperately ill to know when his poor young body was borne away. Finally, after many weeks, she had recovered enough to be carried in a litter to Richmond and later on to London.

In London Catherine and her Spanish household were established in a house on the Strand, until it should be decided what was to be done with her.

For months arguments, between the Spanish and the English, in which she had no part, were bandied back and forth.

The Spanish sovereigns were determined that their daughter's next husband should be Arthur's younger brother Henry, who was now heir to the throne. Members of the English Council raised an objection, quoting the Bible which forbade a man to marry his brother's widow. The Pope could overrule that objection, said the Spaniards, with a dispensation.

Suddenly the death of the Queen left Henry VII a widower and he proposed to marry Catherine himself. Ferdinand and Isabella would have none of that. Catherine must marry the prince, not his father. Henry VII finally gave in. The treaty was signed and a request sent to the Pope for the dispensation.

UNWILLING GUESTS

PHILIP THE HANDSOME "no more wanted to go to Spain than he wanted to go to hell," the Spanish ambassador reported to Ferdinand and Isabella, who had issued the invitation. Much as they disliked the fact that when Juana became Queen, her Hapsburg husband would be King, they had invited the young couple to Spain, to let Philip become familiar with its laws and customs.

After much urging, and after their third child had been born, the Hapsburg playboy finally agreed to make this visit, but it was many months later—before Philip could tear himself away from his gay companions and his latest lady love. Then he insisted on going by way of France, where he was highly entertained by Louis XII, standing enemy of his father-in-law. And despite Juana's objection, he arranged a marriage between their two-year-old son Charles, and the French Princess Claude, who was then three.

Ferdinand and Isabella were to meet Philip for the first time at a family dinner in Toledo. Juana had hoped that in spite of his friendship with the French King, her parents would see how truly wonderful Philip was. She hoped Philip would not show how much he hated Spanish food. He was wearing gold and purple velvet and brocaded satin which, she thought, was most becoming. Then she worried that her parents might think that he was overdressed. They were in plain dark wool.

Ferdinand and Isabella were seated in stiff, high-backed chairs, at a huge carved table lighted with tall, ornate candelabra. Her father, Juana noticed, had lost a front tooth and was beginning to look old. But her mother, although she had been ill, had lost none of that quiet strength that made one feel so inadequate. Juana had to translate all that was said from Spanish into French, and French into Spanish. What her parents were thinking, she could only surmise. Philip, she knew, was bored.

During the next months Philip grew more and more bored. By fall he announced that he was going home. Juana was then expecting her fourth baby and could not travel. When she found that he was going without her, she went to pieces, sobbing and weeping, but to no effect. Philip left, and had such a high time on his way home that it took him almost a year to get there.

First he returned to France, for more gaiety. Then he went on to the Duchy of Savoy to visit his sister Margaret, whom he had sent off in the winter of 1501 to marry a third husband, the Duke of Savoy. The Duke was a brother of her old friend Louise.

In March, 1503, Juana's baby was born, a boy who was named Ferdinand for his grandfather. After that, knowing that she could travel, her spirits revived. When at last she heard from Philip, telling her to come home, she was almost beside herself with joy. She made plans to leave at once and ordered mules for the journey. But she could not go overland because her father was again at war with France.

Juana was then living in an old castle near Medina del Campo. Isabella, who was very ill at the time, in Segovia fifty miles away, sent a Bishop to prevent the impatient girl from starting out on her mules. The Bishop reached the castle just in time—at the very moment when Juana was crossing the courtyard toward the outer gate. As the

Bishop could not stop her with words, he ordered the gate closed and locked, and the drawbridge raised.

Seeing she was trapped, Juana was like a wild animal. She screamed, she begged and pleaded and pounded on the gate until she was exhausted. All day she stood by the gate and all through the icy winter night. Not until the next afternoon would she enter the small guardhouse and sit by a brazier. Then, since no one could do anything more with her, they sent for her mother.

Isabella was far too ill to attempt the fifty miles on horseback, but believed she could endure being carried in a litter and forced herself to make the journey in two days. She found Juana still huddled in the guardroom, disheveled and wild-eyed.

As the frantic girl looked up to see her mother standing there, quiet as a rock, the words she hurled at her in desperation were "words so shameful, so far from what a daughter should say to her mother," Isabella said later, "that had I not seen her mental condition I would never have stood them."

Bishops and doctors advised the Queen that Juana must not be held against her will any longer, and a fleet of ships was assembled to send her to the Netherlands. She went in March, 1504.

Little Ferdinand, then a year old, the apple of his grandfather's eye, was left behind. Unlike his brother Charles, he was to be brought up as a Spaniard in his mother's country.

Reunion with her idolized Philip brought no peace to Juana's sad, foolish heart. One day she came upon a beautiful blonde reading what she was sure must be a love letter from him. She demanded to see it. The young lady tore it to bits and swallowed the pieces. Juana snatched up a pair of scissors, grabbed the girl's long yellow hair, yanked it down, cut it off to the scalp, and sent her rival bleeding and screaming from the scene.

The incident became an international scandal—one more agony for Isabella to endure, which would further sap what little strength the tired Queen and mother had left.

VOYAGE IV

ON THE FOURTH VOYAGE, which began May 9, 1502, Columbus hoped to sail around the world. Ferdinand and Isabella evidently shared his hope, for they gave him a letter of introduction to Vasco da Gama, who was then starting out on his second journey to India. They had also sent out an officer by the name of Ovando, with 2,500 men, to be the new Governor of Hispaniola. Humiliating as it was for Columbus to be replaced, and lose the title of Vice Roy, he still had his share in the gold mines and was permitted to send an agent on Ovando's fleet to look after his interests.

And if he did sail around the world on this voyage it would be the crowning glory of his life! The "High Voyage" he called it.

Ferdinand, who was fourteen, was to go with his father. Among the 140 members of the crew there were a number of other young

304

boys, some only twelve years old, but all big and strong enough to sail around the world, if the way was found. And why shouldn't it be found? Had not Marco Polo sailed home from China? Somewhere, then, there had to be a strait through which he had sailed. Columbus believed that it must be along the western shore of the Caribbean Sea.

By the end of June his four caravels were in the Caribbean skirting the southern shore of Puerto Rico. Just off the harbor of Santo Domingo, Columbus saw signs of a cyclone. Ovando's fleet was then ready to leave on their return voyage to Spain. Columbus sent a messenger to him to suggest that his fleet delay sailing and to ask permission to anchor his four caravels in the harbor until the cyclone was over.

Ovando refused. "Cyclone," he scoffed, and sent out his twenty ships as planned. His only precaution was to put the Admiral's agent, who was taking back 4,000 pesos of gold, on the worst ship in the fleet.

The cyclone struck that night. As the four caravels tossed and twisted in the open sea, Columbus spent the awful hours cursing Ovando and praying to God. In the morning when the sky cleared, Santo Domingo, built of wood and thatch, was flattened to the ground. Ovando's fleet caught by the wind at the end of the island had been battered to pieces on the rocks—all except one. The poorest one, carrying the Admiral's agent and gold, had escaped. Since all four caravels also survived the storm, Columbus was accused by his enemies of having raised the cyclone with the help of the devil!

Sailing west across the Caribbean, Columbus followed the shore of Honduras looking for the strait, in twenty-eight days of continual rain, thunder, and lightning.

"Other tempests have I seen," he wrote, "but none that lasted so long. Many old hands we looked on as stout fellows lost their courage. What griped me most was the sufferings of my son. But our Lord lent him courage that he even heartened the rest and he worked as though he had been at sea all his life. My brother Bartholo-

305

mew was in the worst of the ships and I felt terrible having persuaded him to come against his will."

The storm finally ended, and they followed the Nicaragua coast south, still searching for the strait. Ten days of October were spent in the Chiriqui lagoon in Costa Rica. There Indians told Columbus that nine days' march to the west would bring him to the ocean. That was overland. A waterway was what Columbus was searching for. He was also searching for gold. This, the natives said was to be found in Veragua. Gold was there, to be sure, but the Indians of Veragua were hostile. At sight of the ships, a hundred or more rushed to the ocean's edge, brandishing their spears to drive off the invaders.

From there, Columbus sailed on along the rugged coast, as far as Porto Bello, just beyond the present entrance to the Panama Canal. Here the ships were caught in a winter storm, even worse than those they had already survived. Columbus wrote in his journal that his "eyes never beheld seas so high and angry. Never did sky look more terrible...the lightning broke forth with such violence that each time I wondered if it had carried off my spars and sails."

One day there was an added terror—a water spout which drew up a column of water thicker than a barrel, twisting it about like a whirlwind. Fortunately, Ferdinand said, his father was able to dissolve it by reading from the Bible the account of Jesus stilling the waves on the Sea of Galilee. Then he drew his sword and traced a cross in the sky and drew a circle around the whole fleet, whereupon the waterspout passed by and they were saved.

Utterly exhausted, Columbus was ready to give up searching for the strait and return to Spain, but none of the four ships could make the journey. They were so eaten away by ship worms and so full of holes that with everyone working to bail out the water they barely made it to Jamaica.

There, Ferdinand said, "we ran them ashore and built cabins on the decks where the people might lodge."

Marooned thus on the island of Jamaica the crew, 116 now, out of 140, spent exactly one year, from June, 1503, to June, 1504. A large Indian village lay about half a mile away, and Columbus had to count on the Indians for food while he figured out some way to get home. Without having even a small boat that could be sent to Hispaniola for help, he had to borrow an Indian dugout and in it one brave man, Diego Mendez, set out with six Indians for Santo Domingo. Every month of anxious waiting for their return made the men more irritable. The Indians, sick of feeding uninvited guests, brought in less and less food. Something drastic had to be done.

A book Columbus had with him was one printed in Nuremberg which listed eclipses of the moon for thirty years. Luckily, an eclipse was due in three days. On that day the Indians were summoned to a meeting. Columbus told them God was so angry with them that He was blocking out the moon. The eclipse occurred on schedule and the food problem was solved.

Late in June a caravel arrived with brave Diego Mendez in command to take the survivors back to Santo Domingo, where most of them were glad to stay for a while. Another ship was chartered in September and Columbus, his brother Bartholomew, his son Ferdinand, and twenty-two others embarked for Spain.

On November 7, 1504, the fourth and last voyage ended for the tired Admiral of the Ocean Sea. Instead of being his crowning voyage, it had been the most useless.

But, as Columbus wrote to his son Diego, he had done his best, and if what he had tried was beyond his knowledge and strength, "Our Lord in such cases asketh not more of men than good will." He signed his letter, "Thy father who loveth thee more than himself."

Columbus was in Seville. The court was then at Medina del Campo. He got no summons from the sovereigns to appear. He could not know that while he waited to hear from her, his great and good friend, Queen Isabella, was dying.

OF DEATH, BIRTH, AND TRAGEDY

ISABELLA faced death as she had faced life, with quiet dignity. Her fine mind was clear to the very end, and she worked constantly, writing as long as she could hold her pen. Her great concern was for the welfare of Castile, and most of her will was devoted to wise instructions for its care and government. She urged Juana, Philip, and Ferdinand to "live in peace and concord together." She appointed Ferdinand, who had been King of Castile only as long as she lived, to act as Regent until the new King and Queen should arrive from the Netherlands. If Juana should not be able or willing to rule, her father should continue to rule in her name until her son Charles should come of age. But Ferdinand must swear under oath *never* to try to dispossess Juana or try to rule Castile in his own name.

Isabella knew her husband for what he was—forceful, experienced, and intelligent, but also crafty, sly, and completely selfish. Knowing him so well, she had never expected the impossible, but had brought out the best in him by her unfailing love and great tact.

The will, which she signed on November 21, 1504, three days before her death, began with the wish that her body be taken to the Alhambra in Granada and there laid to rest in the monastery.

"But should the King my Lord prefer a sepulchre in some other place, then my will is that my body be transported and laid where he can be by my side; that the union we have enjoyed in this world and which through the mercy of God may be hoped for again when our souls are in heaven, may be symbolized by our bodies being side by side on earth. I beseech the King my Lord that he will accept all my jewels so that seeing them he may be reminded of the singular love I always bore him and may be encouraged to live more justly and with more holiness."

Scarcely had the Queen drawn her last breath than the unholy struggle for power was on between Ferdinand and Philip, with no regard for Juana, who was soon to be betrayed by them both. The day Isabella died, Ferdinand had Juana proclaimed Queen, but then immediately summoned the Cortes, declared that Juana was ill, unable to rule, and made himself Regent. This done, he looked about for an ally to help him hold this position against Philip, who was sure to contest it. He hit upon his long-hated enemy, the King of France, and lured Louis XII into the bargain by promising to help him conquer Naples.

The bargain was sealed by a marriage—the marriage in 1505 between Ferdinand and Germaine, a young niece of the French King.

The news of this unseemly marriage caused a flurry of speculation in the Netherlands as to what Ferdinand was up to.

Philip the Handsome decided to hurry to Spain at once and be proclaimed King. He would have preferred to go without Juana, but since it was *her* throne, not his, he had to take her along. They had to risk a winter voyage since Louis XII had been forced by Ferdinand to block their passage through France. Philip set forth with 2,000 soldiers and a fleet of 40 ships.

As might be expected, they struck a bad storm in the Channel and were blown into England. It was spring of 1506 before they landed in Spain. There they received an enthusiastic welcome from the nobles who flocked to meet them in great numbers and for various reasons. Most were naturally loyal to Juana as their rightful Queen. Many had been well bribed by Philip to support him. And all had turned against Ferdinand for his untimely remarriage. With so much support, Philip urged Juana to have the coronation ceremony performed at once, but Juana refused to perform any act as Queen before she saw her father and had his advice.

Ferdinand, who saw that he could not oppose Philip without support of the nobles, changed his tactics and invited his son-in-law to a friendly meeting, put an arm about his shoulder like a good father, and had him agree upon one thing—that Juana should never be allowed to rule. Ferdinand then withdrew to Naples with his young wife, to wait until such time as it seemed possible to return and get rid of Philip.

Philip and Juana remained in Valladolid. During all this time Juana had not been allowed to see or talk to her father. She had no idea that both he and Philip were spreading the word that she was out of her mind, unable to be Queen.

One of the nobles who doubted this forced his way in to see Juana, found her sitting alone in a room with the curtains drawn. After talking with her for ten hours he warned Philip that he would fight every effort to have Juana judged unbalanced.

1506

Columbus was also in Valladolid in that spring of 1506. He was then very ill. Otherwise he would have made every effort to see Juana and ask her for the title and income he thought were rightfully his but which had been denied him by her father. Although Columbus had a good income from the gold mines of Hispaniola, he did not have the title of Vice Roy nor as much income as originally promised. As a compromise, Ferdinand had offered Columbus a handsome estate in Castile and a fair amount of money. Columbus was no man to compromise. Now that he was bedridden, he had sent his brother Bartholomew to plead his cause with the new Queen.

Queen Juana! Columbus remembered the first time he had seen her. It was in Cordova when she was about nine, the prettiest of the royal children and the quickest to learn, it was said. The last time he had seen her was when she left for the Netherlands, and he himself was waiting to return to Hispaniola. Bartholomew was then building the new fort at Santo Domingo. Where was Bartholomew now? Had he been unable to see Juana? Why had he not returned? Columbus could wait no longer, signed his will on May 19th, leaving all the property he had to his son Diego, commending to his care the other members of the family, including Beatriz, Ferdinand's mother. He asked that his body be sent for burial to Santo Domingo.

On the following morning he grew suddenly worse. On May 20, 1506, Admiral Christopher Columbus died. At his bedside were his brother Diego, his two sons, Diego and Ferdinand, a few faithful servants, and Diego Mendez, the loyal friend of the last disappointing voyage.

And so, like the great Queen, he had come to the end of a life which had brought the supreme joy of achievement, balanced—as are all lives—with a measure of sadness and disappointment.

In September, 1506, a young life was snapped off. King Philip the Handsome died suddenly after only seven days of illness. Juana was almost frantic with grief, unable to believe that such a thing could happen. He had been perfectly well, playing a game of tennis. A fever set in, caused, the doctors said, by drinking too much cold water when he was overheated. Juana nursed him night and day. When he was gone she clung to him, sobbing and kissing his cold face and mouth until she had to be carried from the room.

One cold, dark night the funeral procession started for Granada where Philip had wished to be buried. Juana would travel only at night. "It does not become a woman who has lost the sun of her life to see the light of day," she said. And she was the Queen; her wishes were not to be denied. So the solemn procession wound its way along the roads under the night sky, monks and priests intoning the office of the dead. Ferdinand, who was four then, walked with his mother behind the hearse. At Torquemada they halted. Juana could go no farther.

There, a few weeks later, on February 14, 1507, her last child was born, a little girl whom she named Catalina for her sister in England. The Queen spent four months in Torquemada.

And there all the wrangling crowd of nobles and prelates who were trying to get control of the government followed her, clamoring for her royal signature on this and that. Juana would do nothing as Queen until her father came, except to dismiss all the Council of Flemish friends whom Philip had appointed so that, when her father returned, he should find the government just as her mother the Queen had left it. And when he did, all would be well; Juana was sure of that.

Ferdinand had kept track from Naples of what was going on at home. Now that the coast was clear and the nobles were well bribed to receive him, he was planning to return to Spain in late August, 1507.

Juana was to meet him in Tortoles. She had chosen for him the best house in town and had tried to make it comfortable. She was busy with the last finishing touches when she heard his horses in the courtyard. Overjoyed, she ran out in her black gown, her mourning veil flying. As he dismounted she flung herself at his feet. She entered the house, with her slim fingers in his big hand and with no suspicion of what the brutal man was about to do.

First he asked her to turn over the government to him, and she did so in perfect confidence, as he had expected. He was not so sure what to expect from the nobles. They might still turn against him and rally round Juana who was actually their Queen. The perfect solution would be to ship her off to Henry VII, who had seen Juana in England and wanted to marry her. But Juana would not hear of that proposal. The only other sure thing was to lock her up where no one could see or talk to her.

The Castle of Tordesillas was the ideal place for that, but at his suggestion that she go there to live Juana flew into a panic. There was a legend that once in every hundred years the Castle of Tordesillas would be the prison of a Queen.

Very well, said her father, she might stay where she was, but she could not keep little Ferdinand with her. He would take his grandson. As Juana ran to the window to see her five-year-old boy being led away, she also saw troops being stationed about the castle. The shock was so great that she never recovered. For days she lay on the floor, seeming not to care whether she lived or died. Worse was to come.

On February 14, 1508, which was the first birthday of her baby, Catalina, Juana was wakened out of her sleep. Above her in the torchlight stood her father's officers, with helmets and pikes. They told her to dress. They had orders to take her to the Castle of Tordesillas, and Philip's coffin to the nearby convent of Santa Clara. She summoned all her wits to resist. She put up every possible excuse for delay. It was of no use. She was led away by the troops to the bleak, gloomy fortress where she was to spend the rest of her life—forty-six years in gathering darkness.

313

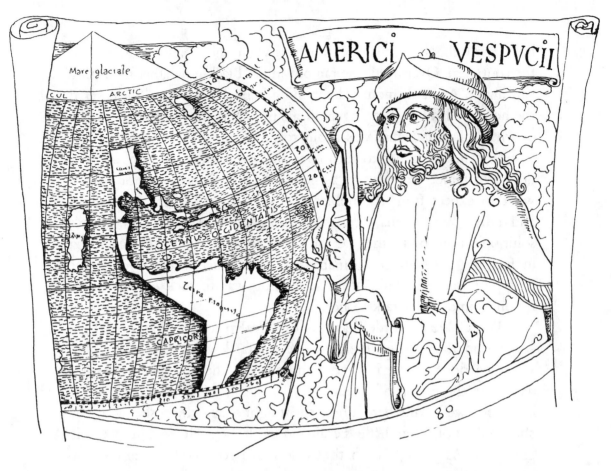

WHY AMERICA?

THE YEAR after Columbus died a map appeared with the name America on it. It was made by Martin Waldseemüller, a German mapmaker in the French town of St. Dié. He was professor of cosmography at the University and in 1507 published a new geography in which the map appeared. Convinced that a new quarter of the world had been discovered, he put the name America on his map saying, "I see no reason why we cannot in full justice call it Amerigo or America, since it was Amerigo who discovered it."

The German got his opinion from a book of letters called *Mundus Novus,* or *The New World,* written by Amerigo Vespucci, or Americus

Vespucius, to one of the Medici, describing four voyages he was supposed to have made to the New World.

Before becoming an explorer, Vespucci had been living in Seville managing a Medici bank, from 1492 until the Medicis were driven from Florence. Out of a job then, he was glad for the opportunity of going on one of the voyages to the New World.

On his first voyage, according to his book, he had sailed from Cadiz on May 10, 1497, and landed on the mainland of South America. But according to the latitude and longitude he gave, he would have had to be either in the Pacific Ocean, or sailing over dry land in western Canada!

His second voyage was made with Hojeda in 1499 to Venezuela. The third and fourth voyages were made in 1501 and 1503 for King Manuel of Portugal, and the letters describing all of them were sent from Lisbon to Florence. In 1505 the book was being published in Venice.

In 1505 Amerigo Vespucci had gone back to Seville. There he had visited his old friend Christopher Columbus, whom he found very ill. As Amerigo was going to court, Columbus gave him a letter to deliver to his son Diego. In it he wrote that Vespucci was "a very honorable man, and always desirous of pleasing me. See what he can do to profit me there and have him do it."

Columbus was not aware that a book by Amerigo Vespucci was then being published which would cause Amerigo to be given the credit of having discovered the New World.

Were the mistakes Vespucci made deliberate or accidental?

Who can say?

It is generally conceded that he did not make the voyage in 1497, but after Waldseemüller had used the name Amerigo, the name spelled in various ways became immediately popular.

In August, 1508, Amerigo Vespucci was made chief pilot of Spain and held the position until his death in Seville in February, 1512.

WARRIOR AND BUILDER

THIS IS JULIUS II, the "Warrior Pope." In 1503 when he was
elected, he was sixty but still full of vim and vigor, and was
quick to say that he "preferred a sword to a book." Most of
his ten years in office were to be spent using the sword waging what
he called "Holy Wars," in which the enemy was excommunicated! In
his first "Holy War," the enemy was Venice. The Republic of Venice
had seized some of the cities that belonged to the Papal State and
Pope Julius was determined to recover them. Needing help, he called
upon the rulers of Europe to join him in a Holy League against
Venice. The members, each with an eye on something to be gained
for himself, were:

> Julius II
> Louis XII of France
> Maximilian, the Emperor
> Ferdinand of Aragon.

316

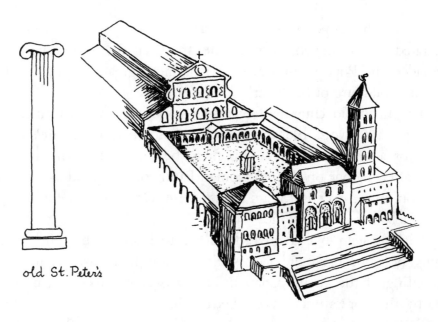

old St. Peter's

By the fall of 1505, war was going well. The Pope had captured, and was making a triumphant entry into, the city of Bologna. With all its pomp and glory this might well have been an old Roman triumph and the hero Julius Caesar himself, instead of his Papal namesake. Magnificent in a gold and purple cape sparkling with jewels, Pope Julius II entered Bologna, carried shoulder-high in a chair of state. Preceded by his cavalry, his men at arms, his military band, officers and cardinals, he was followed by archbishops, bishops, and the papal guard of Swiss from the Vatican. They had or were soon to have gorgeous red and yellow uniforms designed by Michelangelo who was one of the artists now employed by the Pope to beautify Rome.

Pope Julius II, though he had no use for books, took an active interest in art and architecture and was to make Rome what Florence had once been—the center of the Renaissance. He sent for Michelangelo, who had returned to Florence, and ordered him to design a tomb for him more colossal than any ever before built. The excited sculptor drew plans, hurried off to the quarry to select the marble, sent back mountains of it, and began his work, to the joy and the

317

wonder of the Pope, who then changed his mind. Michelangelo, frustrated and outraged, blamed the architect Bramante, who had persuaded the Pope to undertake a still more gigantic project. This was the rebuilding of St. Peter's.

The little old church of St. Peter's, built by Constantine, was now over 1,000 years old and tumbling into ruin. Bramante's plans called for a tremendous new church to be topped by a huge dome copied after the one on the old Roman Pantheon—a grandiose scheme that would take over 150 years to complete. On April 18, 1506, Pope Julius II laid the cornerstone.

Michelangelo in a rage had then fled to Florence, but after much urging he came back and to his dismay was then ordered to paint the ceiling of the Sistine Chapel! This was a barn-like hall built in 1473 by the Pope's uncle, Pope Sixtus IV.

The walls had already been decorated by Botticelli, Pinturicchio, Perugino, and others. To paint the high vaulted ceiling was an almost superhuman task.

Michelangelo, too ill-tempered and nervous to tolerate a helper, erected a scaffold and did it alone, lying on his back, sleeping in his clothes, stopping only to eat. He began in May, 1508. In October, 1512, the scaffold was down, and the hall opened to the public who gazed up in blank amazement. There above them, covering the great vault, they saw the story of Genesis, shown in heroic figures filled with passion and emotion, surrounded by Prophets and Sibyls.

About this time a younger painter, Raphael Sanzio, as charming and handsome as he was talented, came to Rome and soon became the favorite painter of Julius II, though Michelangelo condemned young Raphael as being no more than a "clever imitator." Raphael's first painting was a mural for the room or, in Italian, stanza, in the Vatican where the Pope signed pardons. After that he decorated a series of rooms in the palace now known as the Stanzas of Raphael. The picture of Julius II is from one of these great paintings.

ALDVS OF VENICE

ERASMUS IN ITALY

ERASMUS WAS IN Bologna and saw Pope Julius make his triumphal entry. To Erasmus this was a shocking spectacle. To see the highest priest in the Christian Church so glory in the bloody business of war was something he could never forget. But he was delighted to be in Bologna at last, having had to wait in Florence for weeks until the siege was over. He was now expecting to spend a year of study at the University.

His long-cherished desire to visit Italy had finally been realized. In England the Italian physician of King Henry VII had engaged him to travel with his two young sons who were going home to Bologna, and to act as their tutor for a year. The year at Bologna's famous university was well spent, but tutoring two rather dull boys became boring.

Erasmus was delighted when the year was over and he was leaving for Venice; even more so when he was actually there, seated in a gondola and being taken silently along the winding canals to the house of that printer whose sign was the anchor and the dolphin.

Aldus Manutius, the famous Venetian printer, had agreed to publish a new enlarged edition of his *Adagia*. Erasmus had written to him from Bologna, expressing admiration for the magnificent type which Manutius had designed, especially the very small slanted letters

319

based on Italian handwriting and for that reason called "italics."

On his arrival at the printing plant, the stranger was told to wait. The master was correcting proof and was not to be bothered. When Aldus found who had been kept waiting by mistake, he was most apologetic and more than cordial. He took Erasmus to the home of his father-in-law where the author was to have room and board. The *Adagia* was not yet complete, Erasmus said, "and with great temerity on my part we began to work at the same time, I to write, Aldus to print." To the printer's surprise, Erasmus sat and wrote in the noisy press room, so busy trying to keep far enough ahead that he said he "had no time even to scratch his ears."

At the end of eight months, the author left Venice, pleased with his new enlarged book of adages, but equally glad to be free of the stale bread and bad wine of the boarding house, as well as his very objectionable roommate, a cleric by the name of Aleander, of whom he unfortunately had not seen the last.

From Venice Erasmus went to Ferrara where he met a friend of Copernicus, and to Rome where he was entertained as a celebrity by the gracious Cardinal Giovanni de Medici. He might have stayed longer in Italy had he not heard from England that on April 22, 1509, King Henry VII had died. A letter written in May by Lord Mountjoy was full of enthusiasm for the young King Henry VIII.

"O my Erasmus," he wrote, "if you could see how the world here is rejoicing in so great a prince. Avarice is expelled from the land...our King does not desire gold nor gems, but virtue, glory, immortality. The other day he said to me, 'I wish I were more learned than I am.' 'That is not what we expect of your Grace,' I replied, 'but that you should foster learned men.' 'Yea surely,' said he, 'for without them we should scarcely exist at all.' What more splendid saying could fall from the lips of a prince? The Archbishop of Canterbury is not only engrossed in your Adagia and praises you to the skies, but he also promises you a benefice on your return and sends you five pounds for traveling expenses."

ΜΩΡΙΑΣ ΕΓΚΩΜΙΟΝ

IN PRAISE OF FOLLY

IN JULY, 1509, Erasmus was on horseback crossing the Alps, leaving Italy for England. As he rode along he kept thinking of all that he had seen, read, and observed, and of all the foolishness there was in the world. And yet, how could the world exist without a certain amount of Folly? How could people keep on day after day except by fooling themselves that they were happy, or that what they were doing was worthwhile?

Moria, that was the Latin word for Folly. It reminded him of More, the name of the least foolish man he knew, Thomas More. At the thought of seeing that wise and witty friend again, ideas began to sparkle and play on the subject of "Moria" in a most amusing way.

On his arrival in London, Erasmus went directly to Thomas More's home in the suburbs, and in a few days he wrote a most perfect and delightful satire which he called *Encomium Moriae,* in Latin, or

IN PRAISE OF FOLLY

"An oration of feigned matter, spoken by Folly in her own person."

This was a clever device, by which Erasmus could say things

321

that he would not otherwise have dared to utter without fear of being burned at the stake. Folly, like a jester at a King's court, could speak freely without blame, as if she spoke purely to be amusing.

Dame Folly begins her oration quite properly in praise of herself. She alone, she says, with her two handmaidens, Self-Love and Flattery, keep the world going. Then she describes various kinds of people, showing how each one deceives himself. There is the merchant who relies upon money for happiness, the soldier who thinks bravery in war will bring him fame, the nobles who take false pride in their birth and nothing else matters, lovers who think all beauty and loveliness lie in the object of their affections, and so forth.

After this airy beginning—this light-hearted listing of follies that are relatively harmless—Folly, speaking for Erasmus, strikes out boldly against the true evils of the day, especially the abuses of religion, the sins perpetrated by even the highest dignitaries of the Church. Folly was now saying what thousands of people were thinking but never put into words, the obvious fact that there should be a thorough reform within the Church which had become so corrupt.

This was a dangerous and powerful book, for the very reason that it was amusing and easy to read, and so became very popular and widely read all over Europe.

The illustration on the preceding page is one made by Hans Holbein, when he was barely eighteen. The young German artist who was then in Basle borrowed a copy of the book and covered the broad margins with sketches. Folly, in a jester's cap and gown, is shown lecturing to a class of typical German schoolboys, one wearing donkey's ears.

Martin Luther, who had learned his Latin in just such a school would soon be reading *In Praise of Folly*. A very different man from the intellectual, idealistic Erasmus, who speared the evils of his day with the rapier of satire, Martin Luther, passionate and willful, was to strike at those evils with a hammer.

THE HAPPY HUSBAND, HENRY VIII

O N HIS DEATHBED Henry VII had made young Henry promise to marry Catherine of Aragon. Having delayed six years after the betrothal, the old King had finally given in. He also left a sum of money to secure masses for his soul so long as the world lasted, which it was generally believed would be less than 200 years. Henry VII died on April 21, 1509, and was buried several weeks later in the unfinished chapel in Westminster that was to bear his name. As soon as the funeral was over, Catherine and Henry VIII went across the Thames River to Greenwich Castle.

There, in the first lovely days of June, they were married very quietly in a small chapel close by the Castle wall. This was their favorite chapel, and because of those first happy days of her marriage, Greenwich was always to be Catherine's favorite residence.

Marriage to Henry! It had come at last—what she had longed and prayed for day and night for seven miserable years. After her mother's death, Henry VII had considered her of so much less worth, that her position at court had become almost unbearable. Whenever she saw the King he reminded her that she was only living on charity —that her father still owed him half of her dowry.

"Why does His Highness not keep his word?" he would ask. "You have no claim on us. It is only our good will that makes us give you food to eat."

Catherine wrote her father pitiful letters, asking for help, but she got no reply. Not one gold piece did Ferdinand of Aragon ever send his daughter after she left Spain.

"I have now sold some bracelets to get a dress of black velvet, for I was all but naked," she wrote him in one letter, "till now the dresses I brought from Spain have lasted me. . . ."

Now on this shining June morning of her wedding day those black years of humiliation were behind her. Catherine's heart was full of thanks to God, as she walked along the lattice-covered path from the chapel to the castle. Her handsome young husband towered above her, his golden hair dappled with sunlight shining through the leaves. Henry, having reached the age of eighteen, was nearly his full height of six-feet-four. And he was fairly bouncing with good spirits, delighted to be alive.

The coronation ceremony was set for Midsummer's Day. Henry and Catherine spent the preceding night, according to ancient custom, in the royal apartment in the Tower of London. Next day happy crowds of Londoners lined the way, waiting to see and cheer their young King and Queen as they rode from the Tower to Westminster Abbey. Henry, who sat extremely well on horseback, wore a robe of crimson velvet, furred in white ermine. Catherine was seated in a litter of gold cloth swung between two white horses. Her gown was of white satin, and her golden hair hanging loose was "of very great length, beautiful and goodly to behold." It was a most joyful day for everyone.

The young King was so happy with his Queen that he wrote his Spanish father-in-law, "If I were still free I would choose her for wife before all others."

Catherine, who had remained loyal to her father in spite of his neglect, wrote him of her love for Henry. "Among the reasons that make me love the King my Lord, the strongest is his filial love and obedience to your Highness." And she added, "Our time is spent in continual festivals."

Life at court under the young King was truly one continual festival, the complete opposite of what it had been under the grim old King, with his grinding economy. Henry VIII was now free to do and live as he liked. The coffers full of the gold that his father had hoarded were his to dip into and spend. The world was his to enjoy and he was tireless in pursuing every sport, art, and amusement.

A day spent in hunting might be followed by a masked ball. Another day might bring a tournament, followed by a banquet for a hundred knights or more, and that followed by a concert at which Henry, having jousted and dined with equal gusto, would sing a song he had composed, playing his own accompaniment on the lute. Night after night there would be dancing, in which the King would lead out one lady after another, leaping and cavorting and kicking his heels in the air long after everyone else was exhausted.

The center of life for this rollicking royal playboy was Catherine, his perfect foil, his most appreciative audience. Wherever she might be he sought her out to show her an interesting new book, share an amusing story with her, or relate a fascinating bit of news. He would dash away from his friends, saying, "The Queen must hear this."

Not being overly sure of himself, despite his blustering, Henry often asked her advice. She gave it so smoothly and tactfully that he felt he had made the decision by himself. Being very pious, he heard vespers and compline every evening with Catherine, who often spent six hours a day on her knees in prayer.

All in all, for a marriage that was to end in disaster, this one had a most happy beginning. The crowning joy for both of them would come when Catherine had fulfilled her duty and borne an heir to the throne. Their first child was a little girl, born dead.

But on New Year's Day, 1511, guns boomed from the Tower of London, bells rang out all over the city, streets blazed with bonfires along the Thames. Alehouses ran with wine, and everyone drank to the great good fortune of England. A royal prince had been born, who was alive and healthy! Couriers dashed off to announce the good news to all the courts of Europe.

The infant was christened Henry. In celebration a magnificent tournament was held in Westminster, in which the proud King was one of the chief jousters. Announced as Sir Loyal Heart, he galloped into the pavilion which had been sprinkled with the golden initials of himself and Catherine. The merry-making was contagious and got completely out of hand. Crowds of cockneys from outside broke in and carried off all the gold initials and ornaments they could get their hands on. They ripped the gold lace from the ladies' dresses. They stripped Henry down to his doublet and hose, and some of the knights still further, before the guards succeeded in pushing the unruly creatures out with the butts of their battle-axes. There was still great hilarity, and laughter, as the King and Queen and their disheveled, half-undressed guests sat down for supper.

Meanwhile, at Richmond Castle, the baby boy was dying.

The nobles who had come to Westminster for the tournament in celebration of his birth, stayed on with the heartbroken parents for the funeral of little Prince Henry, 52 days old.

326

LIFE IN SANTO DOMINGO

THE YEAR that Henry VIII became King of England, Don Diego Columbus went to the New World to be the Governor of Hispaniola. He did not, however, have the title of Vice Roy. After his father's death, Diego had carried the fight for this title, originally promised to the Columbus family forever, into the law courts but with no success. Fortunately, he had fallen in love with Dona Maria Alvarez de Toledo, a distant relative of the King, and after their marriage, he had been given the post as Governor. Governor Columbus and his bride sailed for Santo Domingo with a very splendid retinue of knights and ladies, so far the most magnificent expedition to leave Spain for the New World.

Bartholomew and Diego Columbus, the Governor's two uncles, were in the company, also his brother Ferdinand, who was then twenty-one. Ferdinand had been appointed to take charge of building monasteries and churches on the island. But he was not happy there. The things in which he was interested were not to be found in the wilderness. After a few months he got permission to return to Spain. There he began collecting his famous library with the purchase of his first book, a new edition of *The Travels of Marco Polo*.

In Santo Domingo, Governor Diego Columbus began to build for himself a magnificent palace or Alcazar, with walls of stone two feet thick and woodwork of finest mahogany. The original walls are still there, and also there to be seen is the cathedral which he built, now the oldest one in the western hemisphere.

At first, the Governor and his court were located at Concepcion de Vega, which was inland about 100 miles from Santo Domingo. There, one Saturday in November, 1510, a dusty, footsore friar came to pay his respects to the Governor. He said that he and two other Dominican friars had come to Hispaniola to work among the Indians. On Sunday he preached to the Spaniards, describing the glories of heaven and asked them to send their Indians for instruction in the afternoon. Large numbers came and formed a circle around the young missionary who sat on a stool, a crucifix in his hand, and spoke to them through an interpreter.

These Indians sent by the Spaniards were not slaves, in the exact sense of the word. It would have been far better for them if they had been. They were the miserable victims of a system of enforced labor, called Repartimiento, from the word "repartir," which meant to parcel out. A certain number of Indians were parcelled out to each Spaniard to work for him in the gold mines or on his plantation. When they died of overwork, starvation, or abuse, the Spaniard was simply given more to replace them. Had they been his slaves, they would have been valuable property worth caring for. As it was, the average Spaniard treated the Indians less well than their dogs, some actually feeding them to the dogs when they ran short of meat.

Of the peaceful, friendly Tainos who had welcomed Columbus, so many had been exterminated that Indians were being brought in from the Bahamas. In a few years these would also die and be replaced by Negroes imported from Africa.

The three Dominicans were shocked and horrified by the hideous cruelty practiced by the Spaniards. They decided that one of them must preach to their countrymen on the sin of what they were doing. The church was full. Governor Diego Columbus, his wife Maria, and the officers of the crown were all in their pews as Fra Montesino spoke his opening words.

"Ego vox clamantis in deserto—I am the voice of one crying in the wilderness," he said, "and it will prove to be for you the strongest, harshest, most frightful voice you have ever listened to. The voice tells you that all of you are now living and dying in a state of mortal sin on account of your cruelty and tyranny over these innocent people. Have you lost your reason? Have you lost your senses? Continue as you are doing, you will have lost your souls!" This was the gist of his sermon.

That afternoon there was a meeting of outraged Spaniards in the Governor's house. Speaking for the committee, the Governor then delivered an ultimatum to the Friar that unless he retracted what he had said, steps would be taken to bring him to his senses. Unlike most of those Spanish settlers, who resented the sermon, one of them was so moved by the "voice crying in the wilderness," that it changed his entire life.

His name was Las Casas, Bartolomé de Las Casas. He had been living on a plantation in Haiti for about seven years, but had been born in Seville. He was about eighteen, and remembered very well when Christopher Columbus returned in 1493 from his great voyage of discovery, bringing seven Indians, the first ever seen in Europe. On the second voyage his father had gone with Columbus and returned with enough gold to send his son to study law at the University of Salamanca. Bartolomé had also been given an Indian slave, one Columbus had given his father, but who had to be sent back on the next ship. Queen Isabella was very angry that the Admiral should presume to "give her vassals away," and issued a decree that whoever had received an Indian must under pain of death send him back on the next ship sailing for Hispaniola. The next ship at that time was the one on which Bobadilla was being sent out as judge. Las Casas' father went with him. Santo Domingo was then but a few thatched huts around the fort, and there were not more than 300 settlers on the island. Gold, however, was beginning to be mined in such great quantities that in 1502 when Ovando was sent out as Governor, 2,500 men were eager to go with him. One of these was young Las Casas, who had obtained his degree of law from the university and was setting out to seek his fortune.

Las Casas had accepted conditions as he found them in the wilderness, with little thought, until he heard the sermon of Fra Montesino. All the evils he had observed but ignored, he then saw with new eyes. He walked from the church a changed man. Without hesitation he made up his mind to become a priest and to devote his life to the welfare of the Indians. Before the end of the year 1510, Las Casas had been consecrated and had said his first mass, the first mass ever celebrated in the New World.

"For that reason," he said, "it was made the occasion of prolonged festivities by the Governor Columbus, and all those in the city. It was smelting time and great crowds came with their Indians and their gold as they do in Spain on a great market day or a fair."

That was no easy task that Las Casas had taken upon himself—to protect the Indians, to see that they were treated "with Christian love and justice." He roused the antagonism of all the Spanish settlers who benefited from the awful system of Repartimiento. And he had a powerful enemy in Spain working against him—a member of the King's Privy Council, in charge of Indian affairs.

This was Bishop Fonseca, an absentee landlord, who himself had 1,200 Indians working for him in the gold mines and on his plantations. He had no intention of having that income diminished.

Las Casas let no man discourage him. Unwilling to admit that his cause was hopeless, he went back and forth across the ocean, tireless in his fight for compassion and justice.

330

ROMA

SACRED STAIRS · ST. JOHN LATERAN

MARTIN LUTHER VISITS ROME

A JOURNEY TO ROME! In the year 1510 that rare and unexpected opportunity came to Martin Luther. A dispute had arisen among the Augustinian monasteries, that had to be settled by the Pope. Luther and another brother were chosen to represent their monastery at Erfurt. One crisp morning in November shortly after matins, the two monks were starting out, thrilled with the privilege of spending a month in the Holy City. A hundred miles to the south would bring them to Nuremberg; another two hundred miles and they would be crossing the Swiss Alps, halfway to their destination.

There was nothing Martin Luther desired more than to make a pilgrimage to all the various shrines and famous churches in Rome—to see all of the holy relics of the saints; the heads of St. Peter and St. Paul; the bones of the Christian martyrs in the catacombs; the coin Judas had received for betraying his Lord. Most blessed of all

331

were the Sacred Stairs on which Christ had stood before Pontius Pilate in Jerusalem.

Vague rumors had reached the German monks in the monastery at Erfurt of the immorality to be found in Rome among the priests and cardinals. This Luther had taken with a measure of doubt, until he was there and saw the shocking truth with his own eyes. There with his own ears he heard young Italian priests rattling through their solemn masses for the dead, and even making wicked parodies on the sacrament for their own amusement.

The month in Rome brought another unexpected revelation to him. One day he went to climb the Sacred Stairs, fully believing, as he had been told, that anyone who climbed those twenty-eight stairs on his knees would release one soul from purgatory. As he knelt he almost wished that his parents were dead so that they might receive the benefit instead of his grandfather. He added a kiss to each step as he climbed and repeated the proper prayer, being certain that when he reached the top his grandfather's soul would be in Heaven. He stood up. Suddenly, like a streak of lightning, doubt flashed through his mind. To his own amazement he heard himself say, "Who knows whether this is true?"

Could an act such as this really be a substitute for lack of genuine goodness in a person's own life?

On his return to Germany in the spring of 1511, Luther was transferred from the monastery at Erfurt to the Augustinian monastery at Wittenberg. Wittenberg was a small village in Saxony on the River Elbe, with the Castle Church at one end of the main street and the monastery at the other. There the Elector of Saxony, Frederick the Wise, had founded a new university, which was the pride of his heart.

Martin Luther had come to be one of the new teachers. Soon after he began his work at Wittenberg, Luther seemed so overly

Wittenberg

Frederick the Wise

distraught and filled with anxiety that his confessor suggested that he take up the study of the Bible, in which he had then read very little, if any. This was another revelation. He found no mention of purgatory, nor of the power of holy relics as a substitute for true faith and righteousness. Two years later he commenced to lecture on the Psalms, following shortly with lectures on the letters of St. Paul, written to the Romans.

The year after Martin Luther's visit to Rome, Pope Julius was involved in another one of his Holy Wars, but had switched partners for this one. This time Venice was an ally, and the former ally, Louis XII, was the wicked enemy to be reviled and excommunicated. In the previous war the Pope had regained the cities he wanted, with the help of the strong French army, after which he became very fearful that the French were strong enough to take over all of Italy. He called upon Venice, Florence, Ferdinand of Aragon, and Maximilian to help him drive out the now-terrible invader.

Ferdinand, who wanted to get complete control of Naples which Louis XII had helped him to capture, was glad enough to change sides and fight against his natural enemy. Florence refused to join the "Holy Union." The Emperor Maximilian had not been able to make up his mind, before Louis XII sent his powerful army into Italy and the fighting began. The French easily defeated the combined Italian and Spanish forces. But in the battle one of the most gallant of the French commanders, Gaston de Foix, was killed. This disheartened the French so completely that within three months they had abandoned Milan and departed. The victorious allies then began to wrangle over the spoils.

Pope Julius II, hailed as the "Liberator of Italy," was a strict arbitrator and under his direction this was the result.

NAPLES went to Ferdinand of Aragon.
MILAN was given back to Maximilian Sforza, son of Il Moro.
VENICE gained several cities.

Florence, having angered Pope Julius by not answering his call, was forced to turn out the people's government of the last seventeen years, and recall the Medici family, who all of that time had been living in exile.

Pope Julius II died two years later, in 1513. The colossal tomb, which he had had Michelangelo begin, had never been finished except for this magnificent statue of Moses, who was also a priest and a

warrior and therefore had been denied entry to the Promised Land.

Erasmus was at Cambridge University lecturing at Queen's College on the Bible that winter. When he heard of the Pope's death he seized his pen and dashed off a biting satire called *Julius Excluded,* in which Pope Julius appears before the gates of Heaven and St. Peter refuses to admit the priest who preferred a sword to a book.

Life at Cambridge was beginning to bore Erasmus. He had received an invitation which he had decided to accept. It was from Margaret of Austria, who was now the Regent of the Netherlands.

MARGARET AND THE THREE KINGS

MARGARET OF AUSTRIA, in her crisp white widow's cap, was seated in a sunny window of her palace in Malines writing a letter to her father Maximilian. It was a morning in 1512, and she was reporting to him, as she often did, about the welfare of his grandchildren, twelve-year-old Charles and his three sisters who lived in another small palace just across the village street. Among the many and various members of their household, the most important was Charles's tutor, William of Croy, the Duke of Chievres. A Flemish nobleman of great ability and pride, the Duke of Chievres had himself been Regent of the Netherlands from the time her brother Philip had gone to Spain, until 1507 when Margaret had returned from Savoy following the death of her third husband. The Duchess had then been appointed Regent by her father Maximilian, and the

336

very true and enthusiastic welcome from the people had made this homecoming a most heartwarming experience.

The Duke, naturally, had not been happy over being replaced, which was quite understandable. Out of respect for the older man's pride and ability, Margaret appointed him tutor to the young Archduke Charles, the future ruler of the Netherlands.

Charles was then a pitiful-looking, sickly boy of seven who breathed through his mouth, kept it hanging open, and spoke with a thick tongue which made him sound and look rather dull.

The Duke had been most wise and patient in handling the boy, and Charles was utterly devoted to him. Still at twelve he was difficult to manage. Though he was a good student, he was moody and un-predictable and given to temper tantrums. What kind of ruler he would make no one could foresee. One could only hope.

Now, after five happy years at home, absorbed in her work, Margaret had no wish ever to go away again. This palace at Malines was not large, but very pleasant, filled with lovely things that she had chosen—damask-covered walls, hangings of taffeta, a library of rare books and fine paintings by the great Flemish masters. A small dog was curled up on a cushion at her feet, and in the window preening his green feathers in the sun was her parrot. Nearby on a small table flanked by two armchairs lay a chessboard of silver, with knights, kings, and castles of ivory and gold. Margaret loved to play in what few hours she had left from the far more difficult game in which she was now involved on the chessboard of Europe.

Many hours of every day she spent at the Council table, or at her desk. Surrounded by government officials, secretaries, and clerks, she read, wrote, signed documents and letters. Her one aim was to promote the welfare of the Netherlands.

Her greatest concern was to keep on good terms with England, and at the same time get a better deal for the Flemish weavers with the English wool merchants. Somehow or other she must cancel the ruinous contract which her brother Philip had been cajoled into making by that canny businessman, Henry VII. After some thought she hit upon a solution.

Young Henry VIII made no secret of the fact that he wished to revive England's ancient claim to the French crown. If ever, this was the time to try. Louis XII had just dragged his army out of Italy.

Why not continue the war against him on his own territory? Let Henry VIII join those two royal veterans, her father, the Emperor Maximilian, and her former father-in-law, Ferdinand of Aragon, in war against their common enemy?

Maximilian, who had missed getting anything out of Italy, had his eye on two French towns on the Flemish border that he wanted to annex—Therouanne and Tournai. Ferdinand of Aragon was anxious as ever to get hold of Navarre on the Spanish border. Henry VIII wanted no such modest bite, but the whole of France, land, crown and scepter. When the proposal reached England, the young King was so flattered and thrilled by the invitation to join two such seasoned old professionals in the art of war and politics he could scarcely wait to begin the invasion.

Every day he went down to the docks to see the progress of the fleet, decked out as head of the royal navy in what he called "galley" fashion, a sailor's vest of gold brocade, breeches of cloth of gold, and long, bright scarlet hose. About his neck hung an enormous whistle on which, to release pent-up enthusiasm, he blew now and again such a terrific blast as to shatter almost anyone's eardrums. Every blast was music to the ears of the energetic young priest who stood at the King's elbow. This enduring young man was in charge of all preparations for the invasion, which he assured his royal lord would surpass any invasion of France by England in the last hundred years!

Thomas Wolsey was the name of this enthusiast, the youngest priest on the King's Council, and the only churchman who had favored the war. Fiercely ambitious, he expected as his reward to be made bishop, archbishop, and cardinal.

By the last day of June, 1513, all was ready and Henry was leaving London. Catherine, proud of her young husband in his shining armor, accompanied him as far as Dover where 400 ships were waiting. The Queen was to act as Regent in England during his absence. She would write once a week and the courier would bring back a letter from Henry, or from Wolsey if Henry was too busy on the battlefront. Catherine warned him not to be rash, not to get overheated and catch cold, and to have Margaret recommend a physician if he did. She would keep sending supplies of fresh linen underwear, and she and her ladies would make plenty of bandages and banners.

And so Henry sailed for Calais, the one city in France still held by the English. To his complete surprise, the Emperor Maximilian came to meet him, appearing with a most dramatic lack of ceremony, bareheaded, his gray hair touching the shoulders of his black velvet cape, and with no identification but the gold imperial banner with the black two-headed eagle flying over him.

Henry had already sent the Emperor 100,000 crowns in advance and hired some German mercenaries at a price the Emperor said was reasonable. Maximilian now suggested that the best place to begin the campaign was with the capture of the two French towns, Therouanne and Tournai. Henry accepted that advice without question and the siege of the two cities began. Henry loved every minute of it, but only wished there had been an exciting battle. Louis XII, it was learned, had given his officers orders to avoid a pitched battle. But Henry fired one of the cannons with his own hands and rode about in the smoke without a quiver of fear. After one hundred days or so, when both cities had fallen, Henry knighted soldiers on the battlefield and also made Thomas Wolsey a bishop.

Maximilian took no exception to that. But when Henry had himself declared King of France, that was too much, especially as the young King's idea was to push right on to Paris and make good his title! Maximilian had had all he wanted. It was time to call a halt. Finding himself unable to bridle the "young colt" alone, he sent for Margaret to come and help. Margaret replied that she thought it not quite proper for a widow to "trot around visiting armies for pleasure" but would come if she could be of service. She would bring Charles to meet his Uncle Henry. Her ladies-in-waiting were thrilled at the prospect of meeting the young King of England who was so wealthy and notoriously extravagant.

Henry was no disappointment as he came riding to meet them, dressed in yellow satin, on a charger jingling with gold chains and little silver bells. For one month he treated his guests to luxurious feasts and lavish festivities. In return the Duchess, whom he found charming, entertained him at Lille. There an agreement was made to postpone the war until the following spring when it was arranged that Henry's sister Marie, who was seventeen, should marry Charles. Henry was so honest and forthright that Margaret later urged her father not to deceive him.

"I assure you," she wrote, "that there is no hypocrisy in him and therefore the promises made to him should not be broken."

Her appeal was too late. Maximilian and Ferdinand, both having acquired what they wanted, had deserted Henry and made a secret peace with Louis XII. Unaware of their treachery, Henry returned to England heady with success and impatient to tell the story of his triumph to Catherine.

Spring seemed slow in coming, but finally by April Bishop Wolsey was busy with preparations to renew the war. But no signs of war were reported in the Netherlands, nor was there any word about war from Spain. One day an ambassador from France showed up in London with the explanation. Louis XII, not above a bit of doublecrossing himself, had sent the man to inform Henry that his two older allies had been deceiving him. Henry was shocked at the deceit, the lying, the lack of faith on all sides.

Faith? Where was it? "I see no faith in the world," he exclaimed, "save only in me!"

Now that his eyes were opened he was furious at the whole Hapsburg-Spanish crowd, but most of all at Ferdinand, who had made a fool of him before. In his blind rage against her father, Henry hit out at Catherine, even blaming her, as he had never blamed her before, for the fact that they had no living children.

Catherine's grief over this was deeper than his, and her anger at her father's treachery just as bitter. Never again would she listen to him! She had done all she could for Spain. For five years she had been Queen of England; England had her loyalty.

Bishop Wolsey now saw a move that might make him an arch-bishop. He suggested that Henry VIII get into the doublecrossing game himself—make peace with France and seal the treaty with a marriage. Why not have Marie, Henry's pretty sister, who had been promised to Charles, marry Louis XII? The timing was perfect. Anne of Brittany had just died and the old French King was a widower.

Marie was willing, provided, as she put it, that "When the old King dies I may marry as me liketh to do." Henry made her that promise. And in July, 1514, Marie Tudor was married by proxy to Louis XII in St. Paul's Cathedral and was soon on her way to Paris to meet her old bridegroom, who was fifty-three.

RULER OF THE NETHERLANDS

O N HIS FIFTEENTH BIRTHDAY, February 24, 1515, Charles, the Archduke of Austria, was declared of age and took his place at the Council table as Regent of the Netherlands, replacing his Aunt Margaret. This was the work of the Duke of Chievres, who had been opposed to the war against France promoted by Margaret. Under his influence, the States General in Ghent had sent a present of 100,000 guilders to the Emperor Maximilian with the request that he appoint his grandson as their ruler. The Duke's influence over Charles was so great that with his pupil as Regent, he himself was once more practically in control of the Netherlands. And since Charles was also the "Crown Prince of Spain," the Duke of Chievres saw that in time he might also control the government of that country as well.

Hythloday

TWO FAMOUS BOOKS

AND NOW, at almost the same time, two books were being written by two men, an Englishman and an Italian, who had observed the way of the world in which they lived, the faithlessness of men, and the evils of society, and had something to say about it. Niccolo Machiavelli, the Italian, speaking from bitter experience during the tragic events in Italy, wrote a book called *The Prince*. The Englishman, using his imagination, described an ideal society in which the evils might be eliminated, and called his book *Utopia*. The author of *Utopia* was Erasmus's brilliant young friend, Thomas More. He began to write his book in the Netherlands the year that young Charles was made Regent. Thomas More had been sent there by Henry VIII to help in stubborn negotiations between the English wool merchants and the Flemish weavers.

Erasmus was also in the Netherlands and one day in early autumn he, Thomas More, and a few other congenial souls were spending a pleasant afternoon in Peter Gilles' garden in Antwerp. Their conversation started off with a mention of *The New World,* by Amerigo Vespucci, one of the most popular books of the day. This led to speculation about the society and government of those newly discovered islands, and how it compared with that of Europe, which everyone agreed fell far short of being ideal.

In this connection someone naturally quoted Plato's *Republic,* his ideal state being one in which each citizen did the work for which he was best fitted and the rule of the Republic was therefore handled by a philosopher, and everyone benefited.

Thomas More objected. He did not think that in Plato's society all the members of the community would benefit equally. This led him to imagine a society in which there would be equal justice for all. Before he left the Netherlands he had begun writing a book about his own ideal state. Since such a state was "nowhere" in existence, he called it *Utopia,* the Greek word for "nowhere."

Like Plato's *Republic, Utopia* was written in the form of a dialogue. The main speaker was a fictitious character by the name of Raphael Hythloday, who had visited this Utopia, and whom Thomas More imagines being introduced to by... "Peter Giles, a citizen of Antwerp," whom "upon a certain day" he says, "I chanced to espy talking to a stranger who had a black sunburned face, a long beard and a cloak cast carelessly about his shoulders."

"See you this man," says Peter. "There is no man living that can tell you of so many strange and unknown peoples and countries. For this Richard Hythloday, Portuguese born, joined himself in company with Amerigo Vespucci in the three last voyages of those four that are now in print... After departing from Master Vespucci he traveled through and about many countries.

"I turned me to Raphael and when we had saluted each other went thence to my house and there in my garden upon a bench covered with green turf we sat down talking together."

As they listen, Hythloday's knowledge of government and his good judgment soon make such an impression upon both men that they suggest that he should attach himself to some court, since any prince would be delighted to have his advice.

"You are deceived," quoth he. "First of all the majority of princes have more delight in warlike matters and in study of how to enlarge their dominions than on how peaceably to govern that which they already have. If I should propose wholesome decrees, think you not that I should be driven away or else made a laughing stock? Suppose I should rise up and advise the King of France not to meddle with Italy but to stay at home.... This, my advice, Master More, how think you it would be heard and taken?

"So God help me, not very thankfully," quoth I, "Yet if evil opinions cannot be entirely plucked out, that is no cause for forsaking the commonwealth. For it is not possible for all things to be good, unless all men are good, which I think will not be true for many years.

"Wherefore Master More, I consider with myself the Utopians among whom with few laws all things are well ordered. All things being held in common, everyman has abundance of everything.

"But I am of a contrary opinion," quoth I, "for methinks men shall never live wealthily where all things are held in common. For how can there be abundance of anything where regard for his own gains drives not a man to work?

"I marvel not," quoth he, "that you are of this opinion. But not if you had been with me in Utopia."

"Therefore, gentle Master Raphael," quoth Master Peter, "I

pray you describe unto us that island." And so after the three have dined, they return to the garden, and Raphael Hythloday begins to speak of the wonders of Utopia, telling in great detail about this ideal land, ending with the subjects of war and religion.

"The Utopians," he says, "detest and abhor war as a thing very beastly, although by no kinds of beasts is it practiced so much as by men. And contrary to the custom of almost all other nations, they count nothing so inglorious as glory gotten by war.

"There are divers kinds of religion in the island and in every city. But the most and wisest number believe that there is a certain Divine Power, Unknown, Everlasting, Incomprehensible, Inexplicable, far above the capacity and reach of man's wisdom, dispersed throughout the world. Him they call the Father of All. Yet there is no image of any god seen in church so that it may be free for everyman to conceive God after what likeness he will."

On his return to London, Thomas More sent the manuscript back to Erasmus to see about having it published, and Erasmus assured him that he would see that Utopia was produced in handsome form.

This is Niccolo Machiavelli. For eighteen years, while the Medicis had been in exile, Machiavelli had been in the employ of the people's government of Florence. He had seen armies from France, Spain, and Germany descend, as he said, upon Italy "like a pack of wolves." He had seen Naples and Milan captured and recaptured. He had been sent as an envoy to Louis XII, and also to the camp of Caesar Borgia. He had observed how Caesar had made his way by cunning, how his father, Pope Alexander, had succeeded through deceit, and how by his crooked tactics Ferdinand of Aragon had gained Naples.

And he had seen princes who were honorable deposed and ruined. He had been forced to the conclusion that the only way a prince

could survive in such a world was by the use of bad faith and political cunning. This was not an ideal, but a necessary evil.

Machiavelli had been in Florence in 1511 when the Medicis returned to their native city. Pietro, the oldest of the brothers whose haughty, overbearing rule had caused them to be driven into exile, had died. His young son, Lorenzo, became the new ruler of Florence. Two years later, after Pope Julius died, Cardinal Giovanni and his cousin Giulio returned to Rome in order to be on hand for the election of the new Pope. Machiavelli had hoped to get some post in the Medici government, but had failed and been forced to retire to a simple country house outside Florence.

There, one winter night in 1513, he sat writing a letter to an old friend of his more prosperous days, telling how he now managed to while away his time and keep his brain "from growing muddy." For one thing, he said, "I have composed a little work on *princedom,* debating what a princedom is, what kinds there are, how they are gained, how kept, why they are lost."

He drew upon what he had read in the great books of the past, as well as from his own experience.

"Everyone knows," he said, "how praiseworthy it is for a prince to keep good faith and to live by integrity.... But how men live is very far from how they ought to live ... so that anyone who is always good will be at the mercy of the many who are not good. Therefore it is necessary for a prince to learn how NOT to be good and how to do evil if he is obliged to. It is necessary for a prince to know how to imitate both the fox and the lion, for a lion cannot protect himself from traps and the fox cannot defend himself from wolves.

"Where it is an absolute question of the welfare of his country a prince must adopt whatever course will save the nation's existence and liberty."

It was with the existence and liberty of Italy that Machiavelli was most concerned. He had hoped in vain that Caesar Borgia would be able to form a central Italian state strong enough to withstand foreign aggressors. Caesar Borgia was considered cruel, but cruelty, or any other means he used to free and unite Italy, would have been justified. It was now Machiavelli's hope that the Medicis, who had returned to power in Florence could unite and create a strong central Italian state. He therefore dedicated the book to Lorenzo, the new ruler of Florence, appealing to him to rise to the challenge and set Italy free. He also hoped, quite naturally, that he might be recalled to Florence and rewarded with a position in the government.

This "little work on Princedom," as he called it, was to become one of the most influential books ever written in Europe. Many rulers were to study it like a textbook—a practical how-to-do-it book for Kings and Princes. The principle of political cunning and bad faith as a necessary evil is still called *Machiavellian,* just as an ideal state of impossible perfection is called *Utopian.* Each book added a word to the English language.

LEO X

THE HAPPY POPE, LEO X

"SINCE GOD has given us the Papacy, let us enjoy it." So said the new Pope Leo X, shown here with his cousin Giulio in this portrait by Raphael. Never had Rome seen a papal inauguration more lavish than that of Giovanni de Medici, the first of his family to wear the Papal crown. Artists, scholars, poets, musicians, actors—all hailed this as the beginning of a new Golden Age. And as anticipated, the arts flourished and Rome became the center of the most sophisticated and cultured, but also the most sensually self-indulgent society in Europe.

Unlike his predecessor, who preferred a sword, Leo X was a lover of books. Many volumes that had been salvaged by the monks of San Marco in Florence when the Medici Palace had been sacked, were purchased by him and given to the Vatican library. Ancient statues and other treasures were constantly being found and unearthed in and about Rome. The Pope appointed Raphael to appraise and preserve them. He also decreed that no more of the rare old classic temples and buildings of the old Roman Forum, now used as a cow pasture, should be torn down and destroyed. No longer was any marble to be carted away and used for other buildings.

Hunting was Leo's greatest joy. All October was spent entertaining large hunting parties at his country villa where he kept a huge stable of horses and a hundred grooms. One flippant friend remarked that the Pope wore his hunting boots so much of the time no one had a chance to kiss his feet. It was also said that he spent more time in the saddle than on his Papal throne or at his desk in the Vatican. But why not?

Cardinal Giulio, his cousin, was always in Rome to tend to the tiresome details of Papal business. So why should he worry? Why should he do anything but enjoy his splendid position?

Giuliano, the Pope's younger brother, whom everyone had loved as a little boy, had grown up with such a sense of honesty and justice that he proved a little difficult to manage. He refused to use the crooked tactics Giulio insisted upon if he wanted to rule Florence. And he refused to let Leo X rob the Duke of Urbino and give the title to him. So they had him come to Rome and take charge of the Papal forces.

Early in 1515 he was sent to France as ambassador of his brother Pope Leo with congratulations to the new King, Francis I. While there at the French court Giuliano was given a French title, and also a French bride, Philibert of Savoy, a much younger sister of Louise, the King's mother. And so, his young wife being the aunt, Giuliano de Medici became the uncle of the new King Francis I.

THE KING, FRANCIS I

POOR OLD LOUIS XII had lasted only three months after his lively young English bride, Marie Tudor, had come waltzing into his quiet life. Marie was just the age of Louis' own daughter Claude, who had been married five months before to Francis I. Much to Louis' regret, that spoiled, extravagant, frivolous "youngster" was still heir to the French throne.

The King, too old and weary for his years, had done his level best to keep up with his young bride, entering bravely into all the festivities celebrating her arrival. He had tried to dance again, gone hunting in the rain, forced himself to keep awake through long dramatic readings, and dined at the ungodly hour of six, his former bedtime. It was too much for him. He simply collapsed and passed on with the old year. Marie then married, as it pleased her to do, a dashing English soldier, Charles Brandon, and returned to England.

And on the first day of the new year, 1515, Francis, Count of Angoulême, Duke of Valois, became the new King of France.

On January 25, 1515, Francis I, young and glamorous, rode to his coronation in the great cathedral at Rheims "clad in white silk, his horse caparisoned with silver and covered with precious stones." Oriflammes, waving before him, bore his new emblem, the salamander, a symbol of fiery endurance, chosen by his mother.

Louise of Savoy, now the triumphant Queen Mother, had waited many long uncertain years for that glorious day. At last, fairly trembling with joy, she swept into the long-coveted place of highest honor, followed by her aunt, Madame Anne, her daughter-in-law, Queen Claude, and the ladies-in-waiting. That night she wrote in her diary: "On the day of St. Paul Converted, 1515, my son was anointed and consecrated in the Church at Rheims... I have been amply rewarded for all the adversities and annoyances that came to me during my girlhood.... Humility hath kept me company and patience hath never abandoned me."

Young Francis now began a reign of Youth and Gaiety. First he called together all his congenial young companions and formed a permanent royal court. This was a novel idea. Hitherto the French barons had continued to live as they had during the Middle Ages, each in his own fortified castle somewhere in the country. That was now passé. Now the nobles must reside near the King, at Amboise, Fontainebleau, Paris, wherever he might fancy to be. And with their ladies, most certainly, for according to Francis, "A court without ladies was like a spring without flowers." The ladies, needless to say, blossomed under his charm.

Marguerite, his sister, who had always adored her brother, spoke of his "unparalleled beauty," never seeming to see that his nose was far too long. She also vowed that "God alone had endowed him with perfect knowledge."

As to his knowledge, the Venetian ambassador remarked, "One is tempted to say that his wisdom is more on his lips than in his mind yet his bearing is altogether that of a king. Merely to look at him, a stranger would say, 'That is the king.'"

Hunting and making love were the King's favorite pastimes, but whatever caught his fancy was done with style and finesse.

The idea of regaining Milan, which had been lost by Louis XII and given back to Maximilian Sforza, presented an exhilarating challenge and he soon announced his intention to try it, after making an alliance with Venice. During his absence his mother Louise was to act as Regent of France, while his wife Claude, who was dull and meek as a mouse, would keep herself busy as usual saying her prayers and doing needlework. Before the year was half over, Francis was off toward the Alps on his way to Italy, plumes and banners waving, and an army of 40,000 Frenchmen singing:

> "The King goes over the mountains
> Le Roy s'en va del les monts..."

Over the mountains he went, and by a new way, though not from choice. The Swiss soldiers had blocked the only mountain passes it was thought an army could possibly use. Too inexperienced to know what was involved, Francis took the new way. Seventy-two cannon and three hundred pieces of artillery had to be dragged up and down the frozen mountain slopes by hand. It took the army five days but they did it. Then down out of the mountains like an avalanche of men, the French army descended upon Italy.

Swiss soldiers hired by Maximilian Sforza, the Papal forces, and Spanish troops from Naples were gathered to stem the invasion. The one great deciding battle took place at Marignano about ten miles from Milan, a battle which lasted two days and left 15,000 dead on the battlefield. Venetian soldiers fighting on the side of the French helped to win the victory. Then, instead of knighting soldiers on the battlefield, Francis, who had tested his sword in his first battle, let an experienced officer knight him. Calling for Bayard, his most valiant and fearless warrior, "sans peur et sans reproche," Francis knelt before him. Bayard drew his sword and touching both of the royal shoulders, dubbed his lord and master, "Sir Knight."

Milan fell after a short siege of only three weeks. The Duke Maximilian Sforza met Francis I at Pavia and very willingly resigned the Dukedom of Milan. He declared himself sick and tired of trying to hang onto something that cost him so much trouble and money. He was glad to accept a settlement of 36,000 livres and retire to live comfortably in France the rest of his life.

Pope Leo X turned pale with alarm when the victory at Marignano was reported to him. "What will become of us?" he moaned.

The only thing he could do was to go to meet Francis at Bologna and make the best deal possible. To his chagrin he was obliged to return parts of the Duchy of Milan seized by Julius II and added to the Papal State. Francis also demanded that the Pope as supreme authority give him the Kingdom of Naples. Leo X hedged by more or less promising to do so, after the death of Ferdinand of Aragon to whom it now belonged. So the latest war was settled, in a way that would only lead to more wars on the battleground of Italy.

354

1452

1519

LEONARDO'S LAST PATRON

LEONARDO DA VINCI went home with Francis I, happy to accept the young King's invitation. Leonardo was weary. He had gone from Florence to Rome, but there Michelangelo, Raphael, and other younger artists were in high favor and there was little for him. From Rome he had gone to Bologna where he met some of the French officers he had known in Milan. A small, amusing invention which he made caught the fancy of the young King, a mechanical lion that dropped a shower of fleurs de lis at his royal feet.

A devoted young pupil went with Leonardo to France. The King installed them in a small manor house connected by a ramp with the Castle of Amboise. There Leonardo lived the last three years of his life, dying at Eastertime in 1519.

His Mona Lisa, probably the most celebrated portrait in the world, which the painter took with him, now hangs in the Louvre. That and the other paintings which Francis I purchased in Italy started the collection for that great art gallery in Paris.

yo el Rey

THE NEW KING OF SPAIN

ON JANUARY 23, 1516, Ferdinand of Aragon died suddenly in the mountains on a hunting trip. His death threw Spain into a turmoil and the Netherlands into a whirl of excitement. Who should have the crown? Charles, or his mother Juana? Juana was locked up, said to be insane, yet despite that fact, the Spanish nobles insisted that she was the rightful Queen. In the Netherlands, Charles was proclaimed King just as soon as word came of his grandfather's death. The Duke of Chievres saw to that. He immediately began to plan which Flemish noblemen should be on Charles's Council and hold the key positions in the new Spanish government, selling many of them to the highest bidder.

Imagine the fury caused among the members of the Cortes when word of that proclamation and high-handed performance reached Spain!

Cardinal Ximines, the Archbishop of Toledo, was then the Regent. The leading churchman in Spain, he was a true statesman, incorruptible and thoroughly good. Although he was old, in his

yo la Reyne

eightieth year, and very frail, he was still alert and a power in the land. The only solution he saw was for Charles to come to Spain, appear before the Cortes, and have the matter settled. He also wrote Charles begging him to follow the advice of his grandmother Isabella and take only Spaniards into his Council. The Cardinal did not know, though he may have surmised, that Charles did not make his own decisions but was completely under the influence of his Flemish tutor.

It was September, 1517, before "King" Charles reached Spain with his huge Flemish delegation headed by the Duke of Chievres. The voyage was one of those long stormy ones, which finally ended near the small port of Tazones. As soon as Cardinal Ximines heard that Charles was in Spain, the old statesman, frail as he was, set out to meet him. Riding in a heated litter, with a ball of hot metal in his hands, his legs encased in fur, he looked, his jester told him, "like an old greyhound wrapped in wool." It was the firm determination of the old statesman to meet young Charles before he was presented to the Cortes in Valladolid.

The Duke of Chievres was just as firmly determined to prevent that meeting. He kept delaying Charles's journey inland over the mountain roads on one excuse or another, until the old Cardinal became exhausted, was taken ill on the way to meet them, and died.

It was then simple for the Duke to carry out the plan he had for Charles. This was a meeting with his mother, the Queen, in order that before Charles was presented to the Cortes, Juana herself should have resigned the throne in favor of her son.

Eleanor, Charles's sister, who was nineteen and had come with him to Spain, also went with him to visit their mother in the Castle of Tordesillas. It was a cold, dark, dismal day in December as the brother and sister stood waiting in the dreadful, gloomy corridor outside the closed door of their mother's room. The Duke of Chievres had gone in first.

Juana had known the Duke well in Brussels since he had been one of Philip's Council. But she gave no sign of recognition as he entered. She sat there alone, in the half light, her hair disheveled, her gown rumpled. The Duke asked her if she were well, and said that it was a pleasure to see her again. His tone was kind, and she responded enough to ask what news he brought from the Netherlands and if her children were well.

"Well indeed, madam," he answered, "And in truth, madam, in my opinion better children could not be found, so virtuous are they, so wise and so well educated. Would you care to see them?"

Even as he spoke, he had the door opened to reveal the two standing on the threshold. Charles stepped in and made a deep bow. Eleanor, following him, made an even deeper bow. Charles took another step or two forward and recited his speech:

"Madam, we your humble and dutiful children are most joyful to see you, thanks to God, in good health, and for a long time we have been desirous to do you reverence and offer our testimony of honor, obedience and respect."

Juana merely nodded her head and sat for some moments gazing at her two children. It had been so many years since she had seen them. Finally she leaned forward and took their hands.

"But are you really my children?" she said. "How you have grown in so little time. Welcome and Heaven be praised. What troubles you must have had in coming so far. Surely you must be tired. Since it is late, you best seek some rest until tomorrow."

The brother and sister took their leave, bowing their way out.

The Duke of Chievres stayed on to accomplish his purpose, introducing witnesses who could testify that Juana had signed over her throne to Charles. He began by saying, "How fortunate you are as Queen to have so capable an heir as your son Charles. Even now," he added, "Charles is ready and able to take the burden off your shoulders, if you wish him to."

"Yes," said Juana, "let Charles take over."

With those few words, the purpose of the visit was accomplished. Charles could now proceed to Valladolid, appear before the Cortes, and be proclaimed King, in his own right—King Charles I.

There was no chance that silent Charles, with his stumbling speech, would make a favorable impression on the Spanish nobles. Though the Cortes gave him a chilly reception, they granted him the right to rule, but did so grudgingly and only for the time being, saying that,

"If at any time Our Lord in his mercy should restore her reason to the most Serene Queen Dona Juana, his mother, the King shall desist from the governance of Castile."

So Charles was proclaimed King, but at a fatal price to his mother. Only so long as Juana was thought to be mad could Charles rule. After the proclamation, the whole Spanish Council was immediately discharged and replaced by Flemish noblemen. The Duke of Chievres took over the treasury, and his sixteen-year-old nephew replaced the old Cardinal Ximines as the Archbishop of Toledo. Charles, who was very serious and methodical, kept a careful record of all that happened.

MAGELLAN

ON MARCH 22, 1518, while he was in Valladolid, Charles signed an agreement with a refugee from Portugal that was to solve the greatest mystery of his time—the size and shape of the earth.

The Portuguese who came to offer his services to Charles was a short, stocky, blackbearded man who walked with a limp. His Portuguese name, Fernao de Magalhaes, was to become Ferdinand Magellan, as he changed his allegiance from Portugal to Spain.

This change was due to bitterness and disappointment. Magellan was in his late thirties. He had served King Manuel of Portugal for seven years in the Indies. Yet he had received no reward or recognition whatsoever. Not only that, he had been told by the King that, in spite of all his experience, there would be no further place for him in the service of Portugal.

For a year after being dismissed by King Manuel, Magellan had stayed on in Portugal, maturing a plan that was in his mind. He worked in the King's library, where he had access to all the secret charts, sailing directions, and log books of the latest expeditions to Brazil. For now the coast of South America had been explored as far south as the La Plata River. One of the best of those secret maps had been drawn by Martin Behaim, who had made the Earth Apple in Nuremberg. For some years before his death in 1507, Behaim had been employed as mapmaker for the King of Portugal. On Behaim's map Magellan had seen what he was certain was the "Paso" or strait leading through to India.

As Magellan appeared before Charles and his Privy Council, his assurance impressed all—the Flemish Cardinal Adrian, the Duke of Chievres, the Spanish Cardinal Fonseca, as well as the young King himself. Magellan had brought with him a slave Enrique, from the Moluccas, and a slave woman from Sumatra, the first people from the Far East to be seen in Spain, which was also impressive. Although the exact location was not shown on the globe which he had brought with him, the explorer convinced his hearers that he had sure knowledge of where the strait lay.

Magellan was asked to make a written statement of his proposals and Charles I agreed to equip five ships and provide the crew with enough food and artillery to last two years. Magellan was to have 1/20 of all the income to be derived from the venture.

Due to Charles's unexpected interest, arrangements for the expedition began without the usual delay. On March 22, 1518, the agreement was signed. On August 10, 1519, Magellan and his five ships sailed from Seville on their voyage around the world.

By that time Charles and his Council and court were in Barcelona.

APOSTLE TO THE INDIES

An epidemic was raging in Barcelona when Charles arrived, so he took up residence in a castle a few miles away. In the nearby village was a church where he and the members of his court attended Mass. One Sunday a Franciscan friar who had recently returned from Hispaniola was invited to preach the sermon. What he told about the cruel oppression of the Indians so impressed young Charles that he asked the friar to be present at an audience which he was to hold a few days hence, on that very subject. As the friar entered the hall of the palace he found himself in a most distinguished company, all titled gentlemen of Church or State, except one. That one was Bartolomé de Las Casas—the well-known "Apostle to the Indians."

As they took their places, the friar was on the far side of the circle

362

facing the King's throne, the members of the panel being seated according to this diagram.

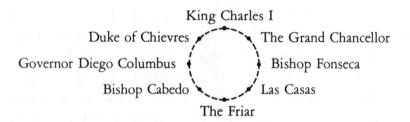

King Charles I
Duke of Chievres — The Grand Chancellor
Governor Diego Columbus — Bishop Fonseca
Bishop Cabedo — Las Casas
The Friar

The Bishop of Cabedo took no notice of the lowly friar, keeping his head proudly turned away.

The meeting opened with ceremony. With most meticulous regard for etiquette, the Chancellor and Chievres each knelt on one knee to confer with Charles, and be apprised of his desire. It was then announced that His Majesty desired that Bishop Cabedo speak first.

Bishop Cabedo replied in a haughty tone that he wished to speak to his Majesty in private. It was evident that he felt above entering into any discussion or conversation with the lowly friar, next to whom it was his misfortune to be seated. Charles insisted, saying that everyone there had come upon invitation. So, forced to do so, the Bishop, after introducing himself, gave his devastating appraisal of the Indians.

"Sire, the Catholic King, your grandfather, having desired to make a settlement on the mainland of the Indies, petitioned the Holy Father to make me the first bishop of that colony. As to the Indians of the country . . . I say that they are SLAVES BY NATURE."

Las Casas, who was asked to speak next, took fire at the Bishop's last remark but controlled himself enough to begin calmly.

"Most powerful and most high lord and King, I am one of the oldest immigrants to the Indies . . . where I saw with my own eyes the cruelties inflicted on those peaceful and gentle people. . . . Those people of the new world are not only capable of understanding the

Christian religion but also of practicing good morals and the highest virtues. The Bishop of Cabedo has told you that they are 'slaves by nature.' Our holy religion adapts itself to all nations of the world. It embraces them all and deprives no human being of his natural liberty, under the pretext that he or she is 'Servus a natura,' a slave by nature as the Bishop, if I understood him, would have you believe. . . .

"His Catholic Majesty, your grandfather, promised me that measures would be taken to correct the evils. But he died and his royal will in behalf of the Indians was frustrated. I next applied to Cardinal Ximines and also to Cardinal Adrian. They acted promptly but the persons sent to execute the laws proved unfit for the task. When I heard that your Majesty had come to Spain, I hastened to renew my representations to you. . . ."

The Friar spoke next. He told how he had had to take a census of Hispaniola and what a shocking percentage of native people had perished. "I beg and beseech your Majesty to put a stop to that torrent of crime and murdering people that the anger of God may not fall upon us all."

Diego Columbus, the Governor, was called upon last. It was not an easy situation for the Governor. Although he himself had made no vast fortune out of mistreating the Indians, the evils had been perpetrated with his knowledge, if not with his active approval. He made no attempt to excuse or defend himself, but out of an innate sense of justice asked Charles to intervene.

"Sire, the crimes which have been and are yet perpetrated in the Indies, of which these reverend fathers have spoken, are well known. Priests and friars as you see have come here to denounce them. However much your Majesty may suffer by the destruction of those people I shall suffer more, because even though all your dominions beyond the seas should be lost you would still be a great lord, whereas I would be left without possessions of any kind. Therefore I came to inform the Catholic King Ferdinand (May he rest in peace) and I am waiting on your Majesty now to beg you to please look into this weighty affair and find a remedy for these evils."

And so the meeting ended. Afterwards Las Casas told Governor Columbus about his latest plan for an Indian reservation in South America which he hoped the King would approve. All of Las Casas' efforts were now centered on saving the Indians in South America since it was too late to save the natives on Hispaniola and the islands. Three-fourths of those gentle, friendly Tainos had been wiped out. Las Casas now planned to establish a reservation on the Gulf of Venezuela where the Indians would be protected and taught. He knew that Columbus had come to Spain to see about the lawsuit regarding the hereditary title of Vice Roy and the larger income promised to his father. Since there was no prospect of this being settled soon, Las Casas suggested a plan by which Diego might increase his own income and also help with the expense of the reservation. He was to ask the King for the exclusive right of trading with the Indians of South America, promising in return to erect fortresses and maintain soldiers to protect the Indians on the reservation while the friars taught and converted them.

Diego said he would take the proposal to his brother Ferdinand who was a scholar and whose opinion he held in very high regard.

Ferdinand's advice was that Diego should also request that the governorship be vested in him and his heirs forever. This was practically the same thing as acquiring hereditary title of Vice Roy, so the whole proposal was rejected.

Las Casas' general plan for the Indian reservation, however, was given royal approval. It was agreed that he should have 260 leagues of coastal region in Venezuela to try out his experiment. The agreement was signed by the King on May 9, 1520, at Coruna. The next day Charles sailed from Spain, bound for Germany where in the past three years tremendously important events had been taking place—events that would change his own life and the world in which he lived.

St. Jerome

Erasmus by Dürer

A NEW NEW TESTAMENT

THE RHINE was the great river highway from the Netherlands to Switzerland. In the spring of 1514 Erasmus was making his first trip up the river to the Swiss city of Basel, stopping at various German cities along the way. Everywhere the "great Rotterdammer," as they called him, was hailed by the German scholars as the "ornament of Germany"—"the light of the world"—its undisputed leader in classical learning.

It was the renowned publisher, Johann Froben, that attracted

Erasmus to Basel. Froben had agreed to publish Erasmus' version of the New Testament, taken from the original Greek sources, on which he had been working for fourteen years. Ever since he had first heard Colet lecture on the Bible at Oxford, and had then taught himself Greek, Erasmus had been working on his translation. All the way to Basel he never took his eyes off of the old black handbag which held the manuscript. He had had a horrible experience on the boat from England. Halfway across the Channel he discovered that his handbag was missing. It was nowhere to be found. He was frantic. To his immense joy, after hours of despair, he found the manuscript safe ashore on the other side, the handbag having been put on another boat by mistake.

For some time Erasmus had been in correspondence with Froben, and was eager to meet him. Upon reaching Basel, he hastened to the printing house and for fun pretended to be just a friend of Erasmus delivering another letter.

"I said I was also entrusted with the publishing of his works, so that whatever I did would stand as if done by Erasmus himself. At last I added that I was so like him that whoever saw me saw Erasmus. Froben then broke into a laugh as he discovered the hoax." As he had been in Venice working with Aldus Manutius, Erasmus was soon as hard at work in Froben's printing plant in Basel, delighted to be surrounded once more by the clatter of presses and the sharp smell of ink. In March, 1516, the first edition of the New Testament in Greek was completed. It was followed shortly by other editions which contained also a Latin translation for those who did not read Greek.

Erasmus dedicated his version of the New Testament to Pope Leo X. Although it differed widely from the translation made by St. Jerome in 386, which was still used by the Church, the Pope was open-minded and pleased to accept it.

With publication of this work, Erasmus, already famous and

respected as the leader in classical learning, became still more famous as the leader in the new scientific study of the Bible.

He had grown famous, but not rich. The task in Basel finished, he had to face the question of where to go next, which invitation to accept. He had a wide choice.

The Bishop of Paris wrote that his King Francis I would present Erasmus with a generous income from Church property if he would come to the University of Paris.

Cardinal Wolsey wrote him of the welcome from Henry VIII and honors awaiting his return to Oxford or Cambridge.

Good Cardinal Ximines, before his death, had invited Erasmus to come to the University of Alcala in Spain.

George the Bearded, Duke of Saxony, offered the "great Rotter-dammer" a chair at his University of Leipzig.

Accepting none of these flattering offers, Erasmus returned to the Netherlands to be professor of Theology at the University of Louvain. "Until I decide," he said, "which residence is best suited to an old age which is already knocking at the gate."

At Louvain he was overwhelmed with letters.

From Switzerland, Zwingli, the great religious reformer, wrote, "The Swiss account it a great honor to have seen Erasmus."

One most respectful letter came from Wittenberg, from the Secretary of Frederick the Wise, the Elector of Saxony, who wrote:

"We all esteem you here most highly; the Elector has all of your books in his library and intends to buy everything you may publish in the future." But he also begged to say that an Augustinian friar there at Wittenberg, who was a great admirer of Erasmus, wished to call his attention to one error. In his version of St. Paul's epistle to the Romans, Erasmus had paid too little attention to original sin.

The humble friar at Wittenberg, with convictions so strong that he dared to take issue with the foremost scholar of his day was Brother Martin Luther, who was making his own serious study of the Bible.

MARTIN LUTHER'S HAMMER

O N HALLOWEEN, 1516, the small town of Wittenberg was crowded with peasants from the surrounding countryside who came, bringing money, to view the relics in the castle church and share in the indulgence that Frederick the Wise was allowed to offer once a year on the Eve of All Saints. The money collected in this way was used to support his castle church and the university where Martin Luther was teaching.

Frederick the Wise was proud of having the best and largest collection of holy relics outside of Rome. A catalogue, illustrated by Lucas Cranach, listed 5,005 articles, among them one tooth of St. Jerome, a wisp of straw from the manger at Bethlehem, and a twig from the burning bush of Moses. All together, the indulgence given for viewing them would reduce one's sentence in purgatory by 1,443 years. The reservoir of good accumulated by the saints could be shared by all those who had properly confessed and sincerely regretted their sins. That was the proper interpretation, and Frederick the Wise, who was an honest, sincere man believed this to be true, as sincerely as had Martin Luther before his visit to Rome.

Young Albert of Brandenburg was the Elector of Mainz—the city where the first indulgence ever to be printed had been made in 1454 by Johann Gutenberg. Young Albert, who was twenty-one and full of ambition, had his heart set on being made Archbishop of Mainz, which he knew would cost him a large sum of money. However, Pope Leo X, who would confer the title, never had enough money for his own luxuries, to say nothing of the vast amount needed to carry on the building of St. Peter's, which Pope Julius had started. After some bargaining between Albert and the Pope, the sum agreed upon was 10,000 ducats to be paid at once. Albert borrowed the money from Fuggers, the famous bankers of Germany. To help him pay back the loan, the Pope granted him the privilege of selling an indulgence in his territory for the next eight years, and keeping half of what he collected. The other half was to go toward the building of St. Peter's. And so far as the buyers were to know, all the indulgence money was to be used for that worthy cause!

Tetzel, a Dominican monk, an experienced peddler with a loud voice and slick tongue, was given the sale of the indulgence. At every town he was met by the Burgomaster. In solemn procession the indulgence was then borne aloft on a gold embroidered cushion to the market square. There, under a cross bearing the Papal arms, Tetzel began his sale with his cry of attention:

"Listen now, God and St. Peter call you! Consider the salvation of your souls. . . . Listen to the voices of your dear dead relatives calling you from purgatory . . . Listen! Consider! Remember:

> "As soon as the coin in the coffer rings
> A soul from purgatory springs."

Not a word was said about sin or repentance. Pay your money and your record would be clean; your soul saved from purgatory!

Frederick the Wise was alarmed that this indulgence sale for St. Peter's would affect the yearly revenue for his own Church of All Saints. He therefore forbade Tetzel and his salesmen from crossing the border into Saxony. That did not prevent them from coming as close as possible. Martin Luther was then preaching on Sundays in a parish church near the border, so near that his parishoners kept crossing over to spend their money for the great bargain that Tetzel was offering. It seemed shameful to Luther. To tell a man that he could buy his way out of purgatory was false. Not only that, it was damaging to a man's soul to believe that his sins would be wiped out by merely paying a few coins.

On Halloween, the Eve of all Saints, 1516, Luther preached a sermon against the whole theory. Since that was the very day when the people came to Wittenberg for the yearly indulgence, offered by Frederick the Wise, that good Prince was naturally dismayed. How-

371

ever, he had great respect for Luther's ability and knowledge; he was slow to anger and happy to see that his people were not affected by the sermon.

A year passed, during which the indulgence sale for the building of St. Peter's continued to flourish. It was again Halloween in Wittenberg, October 30, 1517. Again the little town was filling with people coming to view the relics.

Early in the morning Martin Luther was on his way from the Augustinian monastery at one end of the street to the Castle Church at the other, his long monk's robe blowing about his thin legs as he strode along. In one hand he had a roll of paper; in the other, a hammer. At the door of the Church he stopped and nailed up the paper. This was not unusual. The doors of the Church served as a bulletin board for the University. Debates by faculty members or students were often advertised. Martin Luther proposed a debate on the subject of Indulgences. On his paper was a list, in Latin, of Ninety-five Theses, or topics, to be upheld or denied in the debate.

Why, for example, should Germans pay for the rebuilding of St. Peter's Church in Rome, which would be of no use to them?

What power could the Pope have over purgatory?

No one was more surprised than Luther himself by the interest and excitement aroused by his theses. So many people wanted to read them that soon the University printing house could not keep up with the demand. In a little over two weeks they had spread all over Germany and inside of a month, all over Europe. Erasmus sent a copy to Thomas More. Luther himself sent a copy to Albert, the Archbishop of Mainz, with a letter which began:

"Father in Christ, Most Illustrious Prince, forgive me that I, the scum of the earth, should dare to approach your Sublimity."

After this overly humble beginning, Luther struck out with harsh words against Tetzel's false preaching, and the Archbishop's lack of responsibility for the "souls entrusted to his care."

"God on High . . . I can keep silent no longer . . . Christ did not command the preaching of indulgences, but of the gospel. It is high time you looked into the matter." The letter was dated: Wittenberg, 1517, on the Eve of All Saints, and signed,

Martinus Luther d.

"Martin Luther,
Augustinian Doctor of Theology."

Albert of Mainz sent the theses on to Rome. Pope Leo made some casual comment—that it was probably just a squabble between the Dominican Tetzel and the Augustinian Luther, over the way indulgence should be explained. The Pope could not be bothered then to define how indulgences should be interpreted—not until the following spring. Then it was too late.

The only thing that seriously disturbed Pope Leo's enjoyment of life was his fear of the Turks. The new Sultan Selim I, grandson of the conqueror Mohammed II, had now invaded Hungary and was threatening Italy and also southern Germany. Pope Leo had sent an appeal to the Emperor Maximilian asking him to raise money from the German Princes for a Crusade against the Turks. In reply, Maximilian sent a letter to the Pope asking him first to silence Martin Luther. The monk's attack on the indulgence for St. Peter's might have such an effect upon the German Princes that they would refuse to finance a Crusade. A combined effort was agreed upon.

Maximilian was to summon the German Princes to a meeting at Augsburg early in October, 1518. There, Cardinal Cajetan, the Pope's ambassador, would present his appeal for a Crusade against the Turks, and also interview Martin Luther. The Cardinal was to persuade the troublesome monk to recant, if he could. If Luther refused, he was to be seized, bound, and sent to Rome to be punished as a heretic.

Martin Luther, notified to appear, set out in fear and trembling for Augsburg. He could see himself condemned as a heretic, burned at the stake as the Bohemian Jan Hus had been 100 years ago. A disgrace to his old parents! What if I *am* in error, he thought. Can I alone be wise? Here he was, a mere monk, opposing the two greatest powers in his world—the Emperor and the Pope!

Any respect he might have had for the Pope's ambassador, however, vanished in their first stormy encounter. Luther declared that the Cardinal was "no more fitted to treat the case than an ass was to play the harp." The Cardinal retorted that Luther was "a leper with a brain of brass and a nose of iron."

Friends of Luther in Augsburg now feared that the angry cardinal might have him arrested. One night when they saw special guards being placed at the city gates, they rushed to wake the monk and help him to escape. Having no time to dress, it was said, "He had to ride horseback in his cowl, without breeches, spurs, stirrups, or a sword." By Halloween, 1518, he was safely back in Wittenberg.

Now Frederick the Wise was truly embarrassed. The good man asked himself again and again what he should do, how he should act. He believed in the power of the holy relics. But he also had faith in Luther's knowledge of the Holy Scriptures. What, he asked himself, was his duty as a Christian Prince?

THE LAST KNIGHT RIDES AWAY

THE EMPEROR MAXIMILIAN had called the Diet of Augsburg, not only to place before the German Princes the Pope's request to finance a Crusade, but also to influence the electors to vote for his grandson Charles as the next Holy Roman Emperor.

The German electors numbered seven, and their votes were for sale, except that of Frederick the Wise, who could never be bribed.

By the time Maximilian arrived in Augsburg, five of the seven electors had promised to vote for Charles. But promises are made of air, and in the end the Emperor knew that the ancient crown of Charlemagne would go to the highest bidder.

Francis I was the other leading candidate. Francis based his claim on the fact that he was the ruler of France, the original kingdom of the first Emperor Charlemagne, who had been King of the Franks. Louise of Savoy, Francis' doting mother, was ready to spend her whole fortune in bribing the electors, for the added joy of seeing her darling, head of the empire of Christendom. Pope Leo also favored Francis I as being better suited to lead a Crusade against the Turks than young Charles who had never set foot on a battlefield.

As to the Crusade, Maximilian, still the medieval knight in his imagination, had thought of leading the Crusade himself. He had conceived a grandiose scheme in which not only would the Turks be driven out of Europe, but Constantinople would be recaptured, Jerusalem liberated, and the entire Holy Land freed from the domination of the Moslems. What a dream!

The practical, hard-headed German Princes failed to share it. Nor did they intend to furnish soldiers and levy enormous taxes on themselves to pay for any Crusade whatsoever. As Maximilian had predicted, Luther's courageous stand against the sale of indulgences had had its effect upon the Princes. Even if they should raise the money, they saw no more reason to think it would be used for a Crusade than that all the money raised for the building of St. Peter's would be used for the purpose for which it was intended.

Maximilian was disappointed about the Crusade, but he still had high hopes for the election. He kept writing to Charles in Spain to send on more ducats, not to be so stingy, to keep up with Francis in bribing the electors. The final vote was to be taken at the next meeting of the Diet which was to be held at Frankfurt in June.

The Emperor would not be there.

In January, 1519, Maximilian died quite suddenly of a stroke—but in a happy way, doing something he enjoyed most, hunting the fleet-footed chamois in the Tyrol Mountains.

What people remembered most about this joyous hunter was his unfailing charm and personality. The citizens of Augsburg remembered how he called himself a "burgher of their city, the merriest town in Europe." Merchant princes like the Fuggers spoke of how he would lay aside formality when he came to their homes and dance with the rest of the company. Peasants remembered how, passing them on a country road, he would stop his horse and visit with them, asking about their villages, their crops, their families. "Kaiser Maxi," they called him. Soldiers remembered how in one campaign he had talked with seven foreign commanders, each in his own language, speaking Latin, Italian, French, Spanish, English, Walloon, and Flemish, as well as German. Musicians, writers, artists, and scholars recalled the encouragement he had given them.

He wrote a book about himself which he called *The Dangers and Adventures of the Valiant Knight Sir Teuerdank*. This was an allegorical poem describing his adventures on the way to marry Mary of Burgundy —a blond-haired knight in silver armor who came to the rescue of his lady love.

At the Diet of Augsburg, Albrecht Dürer, who was the Court Painter, made his well-known portrait of the Emperor. On it he wrote, "This is Kaiser Maximilian, whom I, Albrecht Durer, portrayed at Augsburg in his little room high up in the palace."

After the Kaiser's death, Albrecht Dürer finished a spectacular woodcut the size of a billboard, which Maximilian had conceived and ordered. Here the Emperor is shown in a triumphal procession riding in his car of state, accompanied by all the virtues in the form of lovely ladies crowning him with wreaths of honor. So we shall remember him, the last knight of the old order, the final rider in the gorgeous pageant of the Middle Ages.

OPINIONS VARY

IN WITTENBERG it was reported that "Erasmus of Rotterdam gave Doctor Martin Luther great applause for the stand he had taken at Augsburg, as did almost all the University of Louvain." This report was slightly exaggerated, to say the least. The professors at Louvain University were so extremely hide-bound that they were even critical of the moderate teachings of Erasmus. As for Erasmus, annoyed as he was by the backward monks of Louvain, he was equally alarmed by Luther's loud words and coarse tone. When he heard from Basel that Froben had printed the collected writings of Luther and had exported hundreds of copies of the book to France, Spain, and Italy, Erasmus truly took fright and wrote Froben not to publish any more. In March, 1519, Erasmus received an unexpected letter from Luther himself, which began:

"Greeting. Often as I converse with you and you with me, Erasmus, our glory and our hope, we do not yet know each other. It is not extraordinary. For who is there whom Erasmus does not teach, I mean of those who rightly love learning. I am compelled to acknowledge your noble spirit which has enriched me and all men even though I write a barbarous style. Wherefore, Dear Erasmus, learn if it please you to know this little brother in Christ also; he is assuredly your very zealous friend. May the Lord Jesus himself keep you forever, excellent Erasmus, Amen . . . Brother Martin Luther.

"Philip Melancthon prospers, except that we are hardly able to keep him from injuring his health by his great rage for study."

Philip Melancthon, whom Luther mentioned, was Germany's foremost classical scholar, who had recently joined the faculty at Wittenberg where to the great joy of Frederick the Wise, his lectures were attracting many more students to the University. Erasmus had known Melancthon as a youth and recognized how unusually brilliant he was and what promise he had. After hearing from Luther, Erasmus wrote to Melancthon saying that, "No one disapproves of Luther's life; of his doctrines there are various opinions."

In April Erasmus also sent a letter to Frederick the Wise. Luther's writing, he said, had given the Louvain monks plenty of reason to cry out against all scholars and all enlightenment, but that was no reason to condemn Luther for heresy. "None of us is free from error. May the Duke prevent an innocent man from being persecuted under the cloak of piety. . . . This is also the wish of Pope Leo—that innocence be safe."

On May 30, 1519, Erasmus wrote directly to Martin Luther, saying: "Dearest Brother in Christ, your epistle was most pleasing to me. I cannot tell you what a commotion your books are raising here at Louvain. These men cannot be disabused of the suspicion that your works are written by my aid. I have testified that you are entirely unknown to me. I try to keep neutral, so as to help the revival of learning as much as I can. It seems to me that more is to be accomplished by civil modesty than by impetuosity."

The young Archbishop Albert of Mainz also had a letter from Erasmus saying that he had warned Martin Luther not to write anything arrogant or fierce against the Pope, but to preach with a sincere mind and all gentleness.

Erasmus was now on that ever-dangerous middle ground between two extreme positions. Soon the reformers, violent and hasty, would be blaming him because he would not support them, while the theologians at Louvain, narrow-minded and bigoted, accused him of starting the reformation. One priest had said: "Erasmus laid the egg and Luther hatched it."

Erasmus retorted that the priest had neither learning nor fairness nor piety. "I laid a hen's egg. Luther hatched a very different breed of bird."

The summer of 1519 brought two important events—the Diet of Frankfurt which elected Charles V Holy Roman Emperor, and the Debate of Leipzig which convicted Martin Luther.

After her father Maximilian's death, Margaret of Austria, once more Regent of the Netherlands, had spent vast sums to make sure that her nephew would be elected Emperor. On the first vote, the election went to Frederick the Wise, who was not even a candidate. This was due to the influence of Pope Leo X, who did not care to have either Francis I or Charles I become any stronger than they were by being made Emperor. Also he thought with this honor he might induce Frederick the Wise to send Luther to be tried in Rome. To his surprise the Pope found that he was dealing with a completely incorruptible man, no more tempted to sell his integrity for honors than for money. Although the old statesman was taken by surprise and overawed by the honor, he refused the high office, saying he felt in all honesty unequal to its responsibilities. He gave his votes to Charles. And on June 29, 1519, Charles, nineteen, who was Spanish,

Flemish, and Austrian, was elected by the Germans to be "King of the Romans"! And so, the next Holy Roman Emperor.

Meanwhile, on one of those last days in June, an odd procession was starting out from Wittenberg for Leipzig, forty miles away. Two hundred Wittenberg students wearing helmets and bearing battle-axes, trudged along beside a country cart carrying their teacher, Martin Luther, to the University of Leipzig. There, on July 4th, he was to defend himself in a debate against a very strong opponent, a monk by the name of Eck, who had won international fame for his skill and eloquence debating at the University of Bologna.

Eck had challenged Luther to speak on the Power and Authority of the Pope.

The University of Wittenberg was younger and smaller than the University of Leipzig, where the debate was to be held. Leipzig belonged to George the Bearded, Duke of Saxony, who divided Saxon territory with the Elector Frederick the Wise. To the students of Wittenberg, Leipzig was enemy country, and they would not let their good Doctor Luther go there unprotected. They found Leipzig also prepared for trouble. The Duke had stationed a great guard of burghers in armor around his castle to maintain order during the debates.

The university had no hall large enough to hold all the people who wanted to attend, so George the Bearded had lent his huge banqueting hall for the occasion. Chairs and benches were decorated with tapestries. Those of the Lutherans displayed the emblem of St. Martin, and the Eckites that of St. George the Dragon Killer. There was a preliminary bout of words by two lesser protagonists preceding the main event. Then, as a shiver of excitement passed over the audience, the two main contestants rose and faced each other; both were peasants, the son of a miner, the son of a butcher.

Eck, who had a huge, stocky frame and a booming voice, showed immense confidence in himself, and in his speedy victory.

Martin Luther looked thin and almost pale compared to Eck.

His voice was clear and distinct, but he carried a bunch of flowers which he looked at or smelled when the discussion became heated.

Eck's obvious intent was to force his opponent into a corner where he would have to make some statement that would prove him to hold the same ideas as Hus, the Bohemian heretic.

Eck challenged Luther's assertion that in the early days the Roman Bishop, or Pope, had not been above the others, that the Bishops of Athens, Constantinople, Alexandria, of all the cities, had originally been equal. Actually, this was true. That was why the Greek Church had never accepted the supremacy of Rome. All through the Middle Ages, however, the Roman Church having become powerful, had claimed to be the original church founded by St. Peter, and for that reason its power was of Divine origin. This was the claim that Eck clung to and upheld.

"But I see that you, Martin Luther," he shouted, "are upholding the damned and pestilent errors of Hus."

"I deny the charge," retorted Luther. "Not all the doctrines of Hus were judged to be heretical."

"None of them was called Christian," roared Eck. "And if you defend them you are a *heretic*." Triumphant that he had forced Luther to damn himself by defending Hus, Eck had rushed in for the final blow. Now all that was needed was the papal decision against Luther and the world would be rid of another heretic!

Even so, the debate continued. It went on and on for over two weeks, to a capacity audience. "It might have gone on forever," said one of the listeners, "if Duke George had not intervened." Hospitable George the Bearded needed the banquet hall to entertain the Margrave of Brandenburg, one of the Electors who was on his way home from the Diet at Frankfurt, with news of the election.

Eck, proud of his victory in the debate, went off to Rome to report another heretic. There in December, Martin Luther's books were publicly burned in the Piazza Navona, while a Bull threatening him with excommunication and punishment was being prepared.

CLIMAX ON THE RHINE

Nine months went by after Charles I received news of his election as the Holy Roman Emperor Charles V before he was able to leave Spain for the coronation. He had found it all but impossible to get the Cortes to furnish money for the journey. Diego Columbus loaned him several thousand ducats and was rewarded with the title of Vice Roy, although Charles still did not make the title hereditary. Both Diego and his brother Ferdinand were among the friends and retainers who were to accompany the newly-elected Emperor to the Netherlands, and from there to the German city of

383

Aachen for the coronation. On May 20, 1520, the day after Charles signed the agreement with Las Casas for the Indian reservation, they sailed from Coruna.

Ferdinand Columbus looked forward with pleasure to purchasing books in the various cities of the Netherlands and Germany. So far the books he had purchased outside of Spain had been in Rome where he spent several months in 1512 while Julius II was still Pope. He had been there again in 1516 and 1517 when it had been a joy to find the interest in books stimulated by Pope Leo X and the Vatican Library largely increased by the Medici collection.

Not long after Charles and his court were established in Antwerp a Cardinal named Aleander arrived as ambassador from Pope Leo X, bringing a copy of the Papal Bull against Martin Luther. This had been signed on June 15, 1520, about a month after Charles had left Spain. Cardinal Aleander had his instructions to deliver the Bull first "to our beloved son Charles, Holy Roman Emperor and Catholic King of Spain," and then to spread copies throughout the Netherlands and southern Germany.

Eck, meanwhile, was to deliver the Bull to Martin Luther in Wittenberg and post it throughout the German States of the north. Since the number who sympathized with Luther was growing rapidly, neither ambassador relished the assignment. It was too much like stirring up a hornet's nest.

Cardinal Aleander was well received by Charles, and with proper words for the occasion placed in his hands a copy of the Bull, signed by Pope Leo X, sealed with the papal ring and bearing the arms of the Medici. Charles opened the handsome cover and read the first words, "Arise O Lord, a wild boar has invaded thy vineyard." "Surge Domini, Arise O Lord," were the words by which the Bull was to be known. The text, which was fairly long, stated that Martin Luther was to have sixty days either to retract what he had written and be forgiven, or be excommunicated and punished as a heretic.

Charles promptly issued a decree against all Lutherans in the

Netherlands. And Cardinal Aleander went on to Louvain. There, Luther's books were solemnly burned to ashes in a square near the university, which afforded grim satisfaction to the faculty members. The one outstanding exception was Erasmus, who decried it as an act of barbarism, a tragedy arising "out of hatred of good learning and the stupidity of the monks. They can burn Luther's books," he said, "but they cannot refute them."

The university was then making life almost unbearable for Erasmus. Cardinal Aleander, the same irritating Aleander who had roomed with Erasmus in Venice, ten years ago, now attacked him in a violent speech on Monday, October 8th, the day Luther's books were burned. On Tuesday Erasmus was dismissed from the faculty.

On Sunday, the day before the fire, Erasmus autographed for a most appreciative guest a copy of his *Antibarbari,* his earliest book, the one in which he had lashed out for the first time against the barbarism of ignorance and superstition, of which this burning of books was striking evidence.

The guest was Ferdinand Columbus, and the most prized possession which he took back with him to his library in Seville was this present from the most famous scholar of his age. On the flyleaf Ferdinand wrote, half in Latin, half in Spanish: "The author gave me this book as appears on the eighth page. ERASMUS ROTERODAMUS gave this as a present to Don Ferdinand Colon. Louvain. On Sunday, October 7, 1520. Erasmus himself wrote the first two lines here with his own hand."

Three weeks later, on October 22nd, Ferdinand Columbus was entering Aachen, the old capital of Charlemagne, with Charles V.

Five German electors rode to meet the new Emperor outside the city gates. At sunrise of the following day, October 23, 1520, as bells rang from every tower, he was escorted to the door of the cathedral where three archbishops waited to bless him as he entered.

The lofty cathedral, lighted by a thousand candles and torches, was filled with princes, attired in cloth of gold, with massive gold chains set with precious stones about their necks. On a platform hung with gold and silver tissue sat the royal ladies, Queen Claude of France, Louise of Savoy, and most distinguished among them in her widow's cap, Margaret of Austria, Regent of the Netherlands.

Long ago, her grandfather, Emperor Frederick III, had devised this motto from the initial letters, A E I O U:

"All the world is subject to Austria."

Here on this day in the coronation of her nephew Charles V, Margaret of Austria was seeing the fulfillment of that motto.

During the solemn consecration, Charles lay prone on the altar steps, his arms outstretched in the form of a cross. After being anointed and taking his vow, he was clothed in the coronation robe. Then, with a sword at his side, the scepter in his hand, he was seated on the old stone throne and the ancient iron crown of Charlemagne was placed upon his head. Albert, the Archbishop of Mainz, read a letter from Pope Leo X, according Charles the title, "King of the Romans —the Emperor-Elect."

Later Charles V was to have his title of Emperor confirmed in a coronation by the Pope, which also had been the custom for seven centuries—ever since Pope Leo III had crowned the Emperor Charlemagne in the year 800.

But, as Charlemagne had been the first German Emperor to be crowned by the Pope, Charles V was to be the last.

For the Middle Ages were past. The Roman Church which had ruled and united western Christendom for 1,000 years had come to the breaking point. It had destroyed itself through corruption. A reformation within the Church was to come, but not before it was too late—not before "God allowed this chastisement to come upon his Church because of the sins of priests and prelates."

Those were the words of Cardinal Adrian, the sincere, devout churchman from the Netherlands, who was to be the next Pope. He was now acting as Regent in Spain during the absence of the young Emperor.

Frederick the Wise, Elector of Saxony, "Uncle Frederick," as Charles called him, missed the coronation. On the way to Aachen he was laid up in Cologne with an attack of gout. As he was a key figure in the fate of Martin Luther, both Charles and Cardinal Aleander came to Cologne to see him.

On Saturday, November 3rd, "Uncle Frederick" brushed his bushy whiskers with extra vigor, put on his velvet hat, and leaning on a silver-headed cane limped over to the cathedral to meet the young Emperor in the sacristy. He asked Charles to promise that in regard to Luther he would follow the way of the law and have him given a fair trial. Charles gave his solemn promise.

On Sunday, November 4th, Cardinal Aleander called upon the old statesman at his lodgings in the Square of the Three Kings. He demanded that Luther be handed over for punishment without a trial, as guilty of heresy. The old Prince replied that he would not protect heresy. But neither would he deliver up any man for punishment without a fair trial.

On Monday, November 5th, Frederick the Wise sent for Erasmus who, as he knew, had come with Charles to Cologne. He wanted to make a first-hand appraisal of this famous man who was so inscrutable, so irritating to violent men on both sides.

Erasmus, who had high regard for the benign, incorruptible old statesman, accepted the invitation gladly. A large open fire was burning as he entered. Erasmus stood with his back to it, warming his hands behind him as he spoke. Frederick asked him first if he thought Luther had erred. Erasmus waited a moment, then with an odd smile, said that Luther had erred on two points: "In attacking the crown of the Pope and the bellies of the monks."

Frederick laughed. Then Erasmus went on to say that Luther had been much too violent, that the honor of the Pope demanded this, but the cause of truth demanded that, until at the end of the interview he left his good host no less perplexed than when he had come.

"What sort of man is Erasmus anyway?" said Frederick the Wise to his secretary Spalatin. "One never knows where he stands."

Meanwhile the bitter smoke of burning books had reached Wittenberg. On October 10th, Eck had put the Papal Bull in the hands of Martin Luther who, believing in "an eye for an eye, and a tooth for a tooth," declared, "Since they have burned my books, I shall burn theirs." On December 10th, his firm friend Melancthon issued an invitation to the students and faculty of the University of Wittenberg, to witness a burning of the Papal Bull and books of scholastic theology at nine o'clock in the morning outside the Elster gate. There, on an open space outside the walls, a great bonfire had been laid. When the crowd of students, professors, and townspeople had arrived, one of the professors kindled the pile. Luther first laid on the books, and then solemnly placing the copy of the Papal Bull on the fire, spoke in Latin, consigning them to eternal flames.

He waited until the fire had burned down and then, with his friend Melancthon and fellow monks, walked soberly back into town, leaving the students to dance around the fire singing funeral dirges at the top of their lungs.

Frederick the Wise wrote to one of the councillors of Charles V about this retaliation:

"After I left Cologne, Luther's books were burned, and also at Mainz. I have constantly insisted that his books should not be burned . . . If now he has given tit for tat, I hope that His Imperial Majesty will graciously overlook it."

The first act of His Imperial Majesty Charles V was to summon the Princes of Germany to a Diet to consider the case of Martin Luther. True to his own sense of justice, as well as to the promise made to Frederick the Wise, Charles sent a courteous summons to Luther to appear before the Diet to defend or retract his doctrines.

The Diet was to be held in April, 1521, at Worms, a city on the Rhine about halfway between Cologne and Basel.

hie · stehe ich ·

HERE I STAND

THE GREAT COUNCIL CHAMBER at Worms was so crowded that almost no one but the Emperor could be seated as Brother Martin Luther walked into the hall. Among those princes there was a wide spread of opinion, from that of Cardinal Aleander, who would have had Luther condemned with no hearing at all, to that of Ludwig the Elector of the Palatinate, who was said to "roar like ten bulls" in support of the reformer. On the first day Luther's supporters were disappointed by the rather mild and evasive answers he gave but on the following day, April 18th, Luther spoke with his usual vigor. The Archbishop of Trier, the official examiner, showed the monk a pile of books and asked him, as he had the day before, whether or not they were his.

"Most Serene Emperor, most illustrious princes, most clement lords," replied Luther. "You asked me yesterday whether I would repudiate these books . . . They are all mine, but they are not all of one sort. Some deal with faith and life so simply that my very enemies regard them as worthy of Christian reading. Should I be the only man on earth to damn the truth confessed by friends and foes alike? Some of my works enveigh against the evil lives and—"

"There can be no discussion," broke in the Archbishop of Trier, "lest there be no end to the debate. I ask you, Martin, answer candidly —do you or do you not repudiate your books and the errors which they contain?"

Luther replied, "Since Your Majesty and your lordships desire a simple reply, I will answer. Unless I am convicted by Scripture and plain reason, I do not accept the authority of Popes or Councils, for they have contradicted each other. My conscience is bound by the word of God. I cannot and will not recant anything, for to go against conscience is neither right nor safe. Here I stand, I cannot do otherwise. So help me God. Amen."

Luther was dripping with perspiration as he finished. He had spoken in German—"Hier stehe ich. Ich kan nicht anders. Got helfe mir. Amen." He was asked to repeat what he had said in Latin. Luther repeated the words and then threw up his arms as if with those words he had vanquished an enemy, and left the room.

Next day, the young Emperor called the electors and princes and requested their opinion. They asked for more time to consider.

"Very well," said Charles, "I will give you my opinion." He unfolded a paper which he had written, and read in French:

"I am descended from a long line of Christian Emperors of this noble German nation and of the Catholic Kings of Spain. They were all faithful to the death to the Church of Rome. I have resolved to follow in their steps. A single friar who goes counter to all Christianity for a thousand years must be wrong. I will have no more to do with him. He may return under safe conduct but without preaching or making any tumult. I will proceed against him as a notorious heretic, and ask you to declare yourselves."

All of the electors voted to uphold the Emperor, except two— Ludwig of the Palatinate and Frederick the Wise.

That night placards were posted on the door of the town hall and all over Worms. They were stamped with a Bundschuh—the wooden shoe of the German peasant—a silent warning that if the nobles and the princes condemned Luther there would be a Peasants Revolt.

Unmoved by this, Charles V went calmly and methodically ahead. He told Cardinal Aleander to prepare a final draft of his Edict of Worms, but when the Cardinal brought it back for his signature, Charles took up the pen, then, said Aleander, "He laid it down again saying he must submit the edict to the Diet." There was good reason for this. To take a vote was the legal procedure. The two dissenting voters had gone home, and the approval of the Edict would be unanimous. So it was. And on May 26, 1521, as Aleander reported, "His Majesty signed both the Latin and the German with his own blessed hand and, smiling, said, 'You will be content now.' 'Yes,' I answered, 'and even greater will be the contentment of His Holiness and of all Christendom.' "

The Pope's ambassador and the Emperor then returned to the Netherlands. Where was Martin Luther? That lone monk who defied those two highest authorities in his world—the Pope and the Emperor. He had not been seen since he left Worms. No one had heard from him. Could Martin Luther have been murdered? Could he be dead?

"O God, if Luther be dead," cried Albrecht Dürer, "who will henceforth explain to us the gospel?"

Gradually friends began receiving letters from Martin Luther out of some place which he called, "The Wilderness." This was actually the Castle of Wartburg, an ancient, deserted fortress, to which Luther had been carried away as he was leaving Worms by men in the employ of Frederick the Wise. There, hidden away, disguised as a knight, he was being cared for by a warden and two serving boys. Safe, but unhappy in idleness and solitude, he wrote a friend, "I had rather burn on live coals than rot here."

Gottes wort
bleibt ewig.

Biblia/

Martin Luther finally found a cure for his loneliness and depression in work. He wrote twelve books, and started to translate the New Testament into German. This first German translation was to be most important for it spread the reading of the Bible among the people. It also made the north German dialect, which Luther used, the literary language of Germany.

This drawing, which is from the title page of Luther's Biblia, or Bible, shows God the Father writing the Holy Scriptures, and below his pen, the sentence, "God's word endures forever."

The music is from "A Mighty Fortress is Our God," the most famous of the many hymns composed by Martin Luther.

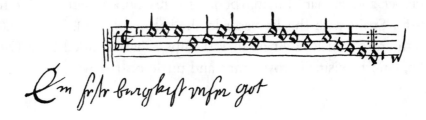

ENGLAND'S "DEFENDER OF THE FAITH"

IN ENGLAND, meanwhile Henry VIII, not to be outdone in piety, had been writing a book which he had dedicated to Pope Leo X and which the Pope had received in 1521 just before he died. Henry's book denounced Martin Luther and upheld the authority of the Pope, as being absolute. Cardinal Wolsey encouraged Henry to exaggerate the Papal authority, hoping that he himself might be the next Pope. Thomas More, who would one day lose his head for defending that authority, suggested that Henry should "Touch it more slenderly." Henry brushed the suggestion aside, declaring that he would "set it forth to the uttermost." Very proud of his book, Henry dedicated it to Pope Leo X, had it bound in cloth of gold, and sent it off to Rome, hoping to be rewarded by a title of some kind.

The Pope thanked the English ambassador and holding the golden book in one of his soft, white hands, remarked with gracious hyperbole:

"We all but welcome Luther's crime since it is the occasion of your noble championship."

Henry won his title as "Defender of the Faith," although twelve years later he was to break that faith, challenge the authority of Leo's cousin Giulio, who had become Pope Clement VII, and as King, declare himself head of the Church of England.

Ferdinand Columbus, who had been in Nuremberg during December and January buying books for his library, left the Netherlands for Spain with the Emperor in the spring of 1522. Taking 2,000 Flemish and Spanish retainers in 150 ships, Charles sailed from Calais for England to visit his royal aunt and uncle on the way.

Henry VIII in his expansive manner gave his sober young nephew a hearty welcome and entertained him with lavish feasts and tournaments at Greenwich, at Windsor, and in London.

Catherine, who had lost her girlish figure, must have looked to Charles like almost any other short, middle-aged lady. She was happy to see her nephew, though he certainly was a peculiar-looking young man with no resemblance to her sister Juana, nor to his father, the Handsome Philip. All the Hapsburgs had that very protruding jaw, but Charles surely had the most exaggerated one.

Little Princess Mary, Catherine and Henry VIII's only child, was then six. Charles acquiesced when Henry bluntly suggested that he "tarry for her and marry her when she is ripe." Charles V also signed a treaty to join Henry VIII in war against Francis I.

So there was the old game beginning over again, with three new players—those three young rival monarchs of France, Spain, and England who now would hold the fate of Europe in their hands.

RETURN TO SPAIN

CHARLES and his huge retinue reached the Spanish port of Santander early in July, when, as he wrote his Aunt Margaret, he "was received with much humility and reverance." This may have been due to the large foreign guard which was there to protect him, rather than to any marked change in Spanish feeling.

Yet there had been a change in Charles. He had grown up a great deal in the five years since he had first come to be crowned King. The Duke of Chievres, on whom he had depended for his every move, was no longer with him. He had died of the plague in Worms. Charles now made his own decisions. Although he had no such magnetic charm as his grandfather Maximilian, nor the driving energy of his grandfather Ferdinand, he was conscientious and methodical, and by his patience and perseverance in time won universal respect.

It would take a full measure of perseverance and hard work to govern such a vast empire as he had inherited, and which steadily increased by conquest and exploration. One great addition was an-nounced in a letter that reached Charles in 1522 shortly after his return to Spain. This was a letter from Hernando Cortes describing in detail his conquest of Mexico. With it he sent one-fifth of all the fabulous captured treasure of the Aztecs.

News of the fate of Magellan also awaited Charles. The ship Victoria returned to Spain in the summer of 1522 with the first men ever to make a voyage around the world. Magellan was not with them. He had been killed in Cebu, one of the Philippine Islands which he had discovered. Though he had not completed the voyage, he had accomplished his purpose, which had been to discover the strait that would take him through to India. Magellan had found it and, after passing through the stormy strait, had come out upon an ocean so comparatively peaceful that he named it Pacific.

Regarding the Moluccas or Spice Islands, some adjustment had to be made with King Manuel of Portugal, since in 1512 the Portu-guese had reached and claimed those islands. Ferdinand Columbus was one of the commissioners appointed to arbitrate with the Portu-guese. And Charles V eventually sold his claim to King Manuel for 350,000 ducats.

Ferdinand Columbus was then in charge of India House in Seville with the duty of examining and commissioning pilots. One of these was Sebastian Cabot who sailed in the service of Spain in 1526 on an expedition to the Spice Islands.

This was the year that Ferdinand began to build his house just outside the walls of Seville, where he had purchased seventeen-and-one-half acres along the Guadalquivir River. It was a most pleasant location. Although there were no trees, he planned to import several thousand saplings from his property in the New World, from which he received sufficient gold to make him a wealthy man.

It was in this home that Ferdinand Columbus, in the last years before he died, wrote the story of his father. By that time the trees brought from America were well grown. The books in his library

Casas de Colón

were in good order and being perfectly cared for by a man from the Netherlands whom he had brought to act as librarian.

In 1537, he received a yearly grant from Emperor Charles V of 500 pesos of gold from the revenues of Cuba to maintain the collection of books, and also another 225,000 maravedis a year, after he had written the Emperor about the need for such a library.

"There should be a certain place in the Kingdom," were his words, "where all books of every branch of knowledge which treat of the Christian world and even outside of it should be collected— something which up to the present time no prince has been known to have ordered to be done. . . . There should be an alphabetical list of the authors and their works, and also a subject index." Much of this work had been done, but Ferdinand wished to be sure that it would continue.

Shortly before his death, further care for the library was recommended in his will. A grille work was to be built around the whole library, six feet from the wall where the books were to be kept in cases, so that no one could touch them. Outside the grille there was to be a bench for readers; inside the grille a stand or holder for the books, and a space large enough for the hands of the reader to reach

Seville

through and turn the pages.... This was necessary, he said, "For we see that it is impossible to keep books from being taken, even if tied up with 100 chains."

Today the books are in the cathedral library at Seville, although no more than 5,000 remain. But among them are those priceless old volumes that played such a part in the discovery of America. There is the volume of Marco Polo, with the marginal notes made by Christopher Columbus during those long years of waiting in Cordova.

The French geography is there, with the note about his hearing Bartholomew Dias tell of the discovery of the Cape of Good Hope. And the old volume of Ptolemy.

There is also the first book which Ferdinand purchased for his library, dated in 1510, the year he returned from Santo Domingo and began the habit of adding, at the end of each book, when and where he bought it and what it had cost.

There is the *Antibarbari*, autographed in 1520 to Fernando Colon, by Erasmus. Of special interest is the note to be seen in a volume of the tragedies of Seneca, the great Roman philosopher who had been born in Cordova in the days of Caesar Augustus.

In his *Tragedy of Medea*, Seneca wrote this prophecy: Tiphys, whom he mentions in the verse, was the pilot of the Argonauts who went with Jason for the Golden Fleece, which he brought back with the help of Medea. This is the prophecy, in Latin:

> Venient annis——
> Secula seris, quibus Oceanus
> Vincula rerum laxet, et ingens
> Pateat telus tiphisque novos
> Delegat orbes nec sit terris
> Ultima tille. . . .

This is the translation:

> An age will come after many years when
> The ocean will loose the chain of things,
> A huge land will lie revealed
> Tiphys will disclose new worlds
> And Thule no longer be the ultimate. . . .

Next to this, in the handwriting of Ferdinand Columbus are the words:

"This prophecy was fulfilled by my father, the Admiral,
in the year 1492."

INDEX

PEOPLE